Queries & Quandaries

Benjamin Franklin

compiled and edited by Kyle D. Frank

DE WARD
PUBLISHING COMPANY

PREFACE

The book is done, and I still wrestle with what to say about this new work. Actually, it is a very old work in a very new form. The idea of this format came to me while gathering materials for the book "Gleanings From a Sacred Field." I kept coming across these little snippets of questions and answers as I rummaged through the dusty files of the *American Christian Review*. Later, while looking in his biography, which had been written by his son Joseph, I ran across a comment by Joel Headington that it would be a very good idea to collect these questions and answers into a form where they could be of the greatest advantage to the brotherhood. Obviously, I agreed. This final work pretty well lays out the wisdom of brother Franklin as he dealt with various queries and quandaries that faced the brotherhood.

As I re-read the manuscript I realized that this book enables one to travel through time. The times we are to visit are from the 1840s until Franklin's death in the fall of 1878. Pardon the rustic, awkward composition of some of the language. Keep in mind that the great majority of correspondents had only a few weeks to months of schooling in the old log cabin schools that graced our nation in those days. Although these people are looked upon as semiliterate, look at the obvious thought and effort put into these calls for light. They were not illiterate, nor were they ignorant, they were merely doing the best they could with what they had. You will especially note the queries that came from the Civil War period. You can almost feel the tension and anxiety of the times coming through the paper. Yet, in all that, you can still see the faith that God was on the throne and the hope that all would be well. May we imitate their faith as we walk through our daily lives.

Kyle D. Frank
Springville, N.Y.
January, 2012

INTRODUCTION

We have occupied the editorial chair long enough to find out that an editor does not *know everything*. There are some questions which we can not answer. There are some which have been answered two or three times during the same year and in the same publication through which the querist desires to put them. In such cases, we desire persons to read a little more closely and find the question and answer the first time they appear. Many questions are asked which would be of no use to a single living mortal, if answered fifty times. Many of this class, we are compelled to pass in silence. Many questions grow out of difficulties among brethren, or in churches. In such cases an editor is no tribunal or court to decide, especially from a one-sided statement of the case, and without testimony of the case, and without testimony on either side. In these cases we are no judge, and prefer giving no decision. Many questions, not exactly in the channel of any of these, might be of profit, if well answered, but we have not at all time to answer, or the authorities to consult. Many persons have no idea of the continual pressure on our attention, preaching once or twice almost every day engaged several hours almost every day in private circles, writing private letters, not only in reference to the REVIEW, but finding fields of labor for preachers, and preachers for fields; reading correspondence, selecting, arranging and preparing matter for the paper. Those who know the amount to which we give attention are not surprised if we *seemingly* neglect some things. We are about as busy as is possible for a man to be, and make this explanation, that persons may see the reason why we do not give attention to more than we do. We desire neither to neglect, nor slight any one.

Benjamin Franklin
Anderson, Indiana
March 12, 1867

TABLE OF CONTENTS

QUESTIONS RELATING TO JESUS

Query–Who crucified the Lord? Was it the Gentiles or the Jews, or both?

Answer–Peter charges the crucifixion on the Jews. But the Jews were only at the bottom of it; they instigated it; the Romans, who were Gentiles, executed him. The Jews were the more responsible party, as they persisted in clamoring for his crucifixion, when Pilate, the Roman judge, wanted to let him go. The Jews premeditated, designed and instigated the crucifixion; the Romans performed the deed, or were tools in the hands of the Jews and executed the will of the Jews.

But when the matter is more fully comprehended the whole world were represented in the transaction. The entire nation of Israel was represented in the Sanhedrim, and the nations apart from the Jews, the Gentiles, were represented in the Roman court, and thus all the world was represented and implicated in the awful act of crucifying the Lord of glory.

The Jews were, as we have said, the *instigators* of the crucifixion, but did not, therefore, have the sole responsibility, as the Gentiles, or the Roman court, had the power to release him and desired to do so, but voluntarily yielded to the wishes of the Jews in giving him up to be crucified, and with their own hands executed him. The Jews had no power to inflict capital punishment without the assent of the Roman court. The Jews were the *instigators* and the Romans the *willing tools to execute their will.*

July 29, 1873, vol.16,#30, page 236.

(Unless indicated, all references are to the *American Christian Review*)

Query–Did Christ inherit the nature which man had *before* the fall; for if the nature which he assumed had been after the similitude of fallen man, then he would have been subject to sin.(?)

Answer—What if he did inherit the nature that men had before the fall? Or what if he did not? There is nothing in that, or in the understanding of it, to make a man any better or happier. The great matter is, for man to believe on the Son of God, hear his sayings, or regard them, and do them. Study what he said and did, and learn what we should say and do, that we may be approved of him.. The matter among us is not to ascertain who can study out, comprehend and understand the deepest, most profound and wonderful mystery, nor who can explain the greatest mystery, but who can *learn* and *do* the will of our Father in heaven most perfectly and faithfully.

7/1/60 vol.3, #31, page 123

Query—Not long since, I had a conversation with a minister of the church upon the subject matter of the following questions. We conversed at some length and parted. I made a minute of what had passed between us, and in looking over it the other day, it occurred to me that I had noticed nothing special on this subject in your excellent paper; and if you think the theme one of sufficient interest, your views upon the following question may benefit many of your readers. How did Christ take on him the nature of Adam before the fall, when the Bible says that he took on him the "seed of Abraham?"

Answer—Christ did not take on him our nature *before* the fall at all, nor till born of Mary.

5/24/59, vol. 2, #21, page 83

Query—How is it possible for Christ to take on him our fallen mortal nature and yet be absolutely pure?

Answer—It is not man's *nature* that is fallen, but man. It is man that is fallen, sinful and mortal. But in his redemption, in his sinless and immortal state, it will be *man* with *man's nature*, just as much as it is man with man's nature now. Purifying man from sin does not make him anything but man, nor take from the nature of man. Sin is no part of man nor of man's nature. Adam was man and had the nature of man before he sinned, as much as we have now. The Word then becoming incarnate, taking upon him the seed of Abraham, did not take upon him sin, but was like his brethren yet without sin.

5/24/59, vol2, #21, page 83

Query—If all the sufferings of Christ were voluntary, did he will to suffer every thing he did suffer, or did he not volunteer to submit himself to a condition where he must necessarily suffer without working a miracle to prevent it?

Answer—*Volition* and *will* certainly amount to very nearly the same thing. That which is voluntary must be willing. The exercise of the will and volition must be about the same. The Lord voluntarily submitted to suffer for us, to shed his blood and die, because without the shedding of blood there is no remission. He was obedient to death, and there is no obedience that is not voluntary or willing. He delighted to do the will of his Father, yet it was a great struggle in this instance, as we learn from the scene of Gethsemane.

5/24/59, vol.2, #21, page 83

Query—If Christ's human nature were immortal when living, dying, and in the grave, in what sense was he made like unto his brethren. (See Heb 2.17) or how could he be our proper representative?

Answer—Christ's humanity was not immortal. He was *man* as well as *God, human* as well as *divine*, but without sin. It is not sin to be human, nor possess human nature, for Adam was human and possessed human nature before he sinned. Sin is the transgression of the law. Christ transgressed no law.

5/24/59, vol.2, #21, page 83.

Query—In the first chapter of John's testimony we are taught very plainly, that the Immerser did not know the blessed Savior, officially until after his immersion, when the Spirit in the bodily shape of a dove, and in an audible voice pointed him out, not only to John, but also to the congregated thousands on the banks of the Jordan, saying, "This is my Son, the beloved, in whom I am well pleased." Query: Why then did John afterward send two of his disciples to the blessed Savior, saying "Art thou he that should come, or look we for another?

Answer—Simply because his understanding was so limited, what had then been revealed so dim, and the amount of what had been explained to him was not sufficient to keep his mind clear, when lying in the darkness and loneliness of a dreary prison, waiting for his martyrdom. We wonder now, after the full-orbed Sun has risen upon us, that John and others did not understand more clearly matters that now appear clear to us. But had we lived then and only had their measure of light, our understanding would be no better than theirs was. When we see the little that is now understood and how many, after we thought they once had their minds clear, fall away and get to groping in the dark, we need not wonder at John the Immerser.

1/60, vol.3, #5, page 18.

Query – Noticing the happy and ready manner in which you have heretofore explained and satisfactorily harmonized apparently difficult passages in the Bible, in reply to various correspondents, I have concluded to desire you to give an explanation through the columns of your excellent REVIEW, of the following seeming discrepancy which I find in reading the Bible,(and I regard it, when rightly understood, the best book ever read by man,) with regard to the following passages: In John 5.31, Christ says: *"If I bear witness of myself, my witness is not true."* And in John 8.18 Christ says: *I am one that bear witness of myself* and the Father that sent me beareth witness of me." According to Mark 14.61–62, Christ does bear witness of himself, for when the high priest asked him, "Art thou the Christ, the Son of the Blessed?" Jesus said, *"I am."* Now, the difficulty which has been pressing upon my mind for years, and which I believe, you can satisfactorily explain and remove, is simply this: When Christ bears witness of himself that he was "the Christ," was his witness true, notwithstanding he says, in another place, "If I bear witness of myself, my witness *is not true?*" Hoping and believing that you can and will make all this clear and harmonious, I respectfully subscribe myself yours, in the bonds of the gospel.

Answer – No man can harmonize the common version, touching the above matter. In John 5.31, we should have two important changes in the translation, required by the original, and the whole matter is free from contradiction, as follows: 1. The original requires a supplement making the verse commence, "If I *alone* bear witness, or testify concerning myself, etc. 2. In the place of the words "not true," at the close of the verse, we should have the words "not to be regarded." It is simply an admission of our Lord, that if he *alone* testified of himself, his testimony was unworthy of credit. But he did, under oath, testify of himself, and is called "the true and faithful witness," Rev 3.14, and his testimony is corroborated by the Father, the Holy Spirit, and all the holy Prophets and Apostles. If it stands alone, it is not worthy of regard, but corroborated as it is, it is worthy of all confidence. By the way, we ought to have had the name of the writer of the above, *not to publish*, but *to look at*.

1/11/59, vol.2,#2, page 7.

Query – What does the Savior mean, where he says, Matt 19.25: "When the Son of man shall sit in the throne of his glory ye also shall sit upon twelve thrones, judging the twelve tribes of Israel?"

Answer – We have seen sundry expositions of the twelve Apostles sitting upon twelve thrones, etc, but are not willing to indorse any that we have seen. We would prefer admitting that we do not know what this passage means to adopting some mere fanciful interpretation.

1858, vol3, #5,

Query – Please notice the following query: "In this was manifested the love of God toward us, because that God sent his only begotten Son into the world, that we might live through him." 1 John 4.9 "For this is the love of God, that we keep his commandments," 1 John 5.3 The sending of his only begotten Son, etc., and the keeping of his commandments, are these things, strictly speaking, love, or are they the result of effect or love?

Answer – God manifested *his love to us* in sending his Son into the world, that whoever believeth on him might not perish, but have everlasting life; and we manifest *our love to God* in keeping his commandments. The love of God resulted in sending his only begotten Son into the world. The love of God in us results in keeping the commandments of God; hence the Scripture says, "He who says he knows God, and keepeth not his commandments, is a liar." No man need deceive himself with the vain conceit that he loves God, who does not keep the commandments of God. "Hereby do we know that we know Him, if we keep his commandments."

8/3/1858, vol.1, #32, page 127.

Query – I have just read the discourse of Bro. Walsh on the subject of "Calling on the name of the Lord." I do not know that I fully understand him; therefore, I wish to add a few scattering thoughts on the subject, with the view of calling him out again. He says in one place, "In this respect there is a marked difference between this exercise and ordinary prayer, or prayer on ordinary occasions." And again, "How beautiful and appropriate that the penitent believer, who is about to be baptized in the name of the Father, and of the Son, and of the Holy Spirit, should go down into the water with his heart lifted up in prayer, and his whole soul engaged in 'calling upon the name of the Lord.' Does Bro. W. mean that *praying* is one thing and *calling* another? If he does, I hope he will make the distinction plain, so that we can understand it. Does he mean that we should call *audibly?* If so, should not all be re-immersed who did not call in that way? The subject under consideration has not only caused contention among the few reformers here, but has actually caused a division in the church. Does not every penitent believer, who understands the design of immersion, pray with his whole heart, when about to be immersed, for the very thing he is seeking, viz., the remission of his sins. I hope, Bro. Franklin, you will write on the subject; perhaps you can afford some light.

Answer–We did not perceive any thing in the discourse of Bro. Walsh that need create any difficulty, nor do we recollect any thing particularly new. That the penitent should come to baptism lifting his heart to Heaven, "calling upon the name of the Lord," is evident; but whether the prayer should be audible or not, we find not one word in Scripture. But we find some instances where the Lord heard audible prayer, and others where he answered prayer that was not audible. We see no necessity for secret prayer being audible. It is simply between the suppliant and the Lord, and the softest whisper is sufficient for the ear of the Lord, or even the inarticulate groaning of the spirit that can not be uttered. The Lord understands the struggling of the spirit, and the Spirit itself maketh intercession or us. Let us not, dear brethren, dispute about empty words, but hold on to the substance-the reality. No matter whether the "calling upon the name of the Lord," be audible or not audible. We have witnessed both, and know not that there is any preference. Some two years ago, as we lowered a young lady into the waters of baptism, she said audibly, "Lord Jesus, save my soul!" This appeared very literally to fulfill the language of Scripture, and was certainly appropriate; but others, no doubt, were as acceptable who uttered nothing audible.

12/7/1858, vol.1, #49, page 195

Query– There are several good brethren here, and I presume there are many at other points, who are not able to reconcile the apparent differences in the genealogy of our Savior, as recorded by Matthew and Luke. I say *apparent* for they cannot be *real*. These brethren have requested me to write to you asking you to make the matter plain. Let us have an essay sufficiently elaborate to make the matter satisfactory to the commonest mind, if it can be done. It will be doing the good cause more service, than almost any thing else that could be done. They also ask that the "Millennial Harbinger" should copy this request, and that our much esteemed and talented brother A. Campbell should devote a sufficient space in his excellent paper to the proper elucidation of this matter. Will he comply, and thus gratify the wishes of his brethren in the Lord?

Answer– One thing that has caused an apparent difficulty touching the genealogy of Christ is, that inquirers are not aware of the fact, that Matthew traces the genealogy of Joseph from Abraham down, and that Luke traces the genealogy of Mary up to Adam. Matt 1. Luke 3. This will account in some degree, for the disagreement in names. They are evidently two distinct lines of genealogy, and the best authorities we can appeal to at present, give Matthew's to Joseph and the other to Mary, and it is clear to any one that one descends and that the other ascends. The best evidence we can command sustains the idea, that Matthew wrote at an earlier date than Luke, and that he took his genealogy from the Jewish records from Abraham to Joseph, as the Jews would be willing to believe their own records, and that when Luke wrote, Joseph had been adopted into the family of Heli, (Eli—the same) Joseph's father-in-law, some years, and consequently Luke copied the genealogy of Joseph through Heli, which was properly Mary's genealogy; up to Adam. There are however, difficulties in these genealogies which we presume no one can reconcile, but Matthew and Luke are not accountable for them, as they simply give these as the commonly received genealogies which those, in the day when they had the records to appeal to, never disputed. Had the Jews been able to involve the apostle and Luke in a contradiction, they, no doubt would willingly have done it, but this they could not do without disputing their own records. We cannot at present go into an elaborate exposition of the subject, as we have not room. We hope the clue we have hinted at will enable the friends to satisfy themselves.

Query–Please notice the following query: "In this was manifested the love of God toward us, because that God sent his only begotten Son into the world, that we might live through him." 1 John 4.9 "For this is the love of God, that we keep his commandments," 1 John 5.3

The sending of his only begotten Son, etc., and the keeping of his commandments, are these things, strictly speaking, love, or are they the result of effect or love?

Answer–God manifested *his love to us* in sending his Son into the world, that whoever believeth on him might not perish, but have everlasting life; and we manifest *our love to God* in keeping his commandments. The love of God resulted in sending his only begotten Son into the world. The love of God in us results in keeping the commandments of God; hence the Scripture says, "He who says he knows God, and keepeth not his commandments, is a liar." No man need deceive himself with the vain conceit that he loves God, who does not keep the commandments of God. "Hereby do we know that we know Him, if we keep his commandments."

8/10/1858, vol.1, #32, page 127.

Query–What became of Christ's body?

Answer–It was changed from a mortal to an immortal body. It was glorified, after which there was no "flesh and blood" about it. By the way, we love questions that look the prosperity of the cause and the salvation of the world, and have but little time for speculative questions. Study now to do the greatest possible amount of good in the shortest time? Time is short, and what is done must be done quickly.

5/8/60,vol.3, #19, page 75.

Query–1.Was Jesus Christ the son of God *before* he was born of the virgin Mary? 2. What was the character of his humanity? Did he inherit the nature which Adam had *before* the fall, or the nature which we have ever since the fall?

Answer–We have not gotten far enough in the book to find the answer to the above questions. We could have answered them twenty years ago, but can't now. We must be excused, and leave them for wiser heads.

5/8/60,v.3, #19, pg.75

Query–If it were not presuming too much, would you please enlighten me as well as many others in this vicinity, through the columns of the REVIEW, in regard to the difference of the account of Christ's pedigree as recorded by Matthew and Luke. Luke, in tracing Christ's descent, differs from Matthew both in number and the names of his forefathers. By throwing a little light on this subject, you will much oblige.

Answer–The genealogies given by Matthew and Luke are not the same. One is the genealogy of Joseph, and the other of Mary. The reason they do not give the same genealogy is, that Matthew wrote early and gave the genealogy of Joseph. Luke wrote at a later period, when Joseph had been adopted into the family of Mary, and he therefore gave the genealogy of her family. Not only so, but these genealogies were probably simply transcribed from the Jewish records, and if they contained any inaccuracy, the sacred writers were not responsible. The Jews regarded and received these genealogies, and that was sufficient for the purposes of the sacred writers.

5/8/60,v.3, #19, pg.75

Query–Where Paul represents Christ as saying to him, Acts 26.16, "I have appeared unto thee for this purpose, to make thee a minister and a witness both of these things which thou hast seen," etc. In what manner do we understand Christ as *appearing* unto Paul? Was it literal? Did he come personally within the range of human vision, and in a bodily form? In other words, did he appear to Paul in such a manner as to be seen by others had they been present? By answering the above, you will oblige a reader of the REVIEW.

Answer–Most certainly the appearing was literal, else Paul would not have said, "Have I not *seen* Jesus Christ our Lord." The Lord, when he appeared to him, said, "I have appeared to thee for this purpose, to make thee a minister and a witness both of *these things which thou hast seen* and of those things in which I will appear unto thee." The Lord appeared to him personally, so that he *saw* him and *heard the voice of his mouth.* We saw nothing in the case to put any person in mind of any other kind of an appearing than a *personal* one. He came in the range of his vision, so that he saw him, and in the range of his hearing so that he heard the voice of his mouth. See Acts chapters 22 and 26. This appearing and that when Stephen saw him standing on the right hand of God, or that when John saw him, in the island of Patmos, are not taken into the account, in that passage; "he shall appear a second time without a sin offering," etc., which is the only instance we now think of, where the term "second," is applied to his coming to raise the dead and judge the world.

4/1/62, v5, #13, pg.2

Query–Why was it necessary for Christ to die in order that man might be saved?

Answer–1. Because it pleased God, as a demonstration of the sinfulness of sin, to grant no remission without the shedding of blood; and, as a demonstration in the universe of the terrible nature of sin against God, it pleased God to make it impossible for sin to be taken away except by the precious blood of Jesus. Sin is so awful in the sight of God, that no offering could take away sin, and make reconciliation, but the one offering in the end of the ages to purge us forever from our sins. 2. Because no offering but the one made could impress the heart of man with the love of God to man. We love God because he first loved us. He so loved the world that he gave his only begotten Son, that he who believes in him might not perish, but have everlasting life. 3. The Infinite One may have many reasons which we can not see or give. We can receive statements of revelation, in regard to the divine procedure, even if we can not understand the reason. There are many things, in the procedure of our Heavenly Father, which we do not understand, which are clearly enough revealed, and which we most devoutly believe. There would be no respect to the divine authority in believing, if everything were demonstrated like a mathematical problem. We would believe things on their own merits. But we believe what our Lord says, *because he says it,* and not *because we understand it,* or the reason of it.

1/27/63, v.6, #3, pg.3

Query–Was not our Lord anointed with the Holy Spirit, immediately after his baptism to be a Prophet, Priest and King? Matthew 3.16–17; Acts 10.38

Answer–1. The first thing in order, is to determine the meaning of the question. What is intended by the words "to be a Prophet, Priest and King?" These words are not clear. They are liable to be taken to mean in two different ways. They might be understood to mean, to be a Prophet, Priest and King immediately, or from the anointing forward. We think the intention of the question is better expressed omitting the words, "to be." Was not our Lord anointed the Holy Spirit, a Prophet, Priest and King, immediately after his immersion? The intention, we take it, is to ascertain whether the Lord did not commence acting and officiating fully in his offices as Prophet, Priest and King, at the time of the descent of the Holy Spirit on him. If we are not correct in this, our worthy brother will correct us. So much for the definition of the question. With this definition, we answer, No. 2. The idea that the Savior was anointed Prophet, Priest and King, with the Holy Spirit, immediately after his immersion, is plausible, and has been received thousands of times for no other reason that its mere beauty and plausibility, Still, we know of no Scripture that teaches anything of the kind. That he was "anointed with the Holy Spirit and with power," we are clearly taught in Scripture. See Acts 10.31. That he received the Holy Spirit—that the Holy Spirit descended on him immediately after his immersion, is equally certain, but that this was intended to anoint him a Prophet, Priest and King, is not proved by any Scripture known to us. We have one clear intimation of the object of the descent of the Holy Spirit on him. John the Immerser said, "I know him not, but he who sent me to immerse said, On whomsoever you shall see the Holy Spirit descending and remaining on, is he." The intimation is clear from this, that the object of this wonderful descent of the Spirit, accompanied by the words of the Almighty Father, "This is my Son, the beloved, in whom I am well pleased," immediately after his emerging from his immersion in Jordan, was to manifest him, as the Son of God to Israel. Hence John the Immerser exclaims, "Behold the Lamb of God who takes away the sin of the world," and not "Behold your Prophet, Priest and King." The intention was to make him known to Israel, as their long-promised Messiah. We must take the divine intention and some modern theorist. 3. He was certainly a prophet, and more than a prophet. He was the Prophet of all the prophets—the one of whom Moses spoke, whom the Lord should raise up and he was a Prophet while on earth, but we know of no evidence that he was ever anointed prophet immediately after his immersion by the Holy Spirit. 4. He was prospectively Priest, not merely a priest, but the great High Priest forever after the order of Melchizedec; but he did not enter into his priestly office, act or officiate, as High Priest, while on earth; nor is there any evidence of his being anointed Priest immediately after his immersion, by the Holy Spirit, or by anything else. Paul says, Heb 8.4, "For if he were on earth, he should not be a priest, seeing that there are priests that offer gifts according to the law." He was the victim himself, the great sin-offering, in the end of the two ages, offered without blemish to God. He died without the gate. He entered not into the most holy place on earth, with the blood of bulls and goats, but into heaven itself, into the true holy place, which the Lord pitched and not man, with his own blood to appear in the presence of God for us and purge us forever from our sins. Here is where he officiates, or acts as Priest for us, and not on earth. No man can find an instance of his claiming to be a priest while on earth, or acting as priest. He waited till the law was ended, dead and taken out of the way, till the old priesthood was removed, when he entered his office as a priest forever; to officiate in the true holy place, in the presence of God. 5. He was prospectively, not only a King, but "*the King* of kings and Lord of lords," but not acting in his office, as King, while on earth, nor when put to death. He explained when on trial before Pilate, saying "My kingdom is not of this world; if my kingdom were of this world, then would my servants fight, that I should not be delivered to the Jews; but now is my kingdom not from hence." See John 18.36—When he died, and his disciples were dispersed, his reign had not commenced, but was only in prospect, and he was put to death to prevent the inauguration of his reign. But he ascended no throne, had no crown on his head but a crown of thorns, and inaugurated no reign while on earth. All done during the period of his lifetime, was preparatory; all the steps taken were incipient, and his own disciples did not understand the nature of the reign at hand, believe or understand the foundation facts of the Institution. They did not believe the Lord when he told them that he would be put to death, nor when he told them that he would rise from the dead. They never preached that Jesus would die, that he would shed his blood, or that he would rise from the dead, or even understood these things, during the Lord's personal ministry. During this whole period, they were expecting an earthly kingdom; and even after he rose from the dead and appeared to them, they said, "Lord, wilt thou restore the kingdom to Israel?" All they said and thought of his being King, was not in view of his being anointed King by the Holy Spirit immediately after his immersion, or any other time while he was on earth, but *prospectively*. They believed and preached as he taught them to do while here on earth, and as he also preached himself, that the *kingdom was at hand*. Consistently with this, he taught them to pray,

"Thy kingdom *come.*" This they never prayed after the kingdom *did come.* Many preachers are maintaining that the kingdom *did come* early in the lifetime of the Lord, and are praying for it *to come to this day!*

8/4/63,v.6,#31, p.122

Query–If the Messiah was not inaugurated King before his ascension, how was the prophecy, "Behold thy King cometh unto thee," (Zech 9.9) fulfilled, as recorded in Matt 21.1–4, and John 12.13–14?

Answer–He was their anticipated King, or their King *prospectively,* or *to be*; but certainly not yet inaugurated, reigning and acting in office of the King. Where had he been inaugurated? When? Let him who says, he had been inaugurated previous to this time, point to the *time* and *place.* Where is the account of any inauguration previous to this time? It is not sufficient to imagine an inauguration and claim it, when we have no account of it, but let it be pointed out.

8/4/63,v.6,#31, p.122

Query–If the kingdom was not set up before Pentecost, how could it be preached and men press into it before Christ was crucified? Luke 8.16

Answer–1. It could be preached precisely as Christ commanded, and as the apostle did preach, that it approached, was at hand, and thus prepare the public mind for it when it should come, and not as he did not command them to preach, as they never did preach, that the kingdom *had already come.* Certainly the Lord did not say, as he does, Mark 9.1, "There be some of them that stand here, who shall not taste of death till they have seen the kingdom of God come with power," knowing that they had already seen it, entered it, and introduced others into it. 2. The "pressing into it," only means *inquiring* into it, and not entering into it, for surely "every man" did not enter into it. Had "every man" entered into the kingdom at this period, we know not where Peter found his three thousand on Pentecost, five thousand in Solomon's portico, and the numerous other thousands still not *in the kingdom!*

8/4/63,v.6,#31, p.122

Query–I heard an old preacher say a few days ago, that "Christ was not now a king"—that he is now Mediator, and cannot act the capacity of

Mediator and King at the same time." Now, I am young in the ministry, have many things yet to learn, but have been in the habit of preaching Christ as Prophet, Priest and King, and if he is not a King, I want to know it. Will you please let me hear from you through the REVIEW.

Answer–The discovery that Christ is not a King, is one of the new and brilliant discoveries of soul-sleepers. Let us look at this marvelous negative discovery: 1. "These shall make war with the Lamb, and the Lamb shall overcome them: for he is Lord of Lords, and King of Kings." See Rev 17.14 This not only affirms that the Lamb, which is the Christ, is King, but "Lord of Lords and King of Kings." Paul says, 1 Tim 6.15. Who in his times shall show who is the blessed and only Potentate, the King of Kings and Lord of Lords." John and Paul, in these words, have substantially the same and evidently are speaking of the same person. John mentions the "Lamb" so that he leaves no doubt who he is speaking of, and John affirms that he is the "King of Kings" and Paul that he is "King of Kings." 2. If he is king he must have a kingdom. The disciples were taught in the lifetime of the Savior, to pray, "Thy kingdom come." They were never taught thus to pray after Christ ascended, and there is no account of their thus praying after that time. The plain fact in the case is, that they were taught to pray for the kingdom to come and did thus pray till it came, but never thus prayed after it came. 3. They were taught to preach that "the kingdom is at hand," while Christ was on earth, but did so preach but were not taught to preach that "the kingdom is at hand," after Jesus went to heaven, and never did, after that time, thus preach. The reason is, that they preached that the kingdom is at hand till it came and then never preached thus say more. 4. Matt 16.23, the Lord says:" There are some standing here who shall not taste of death till they see the Son of man coming in his kingdom." This kingdom was his kingdom— the Son of man's kingdom, and it was to come before some standing there were to die. He was to come, in *his* kingdom before they were to die. This was fulfilled. There is no kingdom without a king. When the kingdom came, he was the King in his kingdom. 5. Col 1.13, Paul says: "Who has delivered us from the power of darkness and has translated us into the kingdom of his dear Son." Paul and those to whom he was writing were in his kingdom when he wrote. They had been translated into it. This kingdom had come. It was Christ's kingdom. He was the King in this kingdom and is now. John, Rev 1.9, says, "John your brother and companions in tribulation, and *in* *the kingdom* and patience of Jesus Christ." Were they "in the kingdom" when there was no King nor kingdom? 6. There is no difficulty in Christ being both King and Mediator, say more than their is in this being both Mediator and Priest. He is certainly our great High Priest, goes into heaven to appear in the presence of God for us. So is he our Mediator and King.

4/9/67, v.x, #15, p.117

Query – Why do Matthew and Luke trace the lineage of Christ to Joseph the husband of Mary? We do not understand that Joseph was the father of Christ by blood relation, but by marriage to Mary which made him stepfather. Was Mary of the tribe of Judah, or some other tribe? Did Christ descend from the tribe of Judah by Mary and Joseph?

Answer – Joseph was the "supposed father" of Jesus, or the accredited father, among the Jews, in whom the lineage was counted. Matthew, in writing for Jews, traced the lineage from Abraham to Jesus. This line, as recorded by Matthew, was probably copied for the Jewish record of genealogy, through Jacob and *Judah.* See Matthew 1–2.

3/18/67, v.x,#13, p.52

Query – There seems to me to be a contention between Matthew and Luke as to who Joseph's father was. One says it was Heli; the other Jacob. A word from your pen on this subject would be interesting to many in this country.

Answer – Heli was the father of Joseph the husband of Mary, but as maintained by Lord A. Hervey, the latest investigator of the genealogy of Christ, the real brother of Jacob the father of Mary herself. The one was, then, the *real* father and the other the *adopted* father. This falls far short of a contradiction. The one was the real father and the other the father-in-law, the one the father of Joseph and the other the father of Mary. If our memory is not at fault, this is one of Paine's contradictions in the Bible. 7/15/73, v.16, #28, p.220

QUESTIONS ABOUT THE SCRIPTURES

Query-Where did Moses become the Advocate for the Children of Israel? Before he crossed the Red Sea, or not till after? Some say before; some say they sang the song of deliverance, and some not till he received the law on Sinai.

Answer—Moses became the leader of the Israelites as soon as they started to follow him. He became their advocate as soon as he took their cause in hand and advocated it before the court of Pharaoh. As their leader and advocate he obtained their emancipation at the crossing of the Red Sea. There "They were all immersed into Moses in the cloud and in the sea." He became their lawgiver when he gave them the law at Mount Sinai, and was then the mediator of the First Covenant, or the Old Institution. An *attorney* is an *advocate*, and he became their attorney when he received a commission from God to go before them and lead them out of the land of Egypt and from their bondage. As such he was also their deliverer, obtained for them their freedom, and made them a separate and independent nation, putting them under a law of their own, and he was their governor or ruler.

July 29, 1873, vol.16, #30, page 236

Query—What are we to understand by 2 Cor 14.18?

Answer—It is not our province to tell any man *how he is to understand*; but we suppose the brother simply wished us to give what we consider the import of the passage to which he has referred. This we are willing to do—The first expression of the passage is, "Be ye not unequally yoked together with unbelievers." This command has been most commonly applied to marriage, but we see nothing in the text or context to confine it to marriage any more than any other inappropriate and unphilosophical relation between believers and unbelievers. The allusions to idols, verse 16, seems to intimate that the relation prohibited, in this passage was in some way connected with idols; yet the whole scope of the apostles reasoning goes to show how unprofitable and irrational any intimate relation with the profane and infidel must prove. Nothing can be more absurd and unreasonable, than for the Holy Spirit of God, to be closely and intimately connected so as to be a chief companion with a profane, immoral and infidel person, uncongenial spirits can never dwell in harmony together. From verses 17 and 18 it will be seen that Christians are commanded to "come out from among them," which goes to show the inapplicability of the passage to the marriage state, as the Lord does not require persons to depart from the state in any case. But they were to come out from some unholy relation, which they were in the habit of entering into, with the idolaters, in order to the assurance that God would be a Father to them, and they would be his sons and daughters. In this passage, there is then, a most solemn admonition to all Christians, not to form any relations leading into evil, with the ungodly and profane, yet, on the other hand, there are relations which we must sustain to wicked men, or else, as the apostle has expressed it, "we must needs go out of this world."

Western Reformer March 1848 vol.6 #5, page 310.

Query—If it is agreeable with your feelings, please give your opinion on the first of John, 2 chap. 10th verse, also 5 chap. 18 verse. And much obliged.

Answer—The foregoing difficulty has perhaps puzzled more persons than any other text, and has been a rallying point, for skeptics to the no little confusion of many honest believers. How is it that he who is born of God *"cannot sin* and at the same time, if any man shall say he hath no sin, he deceiveth himself, &c. This is similar to the difficulty in the case where Christ *could not* perform many miracles in a certain place because of the unbelief of the Jews. Yet when they were the most unbelieving and hard hearted he declared that he *could* command twelve legions of angels to his rescue. There is a certain principle of interpretation which has been almost entirely overlooked, which most clearly settles all such difficulties as the foregoing. Just put the word *consistently* after the phrase *can not*, as being understood or implied, and it will give the exact sense of all such passages. Thus: "He that is born of God—can not consistently sin, that is, he can not sin *consistently with his profession, as a*

Christian. One verse on another subject will fully illustrate and confirm this view of the subject. Then said the rulers—"What shall we do to these men? For that indeed notable miracle hath been done by them is manifested to all them that dwell in Jerusalem and we *can not* deny it." Acts 4.16. That is, we can not *consistently* deny it, for no one thinks for a moment that they had not the power to deny any fact however incontrovertible, had they been as inconsistent as some others were in those days. Hence the word *consistently* must of necessity be understood in all such cases.

Western Reformer August 1849, vol.7, #8, page 502.

Query—Will you be so much bothered as to give, an explanation of Rev 11.3–14? An answer to this will much oblige many brethren.

Answer-We have read the passage cited above many times and now have read it over again, and examined several commentaries on it and all we are willing to say about it is, that we find no explanation that we think, any thing more than mere speculation, nor did we ever pretend to understand it, and of course, cannot explain it. We are inclined to think it is *yet too far over* in the book for young learners. If however, any one can throw any light on it, we will gladly print it.

Western Reformer Oct. 49, vol.7, #9, page

Query—What is taught in John 1.1–3 and 14? "In the beginning was the Word, and the Word was with God, and the Word was God. The same was in the beginning with God. All things were made by him; and without him was not anything made that was made. In him was light; and the life was the light of man * * * And the Word was made flesh, and dwelt among us, (and we beheld his glory as of the only begotten of the Father,) full of grace and truth."

Answer—It is taught that Jesus Christ, the only-begotten of the Father and Son of Mary, pre-existed his existence in the flesh. He was of the seed of David, according to the flesh, which he received of his mother Mary. He was therefore human, like his mother, and as human as she: but as he was declared to be the Son of God with power, by the Spirit of Holiness, and the resurrection from the dead, he is Divine like his Father, and as Divine as He. See Rom 1.3–4. In the flesh, when the Apostles *saw* his glory of the Only begotten Son of the Father, full of grace and truth, Jesus was a *Son*, and as a Son he partook of the nature of his parents; he was, therefore, both divine and human. But before he dwelt among them in the flesh, he was not a Son, and was wholly divine, he was God, and was with God, in the beginning and as he was not created, he was the Creator, all things were made by him and for him. To bring heaven and earth together, we need a mediator, who is equally, in nature and experience, allied to both; in other words, we need the Word made flesh. To avoid all complaint and misunderstanding as far as possible, we should express ourselves in scriptural terms and be especially careful not to push aside a sacred phrase for one of modern coinage. The Scripture expressions are current, and also intelligible—more intelligible than any I have seen, and they are authoritative. I can see nothing gained either to God or man by undervaluing the meaning of these terms, and depreciating the true dignity of our common Savior and Lord.

Proclamation & Reformer 1850

Query—I have a query or two to ask you, through the REVIEW, if you prefer to do so, for the benefit of others as well as myself. Previous to my coming here, an idea got into the head of one or more of the brethren, in regard to the Lord's supper, like this: They affirm that because the testimony tells us that "Jesus took bread, and when he had given thanks he *broke it.* And because Paul *broke bread* at Troas, etc., that the primitive custom, and hence the proper mode, is for the administrator to break the bread into little pieces, ready to be eaten. That because the word of Christ, or the Apostles does not say that each one broke it for himself, therefore, from all we can gather, it is not for him to do. A portion of the church adopt this idea, and even practice it, and it has created some feeling, though not an anti-Christian feeling. Will you give us your conclusions and grounds of proof, either briefly or in extenso.

Answer—The above is certainly a small matter, but still matters of no more importance have caused much trouble. The desire to have something new troubles a great many brethren. The above is certainly a mere matter of propriety. We can not endure the idea of going into all the reasons now; but to us, the idea of a brother breaking the bread into small morsels, savors of the Romish custom of putting the wafer upon the tongue, and is ridiculous. It is certainly much more becoming, simply to break the loaf in two, or if there be four deacons, as in some large churches, break it into four pieces.

I presume that when we get a new version of the English Scriptures, that the Greek word *arlos*, translated "bread" in the common version, will be translated *loaf*, as it is in many places. The Lord took a *loaf*, and gave it to the disciples. The idea of breaking it into small pieces is as ridiculous as if, in eating at a friend's table, he would break the bread into small bits. The idea of having more than one loaf, as we have seen in a few instances, is equally absurd. We have one loaf to represent one body.

August 1858, vol1.

Query – Will you please to give, in your next issue, your understanding of Matt 7.6 (?)

Answer – We suppose the intention of this passage is simply to caution the disciples not to attempt to present the pure and holy principles of the gospel before men wholly debased and degraded, who evidently would only despise them and ridicule them to their faces. What would it amount to, should the disciple attempt to present the good things of the kingdom to a company of tippers in a drinking house? What good could result from introducing the good news of the kingdom in many of the dens of dissipation and corruption prevalent, only to have them despised and the disciples insulted and abused? The Lord intended that his disciples should have prudence and discretion, so as not to present the precious matters of the kingdom where it is evident they would only be condemned. This he expresses by the bold and strong figure: "Give not that which is holy to dogs, neither cast ye your pearls before swine, but they trample them under their feet and turn again and rend you."

5/8/60,vol.3, #19, pg.75

Query – I see in your paper that you propose to answer queries. You will please not think it amiss that I ask your views on the third chapter and 9th verse of first John, upon which there has been much division of opinion, and which seems to be a portion of Holy Writ that is very difficult to understand, inasmuch as the first chapter and 8th verse seems to clash, to the mind of a great many persons. We wish your views on the first passage mentioned, which is 1 John 3.9, and taking in consideration the second.

Answer – The import of this Scripture is not that it is an impossibility for them to commit sin, but they can not *consistently with their new relation and confession.*

5/1/60,vol.3,#18,pg.71

Query – Did John, when in prison, deny or forget Jesus? If he did, where is the evidence that he was an inspired man, chosen of God to be the forerunner of Jesus, and to prepare the world for the coming church of the Savior? John 1.29–34, he has the evidence of God. Notwithstanding all this evidence, it appears that John had forgot who Jesus was; for he sent two of his disciples to inquire whether he was the one that should come or they should look for another." See Matt 11.2–3. I am but a boy and my friends could not explain this matter to me.

Answer – John, like all others of that period, was slow to understand, and his inspiration did not give him an understanding to comprehend and interpret revelations, but simply to *make them.* He did not deny Christ nor forget him, but lying in prison, where he saw and heard nothing of what was going on, he became a little unsettled touching the question whether he was actually the promised Messiah, or they should look for another. John was not sent to "prepare the *world*" for the coming church, but to prepare *the way before* the Lord, or to *prepare a people* for him, among the Jews who are called "his own." The fact that any divine messenger does not understand every thing, is no evidence that he has no divine mission. He should understand and be able to fill his own mission, He should understand and be able to fill his own mission, but his not understanding beyond that is divine mission. John prepared a people for the Lord, prepared his way before him, and thus filled his own mission; but beyond that his understanding was very limited, as the time had not yet come for these things to be clear.

5/1/60,vol.3,#18,pg.71

Query – Please explain, through the REVIEW, the meaning of James 5.14–15. What the oil is, spoken of there; and about the prayer of faith shall save the sick, whether they will be healed from their sick bed, or whether that has not reference to their being saved if they should die, and if he have committed sins they shall be forgiven him.(?)

Answer – This has reference to the age of miracles. At that time special judgments were visited upon persons, as in the case of Ananias and

Sapphira, as visible evidences of God's displeasure. In these cases, it was proper to call for the elders to pray for them, and if they confessed their sins, the Lord answered the prayer and raised them up. It is, however, proper now to pray for the sick, but not with the expectation of their being healed by a *miracle*, but for the blessing of Heaven upon them. The Lord will answer the prayers of the righteous still, but not by miracle, and not in particular manner that the suppliant may prescribe, frequently, but in *some way better for them*. The command, "Pray without ceasing," is still in force.

5/1/60,vol.3,#18,pg.71

Query–Please give us your views on 1 Cor 7.14, "For the unbelieving husband is sanctified by the wife, and the unbelieving wife is sanctified by the husband, else were your children unclean, but now are they holy."

Answer–This question only relates to the legitimacy of the children. Some had maintained, that one of the parties not belonging to the church, or being an unbeliever, vitiated the marriage of the offspring, as was considered the case among the Jews.

5/1/60,vol.3,#18,pg.71

Query–In the 15th verse of 1 Corinthians... "But if the unbelieving depart, let him depart; a brother or sister is not under bondage in such cases, but God has called us to peace." What does this mean?

Answer–If the unbelieving husband departed from or left the wife, on account of her religion, in that case she was not bound to him as a husband.

5/1/60,vol.3,#18,pg.71

Query–How are we to understand Luke 16 and 9? "And I say unto you, make to yourselves friends of the mammon of unrighteousness; that when ye fail, they may receive you into everlasting habitations." Is there ambiguity in this language, so as to render it difficult to decide between three constructions? 1. Does the Savior imperatively enjoin on the disciples to secure the friendship of conniving individuals, after the manner of the shrewd but unjust steward, as a means of procuring sustenance for their declining years? 2. Does the Savior interrogate the disciples, for the purpose of distinguishing between the purpose of distinguishing between the characters of crafty, unscrupulous and ungodly sinners, seeking worldly security only, and the upright and pious demeanor of the disciples—whose business it is to lay up treasures in heaven—something after this manner: Do you, my disciples, make to yourselves friend of the mammon of unrighteousness, that when ye fail [become old and infirm] ye also may be taken into the families of your rich neighbors, and board out what should have been in justice paid to their or your creditors? 3. Was it an irony? A discourse with the disciples, in the hearing of the Pharisees, preparatory to administering a cutting rebuke to that proud and self-righteous sect? Please favor us with your views on the above.

Answer—The language is certainly not ambiguous, yet the application of the parable has justly been considered difficult. Still, we think the meaning is surely not the first or second, as act out above. We have inclined to the opinion that the intention was simply an admonition for those possessing wealth, to act wisely in making a good use of it, so as to please the Lord, and thus secure everlasting habitations. Still, we admit that this never appeared entirely clear and satisfactory. On reviewing the connection, we think it highly that it was intended as a most cutting irony, in stating precisely that of which many of those who heard him were really guilty, in a little bolder more unvarnished and glaring terms than they were accustomed to hear, and thus exposing them. The language that follows justifies this. He that is faithful in that which is least, is faithful also in much; and he that is unjust in the least, is unjust also in much. If therefore you have not been faithful in the unrighteous mammon who will commit to your trust the true riches? We admit, however, that the application is difficult.

2/18/62 v.5, #7, pg.2

Query—There is a desire for an answer from you in your paper, to a question or two predicated of the 19th and 20th verses of 1st. Timothy 5th chapter: 1. What is the extent of the power of an evangelist in the building and organization of a church? 2. After a congregation is organized, has an evangelist authority over the officers of the church? These questions may have been often answered in our papers, but a repeated answer may do good.

Answer–1. We do not now recollect anything about the *power or authority* of evangelists, in the New Testament. In the nature of the case, in planting a congregation in a new place, the whole matter begins with the acting evangelist. He acts at first as evangelist, overseer, and deacon. When the time comes for appointing officers, he would naturally be consulted, give advice, and assist in every way in his power, in setting in order the things that are wanting. 2. We know of no ground for evangelists claiming authority over churches in order, with their proper officers. An evangelist has no right to attempt to preach in any congregation in order, or assist them in any way, or meddle with their operations, unless *invited by them so to do*. When evangelists are in the congregation, they belong to the congregation, and must be subject to the congregation. They certainly have no authority over the officers of congregations, but when in a congregation, they should be subject to the officers, and work in co-operation with them. This whole matter is easily adjusted. If officers are disposed to exercise improper authority over an evangelist, when he is in their midst, or make themselves disagreeable to him in any way, all the trouble he need be at, is to seek some more agreeable place to labor. If an evangelist desires to exercise undue authority, and thus renders himself disagreeable, the church can dispense with his services and procure a more congenial spirit. Those Diotrephes who are always in so much trouble about their *authority* and *power*, are the last men who can exercise much authority or power any place among the brethren. They have no use for that stamp of men. They are the material out of which to manufacture arch bishops, cardinals and popes. In the church of God, we have no such consequentials, either as overseers or evangelists.

4/27/62, v.5, #17, pg.2

Query–Who are the foreknown, as found in Rom 8.29–34 inclusive? You will confer a favor by answering the above for your Brother in Christ.

Answer–They were the distinguished persons whom God from the beginning had marked out, through whom, according to his eternal purpose, he would make known his will to man. His purpose was, in the fullness of time, to make known to man his will in the gospel of his Son. This purpose, in a very brief and abridged form was expressed in the promise to Abraham. It was more fully expressed by sundry prophets; but finally unfolded and developed in detail by the apostles. Abraham stands at the head of the long list of those whom God foreknew, predestinated, called, justified and glorified through whom in numerous prophecies, revelations and finally the full and complete glory of the gospel of Christ appeared to man. Numerous prophets fall into the train all along down from Abraham, believing the promise, and in one form or other, speaking of the good things to come, ministering not to themselves, but showing that God had provided some better things for us, during a space of fifteen centuries. After a space of from three hundred and fifty to four hundred years, of intermission in prophecy, John the Baptist, falls into the train of the predestinated, called, justified, and glorified train, of scripture, or *before marked out*, or before designated, or described, as the elect of God, through whom he would bless the world, with a full revelation of his will, in the gospel of his Son. The apostles also belong to the same list, for Paul says, "He hath chosen us in him before the foundation of the world," and "predestinated us to the adoption as children by Jesus Christ to himself, according to the good pleasure of his will." Again he says, "To me, who am less than the least of all saints is this grace given"—this grace of election, or apostleship—"that I should preach among the Gentiles the unsearchable riches of Christ, and to make all men see what is the fellowship of the mystery which from the beginning of the world hath been hid in God who created all things by Jesus Christ.

When Christ rose from the dead, the first born from the dead of every creature, a vast host of these elect persons, ancient worthies, of whom Paul says the world was not worthy, immediately followed him in the resurrection, and he was literally "the first born(from among the dead) among many brethren." These were God's elect, before designated, justified, and many of them, when Paul was speaking of them, risen from the dead, and glorified with their Lord.

According to the purpose of God, to send the Savior, give the Christian religion to the world, the prophets, leading persons and distinguished men, whom the Lord employed in the great work in the gradual unfolding of the divine benevolence to man, were before marked out in the divine mind, in due time called, justified, in God's divine approval of them during their work by miracles, raised from the dead immediately after Jesus rose and glorified. They were not elected for *their own glory* or happiness, but for the benefit of the world as the instruments through whom God made known his will to man.

4/27/62, v.5,#17, pg.2

Query – There is considerable controversy in regard to the analysis of the commission, Matt 28.19. Will you be so kind as to analyze it, and also inform us whether or not you consider it an elliptical sentence? By so doing you will confer a great favor.

Answer – The sentence is certainly elliptical. The words *to do* or *to teach* must be supplied. It is either "Teaching them all things whatsoever I have command you *to do* or "all things whatsoever I have command you *to teach*." The latter is evidently the meaning. The apostles surely did not command the young converts to observe or practice all things which the Lord commanded the apostles *to do*; but all things which he commanded the apostles *to teach* the disciples *to practice*.

4/29/62, v.5,#17, pg.2

Query – We read, Matt 21.44, "Whosoever shall fall on this stone, shall be broken; but whoever it shall fall on, it will grind him to powder." Who were the characters who should fall on this stone? And who those on whom it should fall?

Answer – We do not feel very confident that we understand precisely the force of this very highly figurative expression. There can, however, be no doubt about the "stone," here spoken of, as it comes from the language of Isaiah, which the Lord had just quoted. "The chief corner stone"—the "rock of offense"—"the foundation"—are different forms of expression, amounting to the same. Christ is the rock—the stone of offense—the foundation. There were those among the Jews, well meaning people, comparatively innocent, but so blinded, prejudiced and misguided, that Christ was to them a "stone of stumbling," a "rock of offense." They stumbled at the teaching of the Messiah, and fell. These were probably those who fell on the rock and were broken, or bruised. There were those who were mad and infuriated, who attacked, assailed, maligned and blasphemed the rock—the anointed. On these the rock fell in terrible and awful judgments—crushed them and sunk them in ruin. If anyone has any thing better than this, we are ready to receive it.

4/29/62, v.5,#17, pg.2.

Query – I also wish to call your attention to a passage of scripture, Rom 5.7. "Scarcely for a righteous man will one die. Yet, peradventure for a good man some would even dare to die." Which is the better, a *good* or a *righteous* man?

Answer – Some of the commentators make a distinction, as in the case of Barnes, who makes a *good* man the better. But we doubt whether the apostle intends a different man at all, by the variation from a righteous to a good man.

4/29/62, v.5,#17, pg.2.

Query – I wish that you would be so kind as to explain Luke 23.31–32: "And the Lord said, Simon, Simon, behold Satan hath desired to have you, that he may sift you as wheat; but I have prayed for thee, that thy faith fail not: and when thou art converted, strengthen thy brethren." What did our Savior refer to, by the term conversion? When did it take place, and how does it apply to the present day?

Answer – No doubt, the Savior here had allusion to the time when Peter would deny him. The word "convert," means *turn,* and the Lord says, "when you are turned, strengthen your brethren." The question then is, in what sense did he turn? We suppose he simply turned from his great error and sin, which he fell into when he denied the Savior, and turned from the confidence he had in the Lord being a mere civil ruler, and his kingdom a mere temporal and civil government, to the belief in the Lord as he was, not a mere civil ruler, but a crucified, buried, but now risen Lord, and a kingdom not of this world. The word convert, as the original word from which it comes, means *turn,* and converted, means *turned.* When convert is used in a religious sense, it means *turned to the Lord.* Any person going wrong, who is turned the other way, or turned right, is converted. Indeed, to turn any way is to convert. When Peter, in the case at hand, had turned from wrong to right, he was converted. When a man is turned to the Lord, he is converted. The turning, however, in the case of Peter, was not precisely the same as in the case of some one now turning to the Lord. The turning, in any case, no matter what it may be, is the conversion. In the case of Peter, we simply should examine what sense it was in which he turned, or what he turned from, and what he turned to, in order to understand the sense in which he was converted. The same is true in any other case.

8/26/62, v.5, #34, pg. 2.

Query—Was it the practice of women, (sisters of course) to speak and pray in social meetings of the Saints in apostolic times? Also give us an exposition of the 4th and 5th verses of the 11th chapter of Paul's first letter to the Corinthians, the sort of head covering referred to, and proof of the practice in question. If it was then, the practice, why should it not now be the practice? Please answer through the REVIEW at your earliest convenience, and you will much oblige men of the hyper-critical and *uneasy* on these points.

Answer—It was evidently common for women to pray and speak in the worship, in the time of the apostles, otherwise we can see no reason for the apostle saying what he did about their praying or prophesying the *head uncovered*. It is a fact that the Spirit was poured out on the "handmaidens," and that they *prophesied*. The praying and prophesying with the *head uncovered*, must have reference to acts performed in the presence of others, or in some sort of companies. We doubt not that a vast amount of the worship in the time of the apostles, was conducted in small companies, met in private homes, in underground rooms and the most obscure places they could find. The companies thus met were frequently small, compromising a small part of what was called "the church in Corinth "the church at Rome," etc. Indeed, we find no account of more than one congregation in one city, in the time of the apostles. These did not all meet in the same house, or place of worship. We have no doubt that in some of the small companies, everywhere meeting, two and three times a week, for prayers, exhortation and songs, women prayed and prophesied. But when important questions were pending in the church, discussions in reference to them were in progress and important decisions to make in reference, sometimes, to the most scandalous and disgraceful things that ever occur among the people of God, they were not permitted to speak, nor to arrogate to themselves authority, but if they would inquire anything, ask their husbands at home. In any of our small meetings for prayers, exhortations, songs, etc., the sisters should participate in both the prayers and exhortations; but in the more extended assemblies for the public edification of the people at large, or when church matters are under investigation and important questions at issue, they should be in silence. We doubt that in Paul's time, they had some of those masculine women, like our modern clerical ladies, on a mission of "Woman's Rights," who were repulsive to all refined people and enlightened minds, who were a disgrace to the church of Christ. But these are the whole breadth of the heavens from those holy women, of deep and unfeigned piety, who prayed and prophesied in the first church, or those who participate in the worship in our time.

8/26/62, v.5, #34, pg. 2.

Query–I should be pleased to have you give an exposition of the parable used by our Savior, recorded in Matthew 13 chapter and 33rd verse which reads thus: "The kingdom of heaven is like unto leaven which a woman took and hid in three measures of meal till the whole was leavened." The following deserve attention: 1. What does the "leaven" represent? 2. What do the three "measures" represent? 3. What does the "meal" represent? Please answer through the *Weekly* REVIEW. I heard the following a few evenings ago: 1. The leaven represents Christ. 2. The three measures of leaven represents three measures of time as follows: The first measure embraces all that period of time from Adam to Moses. The second from Moses to Christ, and the third from Christ till the end of time. The meal representing the people during the time of the above named periods. Now, is this the true meaning of the parable, as used by Him that "spake as never man spake?"

Answer–There is no greater absurdity, in attempting to explain the parables of our Savior, than the attempt to find so many points of analogy. The Lord never intended, in any one of His parables, to represent a dozen, or even half that number of features, or points in His kingdom. There was more sense in the saying of Wesley than many think. He said he could explain any text in five minutes, *if he understood it.* Any man can explain the parable of the leaven and meal, or any other parable of or Lord, in five minutes, if he understands it. In these parables there is generally, if not always, but one point of analogy. In what, then, is the kingdom of heaven like leaven hid in three measures of meal? Simply in its tendency to *spread through the world and permeate all its parts*, as the leaven does through the meal. There is nothing else in it. As to the imaginary twaddle about the three measures of meal representing three periods of time, the Patriarchal, Jewish and Christian, it reminds one of the fanciful guessing, imaginary applications and silly interpretations of Baldwin, in his catch-penny appeal to American pride, in his book, styled "Armageddon," or, "The United States in Prophecy." We prefer to admit that we do not know what a prophecy means, sooner than to adopt such loose and idle fancies, subject to no rule of interpretation, or authority in the world.

11/25/62, v.5, #47, pg.2

Query – How, when, and for what purpose did Christ preach "unto the spirits in prison?"

Answer – 1. "In the days of Noah, while the ark was preparing." See 1 Peter 3.20. 2. "That they might be judged according to men in the flesh, but live according to God in the Spirit." See 1 Peter 3.6.

8/26/62, v.5, #34, pg.2

Query – I heard a D.D. (Doctor of Divinity kdf.) a few days ago, explaining the 12th. verse of the 17th. chapter of John's Gospel, and he advocated the doctrine of some being lost by the determinate counsel and foreknowledge of God, saying that of all, God gave Christ, none were lost, but Judas, the son of perdition, was lost, contending that the conjunction "but" indicated this, and assuming that Christ did not die for some part of men. Would you be kind enough to give your views through the columns of your excellent paper?

Answer – 1. A man who does not believe that Christ died for all, does not believe his Bible. That's what's the matter with him, for Paul says, "We thus judge, that if one died for all, then were all dead." 2 Cor 5.14. 2. A man who does not believe that those for whom Christ died may be lost, does not believe his Bible. See the following: "Destroy not him with thy meat for whom *Christ died*." Rom 14.15. "But there were false prophets also among the people, even as there shall bring in damnable heresies, even denying the Lord that *bought then, and bring upon themselves swift destruction.*" 2 Pet 2.1. "Judas *by transgression fell,*" and he was one that was given to Christ. See Acts 1.25. "When the righteous turneth away from his righteousness and committeth iniquity, and doeth according to all the abominations that the wicked man doeth, shall he live? All his righteousness that he hath done shall not be mentioned; in his trespass that he hath trespassed, and in his sin that he hath sinned in them shall he die." Ezek 18.24. This is enough for any man who believes his Bible, and it is no use to quote Scripture to a man who does not believe his Bible.

11/6/63, v.6, #1, p.2

Query– By the request of some of our colleagues, I want you, if you please, to give us a discourse on 1 Cor 16.22.

Answer– The passage referred to, reads as follows: "If any man love not the Lord Jesus Christ let him be anathema maran-atha. This is a wonderful expression and much might be said in reference to it; but we have but little leisure now and can devote but little time to it. Besides, we know nothing of the points on which information is sought. What we say, must, therefore, be said without any idea what the object was in requesting us to discourse on the subject. 1. A portion of this important expression is comparatively lost to the world by the failure to translate it into our own language. The important words "anathema maran-atha," are foreign. We are now from home, and where we have no authority to which we can infer; but our best recollection is, that when the whole passage is fairly rendered, it will read as follows: "If any man love not the Lord Jesus Christ, he shall be accursed when the Lord comes." If we are right in this, the authority the Romanists claim to derive from this, for anathematizing, or *cursing* men, does not have the plausibility of the common version. Paul does not pray that the curse may come upon the man who loves not the Lord; but simply declares that it shall come. 2. The ground of this curse coming is that men love not the Lord Jesus Christ. We take it that this expression is metonymical, or a common figure of speech, in which a part is mentioned for the whole. Love not our Lord Jesus Christ, includes the whole matter of being a devoted follower of Christ. It includes all that pertains to being a Christian. When the Scriptures say the Lord will take vengeance on "them who obey not the gospel," the words "obey not the gospel," include all who are not Christians. They who obey the gospel, love the Lord and comply with all that constitutes the Christian. In the same way, those who love the Lord Jesus Christ, obey the gospel and do everything else that constitutes the Christian. 3. The curses to come upon them who love not the Lord Jesus Christ, is future. It is not something upon them now, but something that shall come upon them in the future. 4. The curse shall come on them *when the Lord comes.* 5. The Lord will come at the resurrection of the dead, and consequently the curse will come on the man who loves not the Lord Jesus Christ at that time. "As by Adam all die, even so by Christ shall all be made alive," or raised from the dead; "but every man in his own order;" that is, when the ellipsis is filled up, every man shall be raised from the dead in his own order "Christ the first fruits"; that is, Christ the first fruits shall be made alive, or raised from the dead; "afterward they who are Christ's at his coming;" or, when the ellipsis is filled; "they who are Christ's *shall be raised from the dead at his coming.*" This shows beyond successful contradiction, that the resurrection of those who are Christ's will take place at his coming. The curse, or anathema, will come on the man who loves not the Lord Jesus Christ, "when the Lord comes." 6. This, then, can be no curse in the present state, unless it shall be the destruction of the of the world by fire, and those who love not the Lord Jesus Christ with it—This may be the case, and the resurrection of the wicked may follow after it, with the final judgment and the second death, when the wicked shall go away into everlasting punishment and the righteous into life eternal. All these things will occur in the right order, at the right time and everything be conducted in the right manner, whether we can understand *how it will be* or not. 7. Men should be careful and love the Lord Jesus Christ ,and do his commandments, that they may avoid this wonderful anathema when the Lord comes. Let us love our Lord Jesus Christ with our whole hearts.

2/3/63, v.6, #4, p.2.

Query–Your hearers last night, have different opinions as to your ideas on one point. Will you please explain briefly? 1st. Did you mean, by change of state or relation, justification? And if so, did you mean by justification a change in the relation of the individual to the Church (or Gospel kingdom of Christ on earth) or to God? i.e. did you use the term justification in an ecclesiastical or theological sense? 2nd. In what order do conversion, repentance, remission of sins, and baptism take place, according to your belief? 3rd. Is baptism an essential antecedent condition of remission of sins? 4th. Please explain Romans 5.1. 5th. Is the doctrine of total depravity as taught by the Methodist and Presbyterian Churches, in agreement with your views of the Scriptures?

Answer–1. I mean, by "a change of state, or relation," as I thought I stated with all possible distinctness and clearness, the transfer from the world into Christ, or into Christ's Church, or kingdom, of the person previously changed in heart by faith, and changed in life by repentance, and that this is equivalent to the transfer into a state of justification. 2. According to the New Testament, the order in turning to the Lord, of the several items, is 1. Faith, 2. Repentance, 3. Baptism, 4. Remission of sins, 5. The impartation of the Holy Spirit. A man is not converted, or in full turned to the Lord, in the New Testament sense, till he has gone through the entire process, or completed the last item.3. According to the New Testament, baptism, is an antecedent, or condition, to be complied with, before man is promised the remission of sins. If any person knows of any *non-essential* antecedents, or conditions, of remission of sins, in the New Testament, I should be pleased to hear them pointed out. 4. The only explanation I can now give of Rom 5.1, is that the justification there mentioned, is not justification by the act of believing *alone*, which would exclude the grace of God and the blood of Christ; but that justification is by the faith of Christ in connection with the grace of God, the blood of Christ and everything else in the Divine process, as found in the New Testament, and not by the works of the law of Moses. 5. The doctrine of total hereditary depravity, as taught by the Methodist and Presbyterian Churches, is not Scriptural. That man is sinful, and that the Lord has included him under sin—in unbelief—that he might have mercy upon all, and that man cannot be saved without his mercy, is true, or that man has gone "very far from original righteousness," is equally true. But this falls far short of *total hereditary depravity*. The foregoing questions were handed to us a few minutes before starting to meeting one evening during our visit in Athens, Ohio, with the request that we should read them to our audience and answer them before preaching. We sat down and hastily wrote off the above answer, and before preaching read the questions and answers to the audience. We knew that the questions were written by Dr. Blair, Professor in the College in Athens, and a Methodist preacher, and spoken of, so far as we heard, as the most talented member of the faculty, if not the most talented preacher of the place. This, connected with the fact that Athens is the Jerusalem of Methodism in this region of country, gives to these questions sufficient importance to demand some additional attention. We do not see any necessity for any fuller answer than we gave on the spur of the moment to the first and second questions. But on the answer to the third question, we desire to amplify somewhat. "Is baptism an essential antecedent condition of remission of sins?" This is a singular question, and appears to have been framed with great labor. If baptism is an antecedent of remission of sins at all, the Lord made it such, and if the Lord made it an antecedent of remission, would Dr. Blair, or any man regarding the authority of the Lord, take the responsibility of placing it subsequent to remission, and decide that it is *not an essential antecedent?* Or, if the Lord has placed it after remission of sins, can any man who respects Divine authority place it before remission of sins, and make it *an essential antecedent?* Or, still farther, and to elicit light, is it essential that the order the Lord has established shall be maintained? Or may we change that which the Lord has made antecedent, and make it subsequent? If baptism is a condition at all, the Lord made it such; and if the Lord made a condition, can man dispense with it, and thus render a condition which the Lord made *non-essential.* In one word, is there not an effort, in the use of the word "essential," to prejudice the case? Is there really anything to inquire into, on the part of the sincere person, who desires simply to know and do the will of the Lord, or are there any questions but the following, touching this matter: Is baptism antecedent to the remission of sins? Is baptism a condition of remission of sins? If it is antecedent to, or a condition of remission of sins, the Lord made it such, and then the only question that this word "essential" involves is whether it is essential that the law of God should be as the Lord ordained, or as the Lord made it. He who says it is not essential that the law of God should be maintained as he made it, admits that man may alter the law of God with impunity. A good and obedient man, when he finds a commandment of God, never inquires whether it is essential. His only question is, doth the Lord command? If the Lord commands, it is right for man to obey, and he who obeys is safe. It is wrong to disobey, and he who thus does wrong cannot prove that he is safe. It is wrong to disobey, and he who thus does wrong cannot prove that he is safe. If, then, the Lord has made baptism antecedent to the remission of sins, or a condition, then it is right that it should so stand in practice, and he who loves and fears God will not inquire whether it is an *essential* antecedent, or condition; but simply whether it is an antecedent, or condition. But "an *antecedent* condition of remission of sins" implies that there may be *subsequent* conditions of remission of sins! If baptism is a condition of remission of sins at all, it is certainly an *antecedent*, and not a *subsequent* condition. Throwing out all useless verbiage, then, we have nothing to inquire, except as follows: *Does baptism preceded remission of sins?* We affirm. Now for the proof. 1. The Methodist Discipline requires the minister, when about to baptize, to supplicate as follows: "We pray for these persons, that they, coming to thy holy baptism, may receive remission of their sins, by spiritual regeneration." We are not certain that we have the precise words, as we quote from memory, being from home; but think we have the substance. Why pray that they, coming to baptism, may receive remission of their sins, if their sins were previously pardoned? 2. Again, the Methodist Discipline says, "Our Savior Christ saith, None can enter into the kingdom of God, except he be regenerate, and born anew of water and of the Holy Ghost." This language is found in the ritual, on the Administration of Baptism, thus applying the words "born of water" to baptism, and making our Savior declare that None can enter into the kingdom of God except he be baptized! What is worse, the Discipline applies this language to infants, and thus represents our Savior as declaring that infants cannot enter into the kingdom of God except they be baptized. Entering into the kingdom of God is equivalent to entering into a state of justification, for all really justified enter the kingdom of God. Then, those infants not baptized cannot enter into the kingdom of God, and, according to the Discipline, must be lost; for it says, "all men are conceived and born in sin." This is a little too strong for us! This makes baptism "an essential antecedent condition" of admission into the kingdom of God, or a state of justification to infants! This we cannot endorse. We object to the application of this language to infants, and move for striking out the word "some" and restoring "a man," as we have it in the "old family Bible." "Except a *man* be born of water and of the Spirit, he cannot enter into the kingdom of God." See John 3.5. 3. But, ceasing to annoy our worthy friend, Dr. Blair, with his Discipline, we invite his attention to the Lord's own words, Mark 16.16: "He that believeth and is baptized shall be saved; but he that believeth not shall be damned." The word, "saved," here amounts to the same as *remission of sins*, or is simply *saved from sin*. Which, then, is antecedent to the other, baptism, or remission of sins? Certainly baptism is antecedent to salvation, or remission, and a condition on which it is to be bestowed. 4. "Repent and be baptized every one of you in the name of Jesus Christ for the remission of sins." See Acts 2.38. Can any man of common intelligence fail to see that baptism is antecedent to remission of sins here? In one passage just quoted, faith and baptism and in the other repentance and baptism, are connected together for the same thing, viz: remission of sins. If, then, faith and repentance are antecedent to remission of sins, baptism is. 5. Ananias said to Saul, "Arise and be baptized and wash away thy sins, calling on the name of the Lord." Acts 22.16. It requires no great amount of intelligence to see that baptism is antecedent to remission of sins, from this statement. Wesley, in his note on this passage, if we mistake not, as we have not the work at hand in his writing, says, "Baptism is administered to real penitents as both a *means* and a *seal* of pardon; nor did God ordinarily, in the pardon; nor did God ordinarily, in the primitive Church, bestow this upon *any except through this means.*" The italics are ours, merely to call attention to certain words. 6. The Lord says, "Except a man be born of water and of the Spirit, he cannot enter into the kingdom of God." See John 3.5. This passage is applied to baptism by Wesley, and Dr. Blair's own Discipline, thus making baptism "an essential antecedent condition of" admittance into the kingdom of God, which is equivalent to making it "an essential antecedent condition of remission of sins." We, therefore, do not hesitate to say that, according to Scripture, baptism is antecedent to the remission of sins; or that baptism is a condition upon which remission of sins is promised to the truly penitent, or proper subjects. The Lord said to Saul, "It shall be told thee what thou must do." When it was told him what *he must do*, he was commanded to arise and be baptized. When the Lord says that anything *must be done*, we leave it for Dr. Blair to decide whether *it is essential.* Does he believe the language of the Lord, "Except a man be born of water and of the Spirit, he cannot enter into the kingdom of God." Does he believe his own Discipline? Does he believe the language of Wesley? Will the Doctor answer these things, that the people may understand him? Dr. Blair came to us, at the close of the meeting, the evening on which the questions and answers were read, and requested us to strike out the word "total," as found in his closing question. This was a little suspicious! We fear the Doctor is not entirely sound, as he desired to get rid of the word *"total"* The word "hereditary" he left out in the first place, and then, his desiring the word *total* struck out, shows that he does not believe the doctrine of total hereditary depravity, as taught by the Methodist and Presbyterian Churches. The devil can be no more than *totally depraved.* If the unregenerate are totally depraved, they are all bad alike, for there can be no degrees in that which is total. We know they are not all bad alike that among unregenerate men there is a difference—that some are worse than others. Paul says, that "wicked men and seducers wax worse and worse, deceiving and being deceived." They could not wax *worse* and *worse,* if they were *totally depraved.* If the Doctor desires to make any explanations, or reply to the foregoing, our columns are at his service. We shall be pleased to let our readers have the finest things he can say, or any of his associates in the Faculty.

2/17/63, v.6,#7,p.2

Query–Peter says, 1 Pet 3.19, "By which also (the Spirit) he went and preached unto the spirits in prison," etc. Will you please explain to me how Jesus preached to the spirits in prison.

Answer–We have had substantially the same question as propounded above, presented for an answer, we think, at least as often as once a year for the past twenty years, and probably as many times given an answer to it, doing so, in many instances, in public. Many other brethren have given answers to the same thing. Still, there are many brethren, recently enlisted, who have not met with any of these answers, and for whom becomes necessary to explain the matter again. One of the most talented, popular, and influential preachers among us, some years ago, stumbled upon this passage, stranded and fell. He soon founded an intermediate system of grace, or a system of grace, or a system of grace between death and the resurrection of the dead, as he expressed it, to give those who did not obey the Gospel in this life, *another chance* to receive Christ, repent and turn to God. He, however, did not stop long at this point, but soon became enlisted in spirit-rapping, and, at last accounts, was pretty low down in the gloomy, dark and doubting regions of unbelief. Many other men, both among the German and French doctors, who, whether they design it or not, are continually undermining the Gospel and destroying its power on the world, are adopting some similar speculations, and publishing them for the gratification of the morbid, vitiated and corrupted appetite of these times. Romanists have tried to draw support from this passage for the nefarious pretense of their priesthood, of delivering souls from purgatory—a false pretense and wonderful deception, by which they have taken from the pockets of the people more of their hard earnings than would found the richest kingdom in the world. This, however, is but one instance, out of many, where wicked and designing men have seized a rather obscure and incidental expression, and perverted it; not only to the most wicked and basic purposes, but to their own destruction. Indeed, there is one thing clearly noticeable, and that is, that corrupt men are better read, and more familiar with, the obscure, more mystical and difficult portions of Scripture to understand, than the clear literal and practical parts. They love to deal in the obscure, the mystical and dark portions. In this work, there is an opportunity to get out of the purview of the people; beyond the knowledge; into the fog, mist and smoke. They then have a double advantage. 1. They can get credit for explaining a mystery, and thus astonish the world with the profundity of their knowledge. 2. They can explain the mystery to mean just what they please, and the masses of the people cannot determine whether they are right or wrong. This suits them precisely. They have a wicked scheme to advocate. To accomplish this object, they resort to obscure Scriptures, dark expressions, and obsolete metaphors, and interpret these to mean the very thing they aim to advocate, and thus claim Divine authority. We press all these with the question why not go to the literal; to the last commission; to the preaching of the apostles under that commission; show the people precisely what the apostles preached; the effect the preaching had on the people; the inquiries they made; what the apostles commanded them to do; what it was to be done for; how it was to be done ; ascertain precisely what the people did, the result that followed, and all about it? We repeat it, why not come here, and make this the main rallying ground? What reason can men have for not coming here, if they desire to know and teach the truth, the whole truth, and nothing but the truth? Here, we find the apostles with a holy commission immediately from Jesus, endued with supernatural power, to guide them infallibly into all truth, and surrounded by the most stupendous displays of miraculous power, confirming their Divine and holy mission, as well as all they said. Here we find a history of what they did, the founding of the kingdom of God, the introduction of the first converts into the kingdom, and everything as at the beginning. The only reason we can see why any man should avoid this all important portion of the Oracles of God, is because he does not desire to come to the light. The matters here are clear, tangible and intelligible. All can readily see the slightest departure from the truth. If a man attempts to deal with the things detailed here, he will at once be detected. But all this is not answering the question at the head of these remarks. The question reads as follows: How did Jesus preach to the spirits in prison? The following is the reading of the passage: "For Christ hath once suffered for sins, the just for the unjust, that he might bring us to God, being put to death in the flesh, but quickened by the Spirit; by which also he went and preached to the spirits in prison, who sometime were disobedient, when once the long-suffering of God waited in the days of Noah, while the ark was preparing, wherein few, that is, eight souls, were saved by water." 1 Peter 3.18–20. The following items we lay down as true: 1. This preaching was done "in the days of Noah, while the ark was preparing." 2. Christ did not do this preaching *in person*, but *by the Spirit*. He was put to death in the flesh, but quickened by the Spirit, by which (Spirit) he went and preached to the spirits in prison. 3. No preaching was ever done by the Spirit without a human agent, through whom to preach. There must, then, have been a human agent, through whom to preach. There must, then, have been a human agent in this case. 4. Was there any human agent; in the days of Noah, preaching by the Spirit? Beyond all contradictions there was. That human agent was Noah. He was a preacher of righteousness, preached by the Spirit, the only preacher of righteousness in his time, and, therefore, the one employed. Christ, then, went and preached by the Spirit, through Noah, a preacher of righteousness, to the antediluvians, who were the spirits in prison alluded to by Peter. Hence the Lord said, Gen 6.3, "My Spirit shall not always strive with man, for that he is flesh; yet his days shall be a hundred and twenty years." The Spirit of God which was in Noah, did strive in them, through Noah's preaching; one hundred and twenty years, at the end of which time God destroyed them by the flood. 5. Their disobedience was in the days of Noah, as is clearly stated, and most certainly their disobedience was when the preaching was done, and consisted in resisting the preaching, and refusing to repent, when solemnly warned. 6. It is a most unlikely thing that the Lord would attempt to reveal to man a dispensation of grace in the intermediate state, in a single obscure expression like this—The thing is wholly incredible. It would be infinitely better to say, *we do not know what the passage means,* than to make it mean an entire system not mentioned anywhere else in the Bible. 7. It is assumed that this preaching was done between the death of the Savior and his resurrection, by those who claim that it was done in the intermediate state. This is not true, for our Lord went to paradise, when he died, as he said to the thief, "To-day shalt be with me in paradise." The wicked dead are not in *paradise,* but in *tartarus,* between death and the resurrection. Here, too, is where the angels who kept not their first estate, and who were cast down to hell (*tartarus),* are reserved in everlasting chains to the judgment of the great day. There is not, then, one scrap of authority for thinking that there will be any dispensation of grace, preaching, or "another chance," to turn to God and be saved beyond this life. The decree of God is, in reference to all who have passed over the boundary line of time, "He who is filthy, *let him be filthy still*; he who is unjust, *let him be unjust still;*. There is *no chance* for reformation, in this. Now is the time for reformation, and all who will fail to turn to the Lord now—in time will find it an everlasting failure. "Behold, now is the accepted time; behold, now is the day of salvation." Let us neither trifle nor be trifled with, in reference to these stupendous and wonderful matters, but listen to the sure and holy teaching of the apostles and prophets.

8/21/63, v.6, #16, p.62

Query–Bro. Franklin, Please say what you think of the 17th and 18th. verses of the last chapter of Mark, in their connection with the two proceeding verses.

Answer–The reading of the passage in question is as follows: "These signs shall follow them that believe: In my name shall they cast out devils; they shall speak with new tongues; they shall take up serpents; and if they drink any deadly thing, it shall not hurt them; they shall lay hands on the sick, and they shall recover." This is a difficult passage, and men, or course have had different opinions respecting it. Some have supposed that the words, "These signs shall follow them that believe," etc., relate to all who believe on Christ. This we do not believe. We do not believe it related even to all who believe on Christ in the time of the apostles, for the following reasons: 1. The promise contained in these words was, we claim, most faithfully fulfilled. Let him deny this who can. 2. All who believed, even in the time of the apostles, did not work miracles, or these signs did not follow them. 3. All who have believed, since the time of the apostles, have not worked miracles, or these signs have not followed them. 4. It is simply a matter of fact, that since the death of the apostles, and all on whom they laid hands, there have been no miracles. All claims to miracles since that time are the most idle pretenses and base impostures. Why did they cease, if the Lord intended their continuation? Why did they not accompany all believers, if the Lord intended they should? Why did the inspired apostle, in the same connection in which he declared that prophesies and tongues should cease, declare that faith should abide? We are of the opinion that the commission, as Mark inserts it, is parenthetical, and that reading the passage without the parenthesis will show who the signs should follow. Let us now copy the whole passage, placing the commission in parenthesis, that the reader may see what we mean at the same time adopting the Bible Union version: "Afterward, he appeared to the eleven themselves as they reclined at the table, and upbraided their unbelief and hardness of heart, because they believed not them that had seen him after he was risen. (And he said to them: Go into all the world, and preach the good news to every creature. He that believes and is immersed shall be saved; but he that believes not shall be condemned.) And these signs shall accompany them that believe: in my name shall they cast out devils; they shall speak with new tongues; they shall take up serpents; and if they drink any deadly thing; it shall not hurt them; they shall lay hands on the sick, and they shall recover. "The Lord, therefore, after he had spoken to them, was taken up into heaven, and he sat down at the right hand of God. And they went forth and preached everywhere, the Lord working with them, and confirming the word by the signs that followed." 1. The *eleven* whom he upbraided for their hardness of heart and unbelief, because they believed not them who had seen him after he was risen, were unquestionably *the apostles*. 2. Where is the antecedent, so the word "them" in the phrase, "These signs shall follow *them* that believe?" It is not the word "he," in the phrase, *"he* that believe." etc., because "them" is plural, and "he" is singular. It is certainly back of the commission, what we have included in parenthesis, it is certainly the eleven whom he upbraided for their hardness of heart, and unbelief. 3. The position just taken is evidently correct, from what followed. Mark says, "The Lord, therefore, after he had spoken to *them* (the apostles), was taken up into heaven; and he sat down on the right hand of God. And they (the apostles) went forth and preached everywhere, the Lord working with *them* (the apostles), and confirming the word by the signs that followed." The following we doubt not, is the true state of the case: 1. The Lord upbraided the apostles for their unbelief and hardness of heart, because they believed not those who had seen the Lord after his resurrection. 2. The Lord promised that the signs described, should follow the apostles. 3. Mark informs us that the promised signs did follow the apostles. 4. The object of the signs was to confirm the word. The apostles went forth, everywhere, the Lord working with them, and *confirming the word,* which the apostles preached, by the signs that followed. The Lord never promised that *all believers, at any period,* should work miracles, nor that any believers, *in all ages,* should work miracles. The miracles were intended to follow the apostles, and the promise was that they should follow them, and they did follow them, to confirm the word. They came at the time and place intended, answered the purpose for which they were intended, and ceased. It requires a miracle to bring the first human pair into existence; but it required no miracle to perpetuate the human race. It required a miracle to produce the first oak tree; but it requires no miracle to perpetuate oak trees. It required miracles to bring the New Institution into existence, and prove it to be Divine; but it requires no miracle to perpetuate it. In one word, everything began by miracle, and is perpetuated without miracle. Nobody now wants miracles but skeptics. They seek signs, follow delusions and are carried about by modern humbuggery. There is but one sure foundation of life, light and knowledge. That is the Bible, confirmed by the most stupendous displays of Divine power, and attestations of its faithfulness ever addressed to the reason of man. He who rejects it is lost. If one would rise from the dead, he would not believe. There is no power in this universe that will save him.

4/28/63, v.6, #17, p.66

Query–Will you give your views on the 14th, 15th and 16th. verses of the fifth chapter of the book of James. Are the Elders here spoken of, the preachers in the Baptist Church, who are called Elders; or Presiding Elders in the Methodist Church; or are they the Elders or Bishops in the Christian Church; or lastly, were they those old men who were called Elders on account of their age, in the age of spiritual gifts, spoken of in 1 Cor 12.30? Was the practice to be continued beyond the age of spiritual gifts, that the same result should follow the practice as then, in all future time, or was it to cease when spiritual gifts ceased?

Answer–"The elders," alluded to, were evidently *seigniors*, but were *bishops*, or *overseers*, also. All bishops were elders, or old men, but all elders or old men, were not bishops. The mere circumstance of being an old man did not constitute a man a bishop, or overseer. There was no Baptist, Methodist, or Presbyterian church in the time of the apostles, nor for fifteen hundred years after that time, and, of course, no officers of any kind, in the sense of any one of those churches. There was no church but the church of Christ at that time. "On this rock I will build *my church*," said the Messiah. All other churches have been built since, without any authority from the great Head of the only true church. We have no doubt about the propriety of calling for the elders of the church to pray for the sick, and for the sick to confess their sins, and ask forgiveness. Prayer, confessing sins and obtaining pardon, do not belong exclusively to the age of miracles, but are common to all ages. Miraculous healing belonged to the age of miracles. Prayer is as much God's appointment, in which for *his people* to obtain pardon *now*, as it was in the time of the apostles, and when they sin *now*, as it was in the time of the apostles, they need pardon as much as they did then. We have of ground to pray for the sick, without expecting any miracle. They may obtain pardon, if they have sinned, and may be raised from sickness without any miracle. Let us be careful and not give anything to the age of miracles exclusively, which belongs to our time as much as it did to the apostolic, especially *acts of obedience.*

5/12/63, v.6, #19, p.74

Query–I see in your paper on the 17th and 18th verses of the last chapter of Mark. In giving your views on it you say: "Nobody wants miracles but skeptics. They seek signs, follow delusions, and are carried about by modern humbuggery." I hope you won't pretend to insinuate that seekers of truth are skeptics, do you? If so, you will find me one also. Will you please to give the public your views on the 28th verse of the 12th chapter of 1 Corinthians, in connection with the 11th verse of the 4th chapter of Ephesians? By so doing you will much oblige your brother in search of truth.

Answer–It is not skepticism to *seek after truth,* nor to seek to understand the Scriptures; but it is skepticism to insist on the necessity for miracles in our time. Miracles had their day, did their work, did it effectually, and it needs not to be done again. They arrested the attention of the world, called it to Christ, his apostles, his Church, and his religion, and proved that Christ came from God, was divine, the Son of God; that the apostles were inspired; the Church divinely authorized, and the religion of Christ true. This being once proved, never needs to be proved again. The same proof that once established it made it credible, and gained for the credence of mankind so largely, only needs to be exhibited to others, in the preaching of the gospel and the practice of the Church, to gain the credence of mankind to the end of the world. When the rich man, in Hades, desired one to go from the dead to testify to his five brethren, the answer was; "They have Moses and the prophets; if they believe not them, neither would they believe though one rose from the dead." We now have Moses and the prophets, Jesus and the apostles, with the record of all the testimony confirming their wonderful missions, and the man who believes not them may seek signs, prate about miracles and follow spirit-rappers till doom's day; but he certainly would not be converted if one would rise from the dead. If a man can not be moved by the trembling earth, the rending rocks, the sundering of the veil, the darkness of the sun, for three hours, when Jesus died; his resurrection from the dead; the resurrection is all probability, of about one hundred and forty-four thousand immediately after he rose, his appearance to above five hundred brethren at one time; his ascending into heaven, in open day, in the presence of his chosen witnesses; the stupendous displays of supernatural power, in open day, in presence of the vast mixed multitudes on Pentecost; the turning from their established religion of three thousand Jews the first day; the turning of five thousand, in a short time after, in the city of Jerusalem, where they had the best opportunity possible to know the truth of all the apostles were saying; the filling of all the cities, towns and country places the whole length of the Mediterranean Sea, and throughout the Roman Empire—we say, if a man will not believe in view of all this, he would not believe if one would rise from the dead. You need not talk of any signs and wonders to convince such a man. The first thing that will reuse his stupefied soul, quicken his calloused heart, and bring him to spiritual consciousness, will be the sound of the trumpet of God, and the imperative summons, "Arise you dead, and come to judgment." Then, and not till then, will such men believe, and, for the first time, commence praying. What a prayer, too, they will pray! "O for the rocks and mountains to fall on us, and hide us from the face of Him who sits on the throne, and from the wrath of the Lamb." Never was there such a grand display of evidence surrounding anything, claiming the credence of man as that connected with Christ and his religion, and never did man take such responsibility as he does in rejecting Christ and his religion. He risks the loss of everything, without the possibility of gaining anything. 1 Cor 12.28, reads as follows: "And God hath set some in the Church; first apostles; secondarily, prophets; thirdly, teachers; after that, miracles; then gifts of healings, helps, governments, diversities of tongues." These were all supernatural gifts in the primitive church. No time had elapsed for qualifying men for these important offices in the Church by ordinary means. For the time being, they were supplied by supernatural means. But in the last verse of the same chapter, after speaking of spiritual gifts, he says, "Yet show I unto you a *more excellent way.*" Eph 4.11, reads as follows: "And he gave some, apostles; and some, prophets; and some, evangelists; and some, pastors and teachers." What did he give these for? "For the perfecting of the saints; for the work of the ministry; for the edifying of the body of Christ." How long? "Till we all come in the unity of the faith and of the knowledge of the Son of God, unto a perfect man, unto the measure of the stature of the fullness of Christ." This clearly implies that there would be a time when these supernatural gifts would cease. That time was, when the Church passed the period of infancy and childhood—its incipiency—came "to a perfect man." This is evidently that to which Paul alludes, 1 Cor 13. After stating that "prophecies should *fail,* and tongues should *cease,*" he says, "when I was a child, I spoke as a child, I understood as a child, but when I became a man, I put away childish things." This also alludes to the incipient state, while all the offices were supplied by extraordinary gifts, or by miracle; but "a more excellent way" was to follow that, when the Church was to come to the knowledge of the fullness of Christ, "to a perfect man," when prophecies and tongues should cease, the necessity for them no longer existing. Men, since then are qualified for all the offices in the church by ordinary and not by extraordinary means. We have no evangelists, shepherds and teachers now, *made such by miracle,* nor have we miracles now in any form, or any use for them, except *in history,* and the fulfillment of prophecy before our own eyes, uttered eighteen centuries ago. We do not see Jesus turn water into wine, heal the sick, open the eyes of the blind, give hearing to the deaf, speech to the dumb, raise the dead, or feed five thousand persons by a miracle; but we have that which shows his divinity equally as much. We have his words, uttered forty years before Jerusalem was destroyed, declaring that the devoted city should be razed to its foundation, not leaving one stone upon another, and trodden down by the Gentiles till the times of the Gentiles be fulfilled, and that the Jews should be carried away captive among all nations. This prediction stands fulfilled till this day, before the eyes of all nations, showing that he who uttered it *knew all things.* Blessed be his name. He who does not believe now is worse than the Jews, for Paul said, "blindness *in part* is happened to Israel," for blindness not *in part* but *in full,* or total blindness has happened to him. We have now the sacred record of the miracles performed in confirmation of and establishing the New Institution, and the fulfillment of prophecies uttered eighteen centuries ago, taking place in our own time. The people of the apostolic time saw the miracles. This we do not see. But we see the fulfillment of prophecies, which they did not see. Thus the evidence is as convincing in our time as it was in theirs.

Query—Please explain Revelation, 13th chapter, 11th to the 18th verse inclusive. 1. What the beast represents? 2. What is the mark he causes all to receive? 3. The name and the number of the name?

Answer—We have some "opinions" touching the Scriptures referred to, but none that we think would be profitable to the public. There are many things which we certainly understand. There are many things which we certainly understand. These we love to teach and enforce. We can do this with all confidence. But we are not certain that we understand the thirteenth chapter of Revelation. We do not, therefore, like to try to explain it. We know two or three men who can explain the entire book of Revelation, with all the prophecies of Isaiah, Jeremiah, Ezekiel and Daniel, *they think,* but we cannot understand their explanations as well as we can understand the prophecies themselves. We are explaining to sinners how to become Christians, explaining to sectarians how to get rid of sectarianism and unite in the "one fold," under "one Shepherd," in "one body," with "one faith," practicing "one immersion," one religion, as the Lord prayed, "that all may be one, as thou, Father, art in me and I in thee, that they may be one in us, that the world may believe that thou didst send me." If we cannot get the people to understand these matters, it is but little difference whether they understand Revelations or not. They will land in ruin. The people must understand what they shall do to become Christians, or they cannot enter into the service of God. They must understand how to obey the law of God after they are Christians, or they cannot serve God. These are the things to preach about and write about, if we would benefit the world. If we would have the people wonder at our knowledge, we may *explain mysteries.* No matter whether the explanation is true or false, many will think it profound, if for no other reason, because *they cannot understand it.*

9/1/63, v.6, #35, pg.138

Query—Will you please explain the following verses, commencing at the 11th of the third chapter of 1 Corinthians, including all as far as the 18th verse.

Answer—We know not where to commence in such a case as the one here presented. We know not what the difficulty is in the mind of the brother who presents this Scripture. We see nothing difficult in the

Scripture referred to. We must have something more than a simple request to explain a Scripture. What does the writer want to know about it? Where is the difficulty? If he will tell us the point of difficulty, and we can, we will explain it, but we cannot explain Scripture, where we see no point, or difficulty.

9/1/63, v.6, #35, pg.138

Query—Please give your views as to the first verse of the sixth chapter of Galatians, to wit: "Ye who are spiritual, restore such an one," etc.

Answer—We are not decided whether it refers to the better, more devout and spiritual-minded brethren, or those possessing supernatural gifts, but are inclined to the former opinion.

10/20/63, v.6,#42, pg.166

Query—What does the Savior mean in the 17th chapter and 21st verse of Luke, when he says: "The kingdom of God is within you?" Does he mean to teach that the kingdom of God was at that time established? The Pharisees demanded of him when the kingdom of God should come. He replies, it is, present time, within you. And, in the 16th of Matthew, he says, I will build my church—future time. Is the kingdom of God and the church of Christ two things? There is something in this that I cannot see as plainly as I desire, and by giving some explanation you may assist in learning *the truth*, and, by so doing, oblige.

Answer—The kingdom was in them, in its incipiency—in its embryo state, but not built, not developed and established in its fullness. It was to come out of them. It was once, in the eternal purpose of God. It was afterward in the promise to Abraham. Then again, in the prophecies of the Old Testament. Then in Christ and the apostles. Finally on Pentecost, it was set up, built, set in full operation, in a complete form, and the King on the throne and crowned in heaven. When he said the kingdom prospectively, only existing in its incipiency; but after Pentecost, it was the kingdom come, built and in full form.

10/20/63, v.6,#42, pg.166

Query—In John 3.8, is not the Greek word, (*pneuma)* which, in the Bible Union and in King James Version is rendered "*wind*," is it not the same as the Greek word (*pneumatos*), which, in the same verse is rendered "*spirit*"? And is not the New Testament Greek word for "*wind*," *anemos*, and not *pneuma*? Eph 4.14, etc. If *pneuma* (verse 8) means "*spirit*" in the *first case, as it does in the second*, have we had as yet a *correct* rendering of the passage in question?

Answer – 1. Certainly it is the same word, and there is the same reason for translating it *spirit* in verse 8th, that there is in the other four occurrences of the same word in the connection. The Bible Union, in its incipient revision, renders it *spirit*, but in the final revision, revised it back to *wind*. 2. *Anemos* is the usual Greek word for wind, and not *pneuma*, in the New Testament. 3. I believe the brethren translate *pneuma*, verse 9th, "spirit," and have no doubt but this is right.

11/17/63, v.6, #46, p.182

Query – You will confer a favor, if you will be so kind as to give in the REVIEW, an exposition of Eph 4.11–13. My reason for making the inquiry is, that some suppose that the evangelists, pastors and teachers, here spoken of, are the same officers as the evangelists and elders we have now in the Church; and that these officers, according to the 15th verse, were to cease, when the unity of the faith and the church should arrive at perfect manhood, or when the revelation should be completed. According to this theory, there would be no use in setting apart officers of the church now.

Answer – We have no apostles, evangelists and pastors and teachers, as direct and miraculous gifts now. Those directly given and miraculously qualified, were for the infancy of the church, till it should arrive at the unity of the faith and to the knowledge of the Son of God, to a perfect man. The word which the Father gave the Savior, he gave the apostles, inspired and sent them to publish it to the world. We have no apostles now, *in the same sense, as they were*. An apostle is, *one sent*. Those sent directly by the Savior, were apostles of Christ. When the word was given to the church, she sends men to preach, and they are *the apostles of the churches*, or, as styled now frequently, missionaries. These men are not supernaturally endowed or qualified, but have good natural endowments and are qualified by reading, meditation and learning in the ordinary way. In the same way, the first evangelists were qualified by *miraculous gifts*, imparted by hands, till time and opportunity should be afforded for men to be qualified in the ordinary way, or by ordinary means. An *evangelist*, is simply a proclaimer, or an evangelizer-a public propagator of the gospel. The first pastors, or overseers, were supernatural gifts, and, indeed all the officers of the church, and though the manner of giving them now is not the same. We have the apostle, or missionary, sent by the church, or apostle of the church. We have also the evangelist, or proclaimer of the gospel. We have also the pastors, or shepherds and teachers, and the work for them. But none of these are now given or qualified by miracle, nor in their work now supernatural work. The Church and officers were brought into the world by miracle and shown to be from God but are not perpetuated or propagated by miracle. Man was brought into the world by miracle, but not perpetuated by miracle.

5/6/62, v.5,#18, pg.2

Query– 1.What is an ordinance of God? 2. Is the United States Government an ordinance of God? See Rom 13.2

Answer–An ordinance of God is simply that which he has ordained or appointed. He ordains or appoints in two ways: 1. Directly, as he ordained the Christian religion, or any one appointment in it. 2. In his providence, as he ordained the Roman Government, as a terror, to evil doers, and, in scripture, required submission to it on the part of Christians. In this latter sense, the United States Government is an ordinance of God.

11/11/62, v.5, #45, pg.3

Query–Paul says that some men's sins are open before hand, going before to judgment, and some men they follow after. Likewise, also, the good works of some are manifest beforehand, and they that are otherwise can not be hid. Please explain what Paul meant.

Answer–We suppose there is nothing more in this, than simply the fact that the sins of some men are very manifest, open and undisguised, and their effect apparent, while others are more hidden, covert and secret. About the same may be said of the good works of men. The good works of some men are manifest, open and visible, to all, and their results readily seen; while others, are more quietly, privately and less openly performed, and their results do not immediately appear, but afterward are open and manifest before all who will see such as there is.

11/11/62, v.5, #45, pg.3

Query–Titus 2.11 reads as follows: "For the grace of God that bringeth salvation, hath appeared to all men." Will you be kind enough to tell your readers through your valuable paper, just what the Apostle has reference to, when he spoke of the term "grace," as found in the above passage.(?)

Answer–The word, "grace," means *favor*. The *favor* of God," in the passage referred to embraces Christ, the gospel and the entire blessings of Christianity. The entire system of religion given through Christ, embraced in "the favor of God." God has favored the world with the gift of his Son and the Holy Spirit, the Apostles, the gospel, the church, the ordinances, facts, commandments and promises; in one word, the entire system for the recovery of man. "Know ye not the grace of our Lord Jesus Christ, though he was rich, yet for our sakes he became poor, that we, through his poverty, might be rich." This favor of God, the gift of his only Son, with the entire new institution, has appeared to all men, or been presented to all men, "teaching us that denying all ungodliness and worldly lusts, we should live soberly, righteously and godly in this present world." The favor of God, the new institution, or the religion of Christ, *"teaches us,"* etc. Many abbreviated expressions of the scriptures include the whole Christian institution, as for instance, "the faith," "the grace of God," "the new covenant," "preached unto him Jesus," "the preaching of the cross." Reading Moses is reading the writings of Moses, or the law, and hearing Moses is hearing the law. Receiving the grace of God, is receiving Christ, or his system of religion.

11/7/62, v.5, #1, pg.3

Query–If the word *psuche* is twice rendered *life* in the 39th verse of the 10th chapter of Matthew, why should it not be translated *life* in the 28th verse?

Answer–Wilson gives us Matt 10.28 as follows: "Fear not those who kill the body, but can not destroy the [future] life, but rather fear him who can utterly destroy both life and body in gehenna." It is painful to impugn the motives of men, but we deem it but just to the cause, to the friends of righteousness, and the world to say, that we never saw more manifest perversity in any rendering of the sacred Scriptures, than we find here. Look at it for a moment: 1. What reason can any man assign for translating the same word (*apoktino*) "kill" (from *apoktino)* in each of its occurrences in the words "Fear not those who *kill* the body, but are not able to *kill* the soul, is used in the same sense? What reason, then, can any man have for translating it "kill" in the former occurrence, and "destroy" in the latter? Certainly none except to obscure, what should be plain. The word *apoktino,* is never translated "destroy" in the common version. But to translate it "kill" in one part of a short sentence and "destroy," in another part of the same short sentence, can have no good design. It has the appearance of trying to destroy the testimony of an opposing witness. 2. What authority has he for inserting the word "future" in brackets? "Be not afraid of those who kill the body, but are not able to destroy the [future] life." His Literal translation reads as follows: "And not be afraid of those killing the body the but life not being able to kill." Where does he not manufacture it, out and out? Why did he not say, "Fear not those who kill the [present] body, but are not able to destroy the [future] life." There is nothing about *present* and *future* in this part of the sentence. The antithesis is not between the present and future, but between what the persecutors *could do* and what they *could not do.* They could kill the body, but could not kill the soul. The testimony of this witness must be destroyed, or soul-sleeping is ruined. This is no blundering but pure perversity, to destroy the force of a wonderful and fearful passage from the lips of Jesus. What does the word "utterly" come from? "But rather fear Him who can destroy both life and body in gehenna." His literal translation reads thus: "be afraid but rather that being able both life and body to destroy in gehenna." Has he not manufactured the word "utterly," out and but? *Psuche* should certainly be rendered *soul* here: as to kill the body is to take the life of the body; but not at the same time, take the life of the *soul.* If any one translate *psuche,* life, Matt 10.39, as some do, such translation makes our Lord teach, that man can kill the body, but is not able to kill the life, thus proving that there is a soul, or life, that does not die when the body dies. This agrees with one of our Lord's statements: "He who lives and believes on me, *shall never die.*" John 11.26. The body *dies,* but the person who dwells in the body shall never die.

3/12/67, v.x, #11, pg.84

Query–Where Paul represents Christ as saying to him, Acts 26.16: "I have appeared unto thee for this purpose, to make thee a minister and witness both of these things which thou hast seen," etc. in what manner do we understand Christ as *appearing* unto Paul? Was it literal? Did he come personally within the range of human vision, and in a bodily form? In other words, did he appear to Paul in such a manner as to be seen by others had they been present? By answering the above, you will oblige a reader of the REVIEW.

Answer—Most certainly the appearing was literal, else Paul would not have said, "Have I not *seen* Jesus Christ our Lord." The Lord, when he appeared to him, said, "I have appeared to thee for this purpose, to make thee a minister and a witness both of *these things which thou hast seen,* and of those things in which I will appear unto thee." The Lord appeared to him personally, so that he *saw him* and heard *the voice of his mouth.* We see nothing in the case to put any person in mind of any other kind of an appearing than a *personal one.* He came in the range of his vision, so that he saw him, and in the range of his hearing, so that he heard the voice of his mouth. See Acts chapters 22, and 26. This appearing and that when Stephan saw him standing on the right hand of God, or that when John saw him, in the island of Patmos, are not taken into account, in that passage; "he shall appear a second time without a sin offering," etc., which is the only instance we now think of, where the term "second," is applied to his coming to raise the dead and judge the world.

4/1/62, v.5, #13, p.2

Query—Once more on the 29th & 30th verses of Matthew. I really thought I gave you the chapter, but I may be mistaken. It is the fifth chapter of Matthew, 29th and 30th verses. Is the language literal, or figurative?

Answer—Figurative—highly figurative, certainly. The right hand, or the right eye, *literally* does not offend the person to whom it belongs. It is some lust, or unlawful desire, that may be dear to a person, like the right eye or hand, which is to be put away. The subsequent language shows this.

4/1/62, v.5, #13, p.2.

Query—Please answer the following: 1 Tim 3.10, Paul says, "But let these also be proved." Does this proving apply elders and deacons, or only to deacons? "The women in like manner must be grave," etc. Does this apply to the women of elders, and deacons or only to the deaconesses? Does "faithful children" Tit 1.6, mean church members? What is meant by holding fast the secret of the faith, with a pure conscience? Is faith now a secret?

Answer–1. Certainly, this *proving* applies to both overseers and deacons. "Let these *also* (as well as the overseers) be first proved. 2. The women of both overseers and deacons must be grave. This certainly applies to the wives of both alike. 3 "Faithful children" may be dutiful, obedient and submissive to parental authority—children in subjection.4. The secret of the faith," is now the faith, or the gospel revealed. It was a secret, but is now revealed. See Rom 16.17–18.

4/9/67, v.x, #15, p.117

Query–Please reconcile this apparent contradiction. 1 John, 3rd. verse reads as follows: Whosoever is born of God doth not commit sin; for his seed remaineth in him, and he cannot sin, because he is born of God. Again: 1 John, 1st. chapter, 8th. verse—If we say that we have no sin; we deceive ourselves, and the truth is not in us. The point we do not understand is this: it appears from reading the 9th verse of the 3rd. chapter of 1 John, that it is impossible, for a person born of God, to sin: but in the 8th. verse of the 1st. chapter, he says: If we say that we have no sin, we deceive ourselves, and the truth is not in us. Again: Matt. 3rd. chapter and 11th. verse, Were not the same persons that were baptized with the Holy Ghost baptized with the fire: Repent and be baptized in the name of Jesus Christ, for the remission of sins. If repentance is for the remission of sins, baptism is for the same purpose. If some persons were to be baptized with the Holy Ghost, the same persons were to be baptized with fire. Were the hundreds that were baptized unto John's baptism, baptized again before they could become members of the Church of Christ?

Answer–Those questions have been answered many times within our recollection. Still, new readers are constantly entering the list, and new converts coming into the church—making it necessary to explain again. 1. Touching the expression, "He who is born of God cannot sin," we find the only difficulty. It *apparently* conflicts with the other passages referred to. We suppose the amount of it is not in the absolute sense, that he *can not* sin; or that it is *impossible* for him to sin, but that he cannot consistently, or in accordance with his being born of God, or his new relation to God. In our common conversation, we say many times, that we can not do things, when we do not mean that it is impossible to do them, but we can not consistently with something else. We say, "I *can not* lend you fifty dollars," when we have the money, not in the absolute sense, meaning that it is impossible to do it, but can not do it consistently with our obligation to pay our tax, which we require the fifty dollars. It is in the sense in which "it is impossible for God to lie." He cannot do it consistently with his character. The man born of God cannot, consistently with his heavenly birth, and divine relation, sin. 2. The same persons were not to be baptized with fire and the Holy Spirit. John addressed two classes, and only predicts what should happen to them. The commandment to "Repent and be baptized," was addressed to *one* class—those who "heard" and were "cut to the heart"— "every one of you." But John used this, "fire," three times in the same connection. Twice out of the three times, he applies it to no class. The first time he used it, he applies it to no class. The first time he used it, he applies it to one class, and the third time; but the second time, the application is not so clear, by itself, but it amounts to the same as the first and third. In Matt 3.10, he says, "The axe lies at the root of the trees; every tree, therefore, not producing good fruit, is cut down and cast into the fire. What does the tree, not producing good fruit, represent? Persons not producing the fruits of righteousness, undoubtedly! There we cast into the fire. They are the subjects of *fire*. Verse 12. He has chaff and the wheat: the chaff representing the wicked and the wheat representing the righteous. *Fire* here is the same as in verse 10 is one case devouring the trees that bear no fruit, and in the other case the chaff; in verse 12, we find this word "fire," again—baptized in *fire*. He has before him the *same two* classes, the trees that do not produce good fruit and the trees that do produce good fruit; the chaff and the wheat. The trees that bear good fruit, the Saints, he permits to stand in his orchard; the trees that do not bring good fruit, the wicked, he cuts down and casts into the fire. The wheat, which represents the Saints he gathers into the granary, the chaff which represents the wicked, he burns with unquenchable fire. The baptism in the Holy Spirit, and in fire, is found in verse 11, between the other two, and for the same classes. The baptism in the Holy Spirit was for the good, and the baptism of fire for the bad. In these three figurative representations, in the three successive verses, 10, 11 and 12, the fire represents the same thing, and is for the same class. It is, when used as a symbol of judgments of God. No man of scriptural intelligence prays for the baptism of fire, any more than he does for the fire that shall burn the trees that bear not good fruit, or the fire that shall burn the chaff. Those ranting, boisterous revivalists, who pray for the baptism in the Holy Spirit and fire, know not what they pray for. If they ever sit down and read and study three verses of scripture, it would be well for them to give the three in question a careful examination. This language is referred to, in several instances, and where the baptism in fire was not present it was omitted. See Acts 11.16. "John indeed immersed in water, but you shall be immersed in the Holy Spirit, not many days hence." The baptism of the Holy Spirit was present, but not the baptism of fire. All any one has to do who thinks for himself, to satisfy him that he never witnessed a baptism in the Holy Spirit, or in fire, is to read Acts, chapter 11 and 10. All Christians receive the Holy Spirit, it dwells in them and strengthens them, but they are not immersed in it. There is a wide difference between the reception of the Holy Spirit, common to all Christians and the miraculous gift of the Holy Spirit, enabling men to do miracles.

5/14/67, v.x, #20, p.156

Query–If ye are the disciples of the Christ, why not follow his plan, laid down in Luke, chapter 9, verse 3?

Answer–We do follow Christ. This is our aim—to follow him most faithfully, and no other leader.

6/4/67, v.x, #23, p.180

Query– "If any man will do His will, he shall know of the doctrine whether it be of God, or whether I speak of myself." How does a man know when he does the will of God that the doctrine is of God? How does this knowledge come by the spirit of God through the Word? Where in the Scriptures shall we find it? If it comes by some abstract teaching of the spirit, what is it, and how shall we know it?

Answer–Can a man know when his hunger is satisfied? when his thirst was slaked? Can a man know when he has the peace of God, that passes knowledge like a river? Can a man know when he has rest?

Can he know when he is happy? Can he know when he finds rest to his soul? Certainly a man does not need a revelation to tell of what matter of personal realization in himself. Revelation brings him the knowledge of God, of the Savior, the Holy Spirit, terms of pardon, the promise of pardon. This is all by faith. The love, joy and peace, fruits of the Spirit, are matters of actual personal realization. The rest to the soul, which the Lord promises those who come to him is the same. Fear is cast out, and the man living and walking with God, in union and fellowship with the Father, and with the Son, God and Christ and the Holy Spirit dwelling in him, the love of God shed abroad in his heart by the Holy Spirit, in the enjoyment, peace, rest and comfort, richly afforded to the Saints, has a personal realization in its adapted end to him, that it is from God—divine—that amounts to knowledge such as the world can not have.

6/4/67, v.x, #23, p.180

Query–Please explain the sentence: There is a sin unto death found in John's first epistle. What kind of a sin is that which is unto death? See 1 John 5.16.

Answer–Such a sin is described. Acts 5.1, 10, case of Ananias and Sapphira, see also 1 Cor 11.29–30. During the age of miracles, visible judgments were inflicted, as warnings to all who should commit similar offenses time to come. Many were in consequence sickly, weak, and some died. In some cases, the sin was to death, as in the case of Ananias and Sapphira.

6/4/67, v.x, #23, p.180

Query–1.Does not the parable of the tares teach that no son of the wicked one can be put out of the kingdom *till* the end of the world? 2. Shall the kingdom of Jesus ever have an end? 3. If not, how are those already in it to have an abundant entrance into it?

Answer–1. The *field*, in which the seed was sown, the Lord explains, Matt 13.38, to be "the world." The good seed are the children of the kingdom, sowed in the field, or the world. The tares or the children of the wicked one are sowed in the same field or world. The tares, or the children of the wicked one, are sowed in the same field or world. The children of the kingdom are not only in the world, but in the kingdom, and the tares are in the world, and among the children of the kingdom, though strictly speaking, not in the kingdom. Gathering "out of his kingdom," if not strictly speaking, gathering out citizens, or any who were really in the kingdom, but *among* the citizens of the kingdom, together in the field or the world, where they will grow together till the harvest, or end of the world. Persons were excluded from the church, or kingdom, but still in the field, or the world, growing among the children of the kingdom, but will be gathered out of the world, and from *among* the children of the kingdom. 2. As an actual *existence*, the kingdom will have no end but the kingdom of Christ in the *present state*, will have an end; but the same kingdom will be delivered up to God, and in that state it is called in contrast with this state "the everlasting kingdom." 3. Those in the kingdom here, by faithful continuance in well-doing shall have an abundant entrance into the everlasting kingdom there. The kingdom here shall end, but the kingdom there shall never end. When we think of the territory here and there, we speak of the kingdom here and there, or of a present and future kingdom, and when we think of Christ the King here, and his giving up the kingdom to the Father, we think of two kingdoms, one here and the other there, one under the Son, and the other the Father.

6/11/67, v.x, #24, p.188

Query–Is it my duty, as a Christian sister, to speak or pray in public? It is urged by some good brethren that it is. What does Paul mean when he says in 1 Cor 14.34, "Let your women keep silence in the churches, for it is not permitted unto them to speak," etc. Please answer through your excellent paper, and very much oblige a sister in Christ.

Answer–That women should not teach, nor usurp authority in the church, is clear from such Scriptures as referred to above. But that women should never participate in social worship, either in talking a few words, or prayer, is another thing. Why should Paul speak of women praying with the *head uncovered*, if women are never to pray in any worshiping assembly? We think there are two extremes— the one not permitting women to open their lips in any worshiping assembly, and the other making them public *preachers* and *teachers*. This latter class generally get to be infidels, and disgrace themselves.

7/2/67, v.x, #26, p.213

Query – Please pardon me for troubling you for an explanation of the following passage of Scripture contained in Matt 3.8: "Bring forth therefore fruits meet for repentance." The Baptists you know, claim this is a "thus saith the Lord," for this custom they have of requiring "candidates" for baptism to give an "experience" before they are received. Please elucidate through the REVIEW at your earliest convenience.

Answer – 1. John the Immerser was not in the kingdom himself, but the least in the kingdom was greater than he. He was one of the agents of the Lord, near the end of the old institution, engaged in preparing a people for the Lord. He was not receiving any into the kingdom, but preparing them for the coming kingdom. 2. John certainly did not mean by the command, "Bring forth fruits fit for repentance," bring forth a *Baptist experience,* for such a thing was never heard of for more than fifteen centuries after John was beheaded. The idea of that novel and strange thing, called "a Baptist experience," consisting of the doubts entertained, the fears endured, the feelings experienced, emotions and impulses of the subject, the dreams had, sights seen, voices heard on the part of the patient, while yet confessedly a sinner, is certainly one of the most absurd these things of these times of apostasy and irreligion. The doubts, fears, feelings, emotions, impulses, and dreams one has before conversion, with all the sights seen, voices heard, etc., are evidently *experience* but certainly not even *Baptist* experience, to say nothing of *Christian.* Whatever experience one has before conversion, though really *experience* is not *Christian's* experience, but *sinner's* experience. Nothing can be clearer, than that there can be no Christian experience till the subject is a Christian. The experience before that is a *sinner's* experience. But John's fruits worthy of repentance did not consist in historical sketches of experiences of a sinner, or anybody else, but a good life—deeds of righteousness. Even these were not required before he immersed them, for there is no account of delay. Not only so, but he immersed them into repentance, or the privilege of repentance, and required them now to live such lives as would evince their sincerity and honesty.

8/7/67, v.x, #32, p. 253

Query – Did Abraham inherit the land of promise? or in other words, was he made heir of the world? "And he gave him none inheritance in it, no, not so much as to set his foot on, though he promised that he would give it to him, when as yet he had no child." Acts 7.5

Answer–The promise of Abraham, which was four hundred and thirty years before the law, that he should be heir of the world, was not to him, or his seed, through the law, but through God's method of justification by faith. Abraham, and others who believed the promise, sought a country, not in Canaan, nor in this life, nor did they provide expensive residences in this world, but sought a country, "looked for a city which has foundations, whose builder and maker is God." See Heb 11.10. "By faith he sojourned in the land of promise, as in a strange country, dwelling in tabernacles with Isaac and Jacob, the heirs with him of the same promise." They desired a better country; that is a heavenly country. The earthly Canaan was only the type of the heavenly Canaan. The promise that God made to Abraham, contained Christ, the gospel, the whole New Institution, its heavenly Canaan, its city with foundations, its New Jerusalem, its new heaven and new earth; in one word, all that God has prepared for them that love him, through Jesus Christ.

10/15/67, v.x, #42, p.333

Query–Please give Romans 8.29–30 a comment in your wonderful REVIEW. "For whom he did foreknow, he also did predestinate to be conformed to the image of his Son, that he might be the firstborn among many brethren. Moreover whom he did predestinate, them he also called: and whom he called, them he also justified: and whom he justified, them he also glorified." Are the persons in question the same as the "saints" spoken of in Matthew 27.52?

Answer–We do not know whether those referred to in Rom 8.29–30 and the "saints" mentioned in Matthew 27.52 are the same or not, and do not see that it would be of much importance to us if we did know.

7/25/71, v.14, #30, p.236

Query–Luke 15.11—Parable of the Prodigal Son—does that apply to the man who has never obeyed the gospel?

Answer–We think it does not, but most probably to the Gentiles and their return to the Lord, when the gospel is preached to them. It may be used to *illustrate* the return of a sinner, or more appropriately, a straying disciple, but not as *strictly meaning* either.

8/1/71, v.14, #31, p.244

Query – Luke 14.16—Parable of the great Supper—does that apply to the gospel?

Answer – The great Supper represents our blessings the Lord has provided for them that serve him, and which those who heed not his invitations shall never enjoy.

8/1/71, v.14, #31, p.244

Query – As to what is the meaning of the word *it* in Acts 2.3, where the apostle says, "And there appeared unto them cloven tongues as of fire, and it sat upon each of them." Is the word *tongues*, in the plural, the antecedent to the word *it*, in the singular?

Answer – The difficulty is wholly in the translation. The word it has no authority but with the King James' translators. There appeared unto them cloven, cleft or divided tongues, and one was seen to sit upon each one of them. Of course the meaning is *one of the tongues* was seen to sit upon each of them.

8/1/71, #31, p.244

Query – Please give your opinion in reference to the *door keeper* or porter, i.e., who he is referred to in John 10.3. Some say he is Christ, others, John the Baptist, others God.

Answer – The porter can not be Christ, for he is the "Good Shepherd" to whom the porter opens. There is no evidence that it is God. No figure of Scripture represents God as occupying a subordinate position to the Son whom he has sent. It is more probable that it is John the Immerser, as he was sent before Christ to prepare a people for him, and as he did point him out, with the exclamation, "Behold the Lamb of God who takes away the sin of the world." We would not be tenacious about this, as nothing of importance depends on determining *who* the porter was. The main person to whom we should give attention, and whom we should *know*, and of whom we should learn, is the "Good "—the Lord Messiah.

10/8/71, v.13, #40, p.316

Query-1. Where did Christ preach to the spirits in prison? 2. Whose spirits were they to whom he preached in prison? 3. What is meant by the prison?

Answer–1. In the days of Noah while the ark was preparing. See 1 Pet 3.20. "Which (spirits) sometimes were disobedient, when once the long-suffering of God awaited in the days of Noah while the ark was a preparing." Christ went and preached by *the Spirit* through Noah, a "preacher of righteousness." See Gen 6.3. 2. The spirits of the people who lived before the flood. 3. They were in prison when Peter wrote—in *Tartarus*, with the angels that sinned, reserved in everlasting chains of darkness till the judgment of the great day.

3/5/72, v.xv, #10, p.83

Query–Please explain through the REVIEW, Luke 23.30. I wish to know who they were that wanted the mountains to fall upon them, etc. Does the passage allude to the destruction of the Jews, or some event that is yet to come to pass?

Answer–We have referred the "calling for the rocks and mountains to fall on them and hide them from the face of Him who sits on the throne, and to the wrath of the Lamb," to the final calamities that shall come upon the wicked.

4/2/72, vxv, #14, pg.108

Query–Our Bible class in Antioch, West Virginia requests you to answer a question touching Acts 3.21: "Whom the heavens must receive till the times of restitution of all things." Are all things restored now? or were all things restored at the setting up of the kingdom? or will they not be restored till the end of time?

Answer–We must inquire into another matter before we can answer the questions propounded. Till the restitution of all *what things*? The passage itself answers this. "All things which God has spoken by the mouth of all his holy prophets." The sum of the statements is, "whom the heavens must retain till the restoration of all things which God has *promised* by the mouth of all his holy prophets." 1. All things promised by the holy prophets were not restored at the setting up of the kingdom. That was not then the time. 2. All things promised by mouth of all the holy prophets are now restored. *Now* can not then be the time. 3. At the end of time all things promised by the mouth of all the holy prophets will be restored. The heavens will not then retain Jesus Christ, but God will send him to raise the dead and judge the world.

6/12/72 vol.15, #25, pg. 196

Query–Please explain, through your paper, the meaning of the following Scriptures: John 21.18–23, also Acts 2.27. Please give us your views in full, as quite a number are anxious to know, of the first, when this transpired, before or after the crucifixion of the Savior, and of the second, whose soul was not to see corruption, David's or Jesus'?

Answer–1. At verse 12, we find the Lord's invitation to "come and dine." Verse 14, John makes the explanation that, "This is now the third time that Jesus showed himself to his disciples *after that he was risen from the dead*. Verse 15, referring to the same dining to which the Lord had invited them, as we have seen in verse 12, which was *after* his resurrection, we have the occasion of the conversation in question. The whole was after his resurrection. The remark, "signifying what death he should die," does not allude to the death of the Savior, but the death that Peter should die. 2. There is nothing in the passage about the soul of any one seeing corruption. Acts 2.27, we have the words: "Thou wilt not leave my soul in hades, neither wilt thou suffer thy Holy One to see corruption." This is quoted by Peter, from Psalm 16.10. It is the soul of Jesus that was not to be left in hades, and it was Jesus who was not to see corruption. David was a representative person, and though applied to him the Savior. This is the case with many prophetic Scriptures. See the whole connection, Acts 2.21–30.

2/11/73, v.16, #6, pg.32

Query–A question has been started here about the Savior going and preaching to the spirits in prison while he was in the tomb. Some think he did, and others argue that he did not. The preachers are divided, as well as the lay members. They take it from 1 Peter 3.19, where he speaks of Noah and his salvation in the ark. If you can settle the matter, so as to put it out of dispute, please do so and oblige yours.

Answer–We have had no doubt about the meaning of the passage in question for many years, but we do not suppose we can "settle it," or "put it out of dispute." Men will dispute until the end of time. Some are young, and their attention is called to it for the *first time*, and the passage is not clear. They are liable to mistake the meaning. Designing men have quoted it to sustain their pet theories. We will give two examples of these: 1. Romanists have quoted it to give countenance to their shameful pretenses to take souls out of purgatory. They claim that when

Jesus died his spirit went to purgatory and he preached the gospel to them there, that they might be delivered from torment. They quote: "By which also he went and preached to the spirits in prison," 1 Peter 3.19, and "thou wilt not leave my soul in hell," Psa 16.10, in support of this. 2. The same Scriptures have been quoted by Restorationists to prove that the wicked will have the gospel preached to them after death, or in hell, and that they will have another chance for salvation. On these theories and the applications of these Scriptures to sustain them we have a few considerations for the reader: 1. The common version of the Scriptures opens the way for both of these theories and theorizers. Three Greek words are translated hell that evidently do not mean *the same*, nor are *they three names for the same place*. The three Greek words are *gehenna, hades, and tartarus*. The word *gehenna*, if we remember, is found twelve times in the New Testament, and is properly translated hell. It means what we now mean by the English word *hell*. It is not in this world, nor in the intermediate state, or between death and the resurrection. It is the place of final punishment beyond the last judgment. Jesus did not, when he died, go to *gehenna* to preach there, or for any other purpose. He simply was not there at all. *Tartaros* is only found in one place in the New Testament. Jesus did not go there nor did any good being ever go there. The angels that kept not their first estate were cast down to *tartaros*. It is more limited than hades. Hades includes the entire state of the dead, good and bad, from death to the resurrection. It includes *tartaros* and *paradise*, the one the abode of the righteous and the other of the wicked between death and the resurrection. Paradise is also called Abraham's bosom. Between the rich man and Lazarus there was a great gulf, so that they could not pass nor re-pass. Lazarus was in Abraham's bosom, and as the rich man was on the other side of the "great gulf," he was in *tartaros*. But they both were in *hades*. The rich man was in torment and Lazarus was comforted. The King James' version has: "Thou wilt not leave my soul in hell," thus translating *hades, hell*. The Bible Union have translated *hades, under world*. The rich man lifted up his eyes in hell. "Hell," here comes *hades*. But he was in the apartment called *tartaros*, and not in *Abraham's bosom* or *paradise*. Between *paradise* and *tartaros* there is a great gulf, so that there is no passing nor re-passing. Jesus went to paradise when he died. Hence, he said to the thief on the cross: "Today shalt thou be with me in *paradise*." Still, there is no account of his preaching there, or anywhere else between his death and resurrection.

But now to the passage in question, 1 Pet 3.19: "By which also he went and preached to the spirits in prison." The verse before this says: "He was put to death in the flesh, but quickened by the Spirit." There can be no misunderstanding about the meaning of the words: "Put to death in the flesh." The word "quickened" means *made alive*. Some have insisted on translating *en, in,* making it read made alive, or "quickened in Spirit." This is obviously incorrect. This is not intelligible. He had not *died in Spirit.* Agency is implied. He was put to death in the flesh, but quickened *by* the Spirit of God. This corresponds with the following: "If the Spirit of him that raised up Jesus from the dead dwell in you, he that raised up Christ from the dead shall also quicken your mortal bodies *by his Spirit* that dwells in you." Rom 8.11. It also agrees with the following: "God was manifest in the flesh, justified in the Spirit, seen of angels, preached to the Gentiles, believed on in the world, received up into glory." 1 Tim 3.16. "Justified in Spirit" should evidently be "justified *by* the Spirit." It implies the agency of the Spirit *by* which he was justified. God raised him up from the dead, quickened him, made alive, justified him *by the Spirit.* The Spirit is the agent *by* which it was done and the agent *by which* he will quicken our mortal bodies, or raise them up. "He was put to death in the flesh, but quickened, made alive, raised up, justified by the Spirit, by which also"—by which Spirit— "he went and preached to the spirits in prison." When was this preaching done? Peter refers to it again in the next chapter: "For," says he, "for this cause was the gospel preached also to them that are dead, that they might be judged according to men in the flesh, but live according to God in the Spirit." 1 Pet 4.6. The apostle says: "The gospel *was* preached to them that *are* dead," thus putting the preaching in the past tense and dead in the present tense. But he gives the reason for preaching to them. That reason is that they might be judged according to men *in the flesh*, but live according to God in the Spirit. The gospel certainly was preached to them before they were judged. They were judged according to men *in the flesh*. When was this preaching, what was this judgment, and when was it? Let us now turn back to the other passage: "By which also he went and preached to the spirits in prison." Who were these spirits? Those "who sometimes were disobedient." When were they disobedient? "When once the long-suffering of God waited, in the days of Noah, while the ark was a preparing." This passage tells when they were disobedient. It was in the days of Noah, while the ark was a preparing. The preaching must have been prior to the disobedience, for they must have disobeyed the gospel which was preached to them. The preaching must have been in the days of Noah, and they did not obey what was preached to them. Who preached in that day? We must now have a little light concerning Noah: "By faith Noah, being warned of God of things not seen, as yet, moved with fear, prepared an ark to the saving of his house; by which he condemned the world and became heir of the righteousness which is by faith." Heb 9.7. God, "spared not the old world, but saved Noah, the eighth person, a preacher of righteousness, bringing in the flood upon the world of the ungodly." See 2 Pet 2.5. Christ, through Noah, a preacher of righteousness, by his Spirit, went and preached to the antediluvians who were dead, "in prison," when Peter wrote. God said: "My Spirit shall not always strive with man, for that he is flesh, yet his days shall be one hundred and twenty years." See Gen 6.3. The Spirit of God, or, which is the same, the Spirit of Christ, did strive with them one hundred and twenty years, through the preaching of Noah. They resisted it, were judged according to men in the flesh, destroyed by the flood, and, at the time Peter wrote, they were in prison—in *tartaros*. Had they, like the Ninevites, who repented at the preaching of Jonah, repented at the preaching of Noah, they might have lived according to God in the Spirit. Noah believed God, prepared an ark and was saved, and thereby condemned the world of the ungodly. The preaching was in the time of Noah, the disobedience followed, and the judgment—their overthrow in the flood. Some have construed the words, "Yet his days shall be one hundred and twenty years," to mean that the ordinary lifetime of man was from that time to be reduced to about one hundred and twenty years, but this did not come to pass then, which demonstrates that such was not the meaning. The Lord was not speaking of the ordinary lifetime of men, but the *time his Spirit should strive with men*. The first declaration was that it should not always strive with man, and next declaration limits it to one hundred and twenty years. That was the limit till the destruction of the world by a flood. The meaning that his Spirit should not always strive with man, for he is flesh, but it shall strive with him one hundred and twenty years. It did strive with man, in the preaching of Noah, till the one hundred and twenty years had expired. This was the end of that day of grace. Judgment came. The long-suffering of God ceased. The day of wrath came, and there was no escape. No matter if the number was believed the true doctrine was small, and the number of the disobedient large, and the Lord saved the *few* and demonstrating that he will condemn the guilty and save the righteous, without any regard to the number on the one side or the other.

2/18/73, v.16, #7, pg. 52

Query–Please give some light on John 10.9: "If any man enter in he shall be saved, and shall go in and out and find pasture." The going in and out is what we want your views on.

Answer–Figures should never be pressed beyond their intention. The ancient shepherds, in taking care of their flocks, brought them in at night for safety and protected them over night and took them out to the grazing lands in the morning. In allusion to this, the Lord, the Chief Shepherd, speaking of his flock, says, "They shall go in and out and shall be saved." No particular stress should be attached to going *in* and *out.* The Lord simply gives assurance, that he will take care of his followers as the shepherd does his flock. They should hear his voice, and follow him in full confidence that he will take care of them.

7/15/73 v.16, #28, pg. 220

Query–Please explain in the REVIEW what is meant by the expression of Paul, 1 Cor 12.13: "For by one Spirit are we all baptized into one body." 2. What was the "one baptism" spoken of by Paul, Eph 4.5?

Answer–We do not know what explaining is desired. We take it as Wesley did, that "by one Spirit" is by the *direction* of one Spirit, we are all immersed into one body. It is clear that the baptism alluded to is the initiatory rite, for there is no other baptism *into one body.* The immersion in the Spirit is not *into one* body, or *into* anything. At the house of Cornelius they were immersed into Christ after they had been immersed in the Holy Spirit. The immersion in the Spirit was to convince Peter and his Jewish brethren that God intended to receive the Gentiles as well as the Jews. Hence, when Peter, in his rehearsal of the matter to his Jewish brethren, when he came to this, exclaims, "What was I that I should withstand God?" The "one baptism" of Paul is the iniatory rite—the baptism of the Commission, connected with the faith and repentance for the remission of sins, and will remain as long as there is one to believe, repent or seek remission of sins. The faith, repentance, confession, immersion and remission of sins stand connected in the gospel of the grace of God, and we see not how any man can be so perverted as to try to evade any one of these items.

7/28/73 v.16, #30, p.228

Query – Please explain, through the Review, 1 John 1.8; 3.9. It seems to be a contradiction in the eyes of many in this part of the state.

Answer – 1 John 1.8 reads as follows: "If we say that we have no sin, we deceive ourselves, and the truth is not within us." 1 John 3.9 reads as follows: "Whosoever is born of God doth not commit sin; for his seed remaineth in him; and he can not sin, because he is born of God." We suppose the clear import of the first passage is, "If we, we *commit* no sin," etc. To say this would be an empty presumption. In the sense of the apostle, *all commit sin*, more or less. He only vainly deceives himself who asserts that he commits no sin. The other passage is different. "Whosoever is born of God doth not *commit* sin, etc. That is, the tendency is not in him habitually to *commit sin*; for the seeds remains in him, and he can not, consistently with his having been begotten of God, *commit sin*. He is not absolutely sinless, or he would need no pardon. He is not absolutely without sin, nor yet habitually devoted to the practice of it. Being begotten of God, and his seed remaining in him, his life is not devoted to sin; and yet he is not so absolutely without sin as to need no mercy-seat. This may not be entirely clear to every one, but certain it is there is no contradiction when the genuine sense of the apostle is reached. We may not understand him, and in our mind there may be some confusion, or even contradiction; but there is no confusion nor contradiction in his language. We shall frequently find passages like those in hand, a little obscure, and but little light can be thrown on them by any one. The works of God are the same everywhere.

10/15/78, v.18, #42, pg.332

Query – 1.What is the day approaching alluded to in Heb 10.25 2. Is not the sinning willfully (verse 26) refusing to assemble, as commanded in verse 25? 3. Do not those who forsake the assemblies of the saints commit the sin spoken of in verse 29? 4. Is the apostle speaking in reference to the same matter, verses 25 to 29? 5. Is it the proper way of observing the command of Christ to "beware of false teachers," for our preachers to take them into the stand and have them introduce the "services—such teachers as Joe Smith, or Mormons?

Answer–1.No particular day is alluded to. It is simply, as you see, the time passing, and the period coming when these opportunities shall all have passed away. 2. If he is not "forsaking the assembling," it is in very close proximity to it. Paul says: "Let us consider one another, to provoke to love and good works; not forsaking the assembling of ourselves together, as the manner of some is; but exhorting one another; and so much the more as you see the day approaching. For if we sin willfully, after we have received the knowledge of the truth, there remaineth no more sacrifice for sins, but a certain fearful looking for of judgment and fiery indignation, which shall devour the adversaries." Heb 10.24–27. If forsaking the assembling is not the sin, it is certainly *one step directly on the way to it.* The very indisposition to assemble is an unfavorable symptom, pointing unmistakably to disease that may prove very malignant. 3. The third question is virtually the second over again. 4. The matters from 5th to 9th verses are more properly results that will follow the neglecting to assemble. The time for a subject to be alarmed and aroused is when persons find they are losing their desire to attend the assemblies of the saints. Apostasy has begun its work in the heart when the desire to assemble is gone, and becoming malignant when apologies and excuses are frequently made for nonattendance; and when becoming less and less frequent till there is none at all, there is but little hope of care. 5. By no means, Beecher found no trouble, many years ago, in being on fraternal terms with "Rev. Theodore Parker" and "Rev. Chapin." More recently he has openly declared that he could "commune with the Pope," and that he could "worship at a pagan altar." By the time he gets through with his trial in the civil court the people of this country can see what his broad-gauge piety and charity come to. Such pranks paid off before the people, in the place of broad charity, only show the want of *principle* in men. The wonder is that intelligent people can be gulled with such hollow and empty pretenses. Any man who is a Christian, or is in Christ, can be received into the fellowship of the Church. If a man is not a Christian, not in Christ, he can not in any consistency be received into the Church or into the pulpit. We would not give much for any man's principles who can set them aside for a little act of *courtesy*, or a little pretense of *liberality*. It is nothing but a sham, an empty pretense and hypocrisy, to receive a man into the pulpit and recognize him before the people, to whom you would not give the right hand of fellowship. It is liberality to allow every man the same liberality you enjoy, but a sham, a pretense and hypocrisy to recognize him as a preacher of Jesus, when you do not believe he is in Christ, and would not give him the right hand of fellowship and take him into the Church. Nor is it *courtesy* to receive such a man into the stand as a preacher, but *hypocrisy*. A man who is in Christ is a brother, and, if a preacher of Christ, may be received as such, in good faith. Such an one has a right to all the privileges of the body of Christ by virtue of being in it. But the man who ignores the law of the King, and recognizes persons who are not in Christ as brethren, Christians and preachers, instead of displaying a broad liberality, an extended charity, shows that he has no settled principles—that he disregards principles and law. Who ever thought a Mason or Odd Fellow was discourteous for not recognizing a man as a Mason who did not belong to the order? Certainly no man of intelligence. They have their initiation, and without it you are not in the order, and they do not recognize you, charitably or uncharitably.

3/9/75, v.18, #10, pg. 76

QUESTIONS ABOUT BAPTISM

Query–Please inform us where and how were the Apostles prepared subjects of the Church referred to in Acts 2.47. And also whether the 3,000 were added to either, to the apostles or the 120 referred to in Acts 2.15, and if either, which, and the testimony in each case.(?)

Answer–1.) The apostles were prepared subjects of the Church in making them *disciples.* 2.) The 3000 were added to the 120, including the apostles, or to the Church, as subsequently called.

6/25/72, vol.15, #26, page 204.

Query–Is baptism administered to a person scripturally valid when he claims he is in Christ before he was baptized, and will contend that his sins were all forgiven him before he submitted to the institution of baptism, and will still further affirm that baptism is not essential in order to remission of sins of any person?

Answer–A man is "scripturally baptized" when he is baptized according to the Scriptures. A man who believes in Christ, repents and is immersed, is scripturally baptized. His misunderstanding about something else could not invalidate his baptism. The Lord says: "He who believes and is immersed shall be saved." Suppose the man misunderstood: thought he was in Christ before he was immersed; or that he was pardoned, would that make void the promise of God? Surely not. He believed with all his heart and was immersed, and thus came to the promise of God, that he should be saved or pardoned. That promise can not fail because he did not understand *when* he was in Christ or pardoned. The work to do for that man in not enough to convince him that what he has done, and *done rightly*, is to be discarded and repudiated, but teach him "the way of the Lord more perfectly," or, in other words, correct his understanding in the things wherein he does not understand, and leave what he has done rightly unmolested. There are evils connected with an ultra course in the above matter that many brethren do not see.

6/25/72, vol.15, #26, pg. 204

Query–May I please have your views of the "Baptism of the Holy Ghost with fire." Is it all past? And if so, when was it consummated; and, if not, is any part of it passed? The problem I have is with the "fire" part.

Answer–This question has been so frequently discussed but in compliance with the kindly words, we say: 1. It is a fact that none but the good were ever baptized in the Holy Spirit. 2. It is a fact that two classes were present, and addressed in the discourse where the baptism of fire is mentioned—the disciples and others saying, "We have Abraham for our father," called a "generation of vipers." 3. Where these "vipers" were not addressed or alluded to, we find no baptism of fire. 4. In Matt 3.7–12, we find both parties present. In this passage the word fire occurs three times, as follows: first, verse 10: "Every tree that bringeth not forth good fruit, is hewn down and cast into the *fire*." Second, verse 11: "He shall baptize you with the Holy Spirit and with *fire*." Third, ver.12, "He will burn up the chaff with unquenchable *fire*." Now that these three passages are three figurative expressions, meaning precisely the same, we think no reasonable man can doubt. Each of these expressions applies, and is addressed, to the same persons. There is no trouble in determining that the "generation of vipers," who say "we have Abraham for our father," the "trees that bring not forth fruit," and the "chaff," are the same. In the first and third instance, the fire is unquestionably for the wicked. It would be remarkable then, if the fire in the second instance did not apply to the same persons. We have, first, fruitful and unfruitful trees, good and bad people, the one to remain in the orchard, the other to be cast into the fire; second, the baptism of the Holy Spirit and of fire, the former for good, the latter for the bad; third, the chaff and wheat, good and bad, the latter for the garner, and the former for fire. No man would pray for the fire to come upon him that is to burn the trees that bring not forth good fruit, or that is to burn the chaff; yet he who prays that he may be baptized with fire, prays for the same fire. This fire is evidently not past, but the *gehenna* of fire for the ungodly.

1857 vol.2,page 246

Query– If those under the law received a just recompense of reward for every transgression and disobedience in this world, will they be punished in the world to come for the same transgressions?

Answer– The subject introduced by a brother in the above question, is one that can not be satisfactorily discussed and answered in a few words; yet we have but a small space for its elucidation now. We, therefore, can not promise full satisfaction. The law of Moses neither could give eternal life, nor punish with eternal punishment. Its rewards and punishments were not spiritual, but worldly; not eternal but temporal; not in the future, but in the present world. The law could not purge the conscience. By the deeds of the law no flesh could be justified in the sight of God. The law offered no heaven, and threatened no hell. A man could conform to the letter of the law all his life, so as to escape all its punishments; or as in the case of Saul of Tarsus, as touching the law be blameless, and yet have no piety towards God, no purification of conscience, or not at all justified in the sight of God. A mere conformity to the law of Moses prepared no person for heaven, or guarantied to no person any thing in the world to come. A man receiving all its rewards— all its promises, its Canaan, its milk and honey, etc. etc.—in this world, was no reason why he should not enjoy heaven. On the other hand, the penalty of that law failing upon its transgressor, was no reason why he should not be punished in the world to come, any more than the penalty of the civil government falling upon a transgressor is a reason why God should not punish him. The truth is, Abraham was justified by faith, in the sight of God, four hundred and thirty years before the law, even while yet in uncircumcision. His faith looked not to the law, its rewards or its promises, but to Him who was the end of the law, who is the resurrection and the life—the Lord from heaven. In receiving the promise, Abraham received Christ, was justified by him, and through him gained heaven. All the justification, from Abraham to the giving of the law, and from them to Christ, was through faith in the promise, or in Christ, the substance of the promise, and not through the law. Abraham, by faith, saw the day of the Redeemer; and through that faith reached beyond the law, beyond all its rewards and punishments, and above them, to a spiritual life, and spiritual world. Upon this promise, and faith in it, rested the piety of Abraham, and all his descendants, to Christ; in it was their hope of heaven and the world to come; through it was justification, and without that faith there was no justification. Without this faith there was no purification of conscience, no purification of the heart, and union with God, though a man had kept the law all his life. But if a man lived without this faith, and died in his disobedience to the law, he certainly died without justification, without his soul being purified, and consequently without any preparation to enjoy God. The mere circumstance of a man being punished for his sins in this life, has nothing in it to purify his soul, purge his conscience, or prepare him for the enjoyment of God. The Egyptians, the antediluvians, the Sodomites and the Jews, had a just recompense of reward sent upon them in this world, but this only sent them down to *tartarus,* to be reserved, with the angels that sinned, to the judgment of the great day, where, we are assured, Sodom and Gomorrah shall appear. Some men appear to think, that if men are punished, to use their own style, as much as their sins deserve, they must necessarily be happy then. But men can not be happy—can not enjoy God, without justification, purification of heart and conscience, and, unless thus prepared for the enjoyment of God, they can not enjoy the world to come. This is a work that punishment can not do. The hurling of angels that sinned, down to hell, the drowning of antediluvians and Egyptians, the burning of Sodomites and slaying of the Jews, did not purify one of them; nor can we see that any punishment will ever purify, or justify one them. If men live in unbelief, commit some capital offence and are executed for it, though this may be a just recompense of reward, it will not purify their souls, and prepare them to enjoy God. When men pass the boundary line of life, they pass all the means, in the economy of God, for preparing them for heaven, and no punishment will ever do what the grace of God could not do.

1857, vol.2, #2, pg.59

Query–What kind of baptism does the apostle speak of in 1 Cor 12.13? I heard a man that is called a "big preacher," say that it is spirit baptism. I do not understand it that way, though I might be wrong.

Answer–This passage, unquestionably, referred to the ordinary immersion in water, which completed their initiation into Christ. The baptism of the Holy Spirit never initiated any persons into Christ. Those baptized in the spirit on Pentecost, were already in Christ, or in his body, when baptized in the spirit. Those at the house of Cornelius were not in Christ when baptized in the spirit, nor did that baptism take them into Christ; but after their baptism in the spirit, the apostle commanded them to be baptized in the name of the Lord. This baptism, which is a command, in which man can be baptized at will, and man can administer, is water baptism and the initiatory ordinance. But the baptism of the spirit, which man can not administer, which is not a *command* but a *promise*, and in which man can not be baptized at will, never was designed to, and never did initiate any person into Christ. But the baptism alluded to in the query, is the one by which "we are *all* baptized *into* one body." This baptism is common to *all*. It introduces them *into* one body.

By the way, it would be hard for our sectarian friends to prove that they have ever enjoyed this baptism, no matter whether it be spirit or water; for it introduced into *one body*; and they certainly have never been baptized into *one body*, by any kind of baptism.

Proclamation & Reformer 1851, vol.2

Query– If you think proper, please give us an exposition of Gal 3.27, in connection with Rom 13.14. The subject is "Putting on the Lord Jesus Christ." 1. Are there two methods of putting on Christ? 2. If so, what are they?

Answer-The passage, Gal 2.27, is "For as many of you as have been baptized into Christ have put on Christ." The passage, Rom 13.14 is: "But put ye on the Lord Jesus Christ, and make not provision for the flesh, to fulfill the lusts thereof." The former of these passages alludes to adoption, or the putting on of Christ in adoption. In our induction, we took the authority of Christ upon us, or the Christian obligation. This was in baptism. But the passage, Rom 13.14, can not refer to the same, because it is a requirement of those in Christ—already baptized. They had, however, been partially drawn away by divers fleshly inducements, and to some extent thrown off the authority of Christ. The Apostle's admonition is simply to return to their Christian obligations, and maintain their position under Christ.

1857, vol.2, page 249

Query– If a person confess and be baptized without considering the importance of what he is doing, and afterwards becomes convinced by hearing the gospel, and reading the word of God, that he did not have the faith and repentance required, that he is yet in his sins, what should he do?

Answer–We know no better that such person can do than to confess Christ and obey right, after he hears and knows the truth. But, then, such things should be done with care, or you may unsettle the faith of many persons whose profession is good and they need only carry it out rightly to be saved. It is not absolutely necessary that a person should understand all about many of the questions of our times to prepare them to obey the gospel. To believe in the Lord with all the heart is indispensable. The thousands on Pentecost did not understand much about it, but they believed in Christ and that they could not be saved except by him and did all they did in obedience to him. Such persons are proper subjects and their obedience is acceptable. They may not understand all about the design of baptism or its importance, but when they have understood enough of its importance to confess and obey, there is but little doubt that all is right, if they continue true to him. A man who is satisfied that he is yet in his sins, of course should reform and try and escape from his sins.

6/12/60, vol.3, #24, page 95.

Query–I would be very glad to have your opinion in regard to 1 Cor 15.29. The verse reads as follows: "Else what shall they do which are baptized for the dead, if the dead rise not at all?" Why are they then baptized for the dead? Please answer soon and oblige.

Answer–The passage referred to above is some-what dark, and we are not confident about the meaning of it. The apostle is, however, discoursing to them about those who denied the resurrection of the dead, and the most plausible view we have seen is that he reasons with them on their own ground. If there is no resurrection of the dead, then Christ is not risen—he is dead. As those immersed are immersed *for him,* they are immersed *for a dead Christ.* The question, "Why, then, are they immersed for the dead?" is in point. There is no sense in being immersed *for* Christ, or *on account* of Christ, if there is no resurrection, for in that case *he is dead.*

We do not claim that this view is very satisfactory, but, though the passage has been *explained at* in our prints ever since we have been reading them, we have seen nothing more satisfactory or better.

10/10/71 Vol.14, #41, page 324.

Query–If the Legislature of Ohio should pass a law that immersion should not be allowed in the state any more, would it be right to preach against that law in the church?

Answer–The magistrates whipped, stoned and killed men in the days of the Apostles, for *being Christians*, and the Apostles and the first Christians did not even then *preach against the laws nor against the magistrates*, but taught the disciples to *obey both the laws and the magistrates*. It is not a sign that a man is very deeply imbued with the Spirit of Christ and his Apostles to find him ranting against the laws of his country. The first Christians did no work of this sort, though they had not half as good laws as we have. We had better thank the Lord for the best human government in the world and try to show ourselves worthy of it, than preach against it. Let those who can preach, *preach Christ*, the wisdom and power of God unto salvation.

1/11/59, vol.2 #2, page 7.

Query–Do three immersions—one into the name of the Father, one into the name of the Son and one into the name of the Holy Spirit, introduce by one spirit into the one body? In other words, does the three immersions of the German Baptist include the one immersion into the name of the Father and of the Son and of the Holy Spirit?

Answer–The above is a hard question. We have received several of the people alluded to; but whether the Lord will accept such corruptions of his ordinance is all in the dark. The Lord will not accept his baptism unless he has the "one immersion." Ephesians 4.6.

11/58, vol.1, # 48, page 192

Query–While the Apostles were acting under the first commission, in what name did they baptize?

Answer–There is nothing said about their baptizing in any name.

6/19/60, vol.3, #25, page 99

Query–What are your views in regard to the propriety of receiving members into the church without administering the ordinance of immersion, on the plea that they have been immersed by any of the *religious sects*, and are satisfied *themselves with their baptism?* I anxiously desire your views on the subject. I believe in "one Lord, one faith and one baptism." I do not believe in a *sectarian* Lord, *a sectarian* faith, or a *sectarian* baptism; but in the Lord of the Bible, the faith of the Bible, and the immersion of the Bible, against all human creeds and those who hold and maintain them. Please answer in the REVIEW.

Answer–The question involved in the foregoing is one of some considerable moment practically. It is constantly coming before us, while the people, in multitudes, are coming from all the parties around us. It is a question, too, that should be treated gravely. We think the subject naturally divides itself into two parts. In baptizing, there are two distinct responsibilities, two acts of obedience and two blessings annexed. One relates to the baptist and the other to the person baptized. The administrator alone is responsible for *his* part of the work, or for *his own* action. The validity of the one can not depend upon the sincerity or the purity of the motives of the other. Those immersed by sectarian preachers, are as sincere as those we immerse; believe as firmly and repent as effectually; and the act, on their part, is done with an eye as single to the glory of God and their salvation. They have the one faith of the gospel, receive the one Lord, in the one baptism, and are entitled to the one hope. They act from the proper motives, with the proper faith, repentance and devotion to the Lord, and perform the proper action, and they have the promise of the Lord. The circumstance that the preacher is a sectarian, acting from his usual partisan motives and feelings, while it renders his action unacceptable to the Lord, does not vitiate nor invalidate the sincere action of an honest soul, simply aiming to obey the Savior of the world. The action of the preacher is not acceptable to the Lord, because *his heart is not right in the sight of God,* but the action of the candidate is acceptable to the Lord, because *his heart is right in the sight of God.*

If the sectarianism or *heresy* in the minister, or any other defect, may invalidate a baptism, there then is no certainty in any man's baptism; for no man can know that all the men from the one that baptized him, in any successions of Baptists back to the Apostles, is perfect. Yet one link out the chain in any one place, no matter if one thousand years back, would invalidate all below it. The truth in the case is, if any man preaches the gospel of Christ, in its purity, *it is the gospel of Christ.* let him be a sectarian or what not. His being a sectarian, can not sectarianize the gospel, nor turn the truth of God into a lie. In the same way, if he administers the ordinances to proper subjects, *they are still the ordi-*

nances of Christ, though he be an Atheist at heart, and the honest soul who receives the ordinances, is acceptable to God; and, if true to the end, will be saved, though the administrator be condemned world without end. The whole theory of official grace is without one particle of foundation. The Bible is divine, if printed and published by infidels for pecuniary gain; the gospel is the power of God unto salvation to every one that believeth, no matter by whom published and preached; and the ordinances are divine, and the blessing of God will attend all who, with proper preparation of heart, receive them, though the administrator be a hypocrite and condemned for ever.

The greatest work of this generation is to call people out from all partyism ; but this does not make it our duty to invalidate what has been done right, *is done,* and it is not necessary that it be done right. What has been done right, *is done,* it is not necessary that it be done again. All those who resolve to go with us in this great work, we hope will keep all they have received from the Lord and do all the Lord requires, and the Lord will receive them.

1858, vol.1 #32, page 127.

Query–For what purpose was Cornelius baptized?

Answer–For the same purpose as all other persons. Baptism has one place, one design, one purpose, in all cases, in the reign of Christ. It can not have one design to one man and another design to another man. It is connected with entering into the kingdom of God. "Except a man be born of water and of the Spirit, he can not enter into the kingdom of God." It is a condition of salvation. "He that believeth and is baptized shall be saved." It is for the remission of sins. "Repent and be baptized, every one of you, in the name of Jesus Christ for the remission of sins, and you shall receive the gift of the Holy Spirit." These and sundry other duties express the design of baptism in the case of Cornelius, and all other cases, till the final amen of time.

12/58, vol.1, #49, page 195

Query–Where in the Bible do you learn that baptism is a condition of pardon? Paul said unto the Jailer, "Believe on the Lord Jesus Christ and thou shalt be saved." If there is any other condition, please tell me where it can be found.

Answer—We find it in the words, "He who believes and is immersed shall be saved"—that is, saved from sins, or pardoned. This makes immersion as much a condition as believing. We find it in the words, "Repent and be immersed every one of you in the name of Jesus Christ for the remission of sins, and you shall receive the gift of the Holy Spirit." This makes both immersion and repentance conditions of remission of sins.

The circumstance that Paul mentioned believing in his command to the jailer, by itself, in the words, "The like figure whereunto even immersion doth also now save us," excludes faith. Peter, on Pentecost, mentioned repentance and immersion, but not faith. Yet the faith was there as certainly as the items mentioned. Ananias, in his instructions to Saul, mentioned immersion and calling on the name of the Lord, but not faith and repentance. Yet faith and repentance were present. So, in the instance of the jailer, the belief is mentioned, by itself, but the repentance and immersion were present, for "he took them the same hour of the night and washed their stripes; and was immersed, he and all his, straightway."

We shall never be able to diffuse a general understanding of the Scriptures till we get rid of these *Scripture scrappers,* who appear never to be able to understand that the whole Scriptures are to be taken together. It is strange that any man of common capacity can not see that the expression, that "we are justified by his blood," does not exclude faith, grace or repentance. It appears that the veil is over their faces—that they are smitten by some kind of legal blindness and fated to perpetual darkness. The Jews were not more given over to blindness and hardness of heart than some of these modern scrap-doctors.

10/71, vol.14, #41, page 324

Query—Did the baptism of John, the forerunner of our Savior, have anything whatever to do with the remission of sins?

Answer—It certainly did. "John did immerse in the wilderness and preached the immersion of repentance *for the remission of sins.*"–Mark 1.4.

9/22/63,v.6, #38, pg.150

Query—My mind has been agitated, rather troubled about baptism for some time, (particularly the *mode,*) sometimes leading me to doubt as to *immersion* being the divinely appointed mode for administering this holy sacrament, as termed. And as my opportunities for obtaining satisfactory information upon the subject were bad, I could think of no better way than addressing you who I believe delights in leading the earnest seeker in the way of truth.

My doubts were particularly aroused from reading a Methodist tract, entitled, "Subject and Mode of Baptism," containing some 36 pages, and which, if you will *answer*. I will send you, at your request. I would, if you please, have you respond to my letter and state some clear instances of immersion in the Bible, and also some strong inferential proofs given in the Bible, and by so doing you may save one from perhaps some fatal delusion, and thus add a star to your crown when you shall wear it in that "better land," as the reward of your zealous labors here in your Master's cause.

Answer–We could not say, till we see the tract, whether it would be worthy of an answer. If it is, by its friends, considered an able document, or anything like a masterly effort, we should take pleasure in answering the finest things contained in it. We should like to see it.

We never saw a production on the subject that contained anything to induce any one to doubt that immersion is valid, especially in a Methodist work. Any Methodist ought to blush at the thought of questioning immersion. Let us sum up a few considerations: 1. The Methodist Discipline has endorsed immersion ever since it came into existence. It says, if the candidate desires it "he" (the administrator) "shall immerse him." It adds, that when he immerses, he shall save, "I baptize thee." If immersion is not baptizing, the Discipline has, for a hundred years, required the preachers, not only to practice falsely, in requiring them to *immerse*, when the candidate desired it, but required them to pronounce a falsehood in the name of the Lord every time they immersed, in requiring them to say, "I baptize thee." What an unscrupulous set of men these Methodist preachers must be, who, after endorsing immersion, in their Discipline, is the General Conference, pronouncing it baptism in the name of the Lord, when they have immersed, ever since they have existed as a people; but now, in the face of all this, turn around and pronounce it not baptism at all! Do they believe this themselves? Not one syllable of it. If they did, they would pronounce those among them *immersed, for baptism*, not baptized at all, and require them to be sprinkled or poured on. This they have 2. Wesley says, commenting on Rom 6.4, "alluding to the ancient manner of baptizing by immersion."

Samuel Clarke says, "In primitive times, the manner of baptizing was by immersion, or dipping the whole body under water." Dr. A. Clarke, commenting on the same words—"buried with him in baptism" says "Alluding to the *immersion* practiced in the case of *adults*." Martin Luther says, "Baptism is nothing else than the word of God with immersion in water." John Calvin says, "The word *baptizo* signifies to immerse, and it is certain that immersion was the practice of the ancient church." We set these names against all who deny that immersion is valid, and they are not a tithe of what we can collect in a few hours. 3. The Greek lexicons, with great unanimity, give immersion, or its equivalent, not as *a meaning of baptizo*, but *the primary meaning.* 4. No Lexicon, now in use, gives *sprinkle, or pour,* as a definition of *baptizo* at all, either primary, secondary or any meaning. 5. No instances have been produced where any scholar has translated *baptizo,* sprinkle or pour. 6. The words, *sprinkle* and *pour,* are found a number of times in the New Testament, but they are from their proper representatives in Greek, and never from *baptizo,* and never used in reference to the initiatory rite, or baptism. 7. The reason we do not find the word, *immerse* in the common version of the Scriptures, is that *baptizo,* the proper word for *immerse,* is not translated, but merely transferred. *Bapto* is translated *dip* in the common version, but it is never used in reference to the ordinance.

But the writer of the foregoing may say, that he does not know anything about those Greek words, or learned authorities—that he only has the common version of the New Testament—that he would like to have evidence from that. Well, we will accommodate him. 1. What then, did they baptize *in,* or *with,* in the times of the Apostles? When Jesus was baptized, he "went up straight-way out of the water." At the house of Cornelius, Peter said, "Can any man forbid *water,* that these should not be baptized?" "Philip and the Eunuch went down both into the water," when about to baptize. John was baptizing in Enon near Salem, because there was much *water* there." These expressions show that *water* was the element employed. On this there is no controversy. All agree that *water* is the element. 2. Is there anything said about the *quantity* of water? There is. In one instance, it is said, they baptized in a certain place because there was *much water* there. They did not *sprinkle* or *pour* water on persons in Enon near Salem because there was *much water there.* 3. Where did they find the water in which they baptized? Did they find it in a cup, bowl, basin, in a house, or where? Did they send any body to bring it? No account of any thing of this sort in all the New Testament. Where, then, did they find the *water*. They found it in Enon, in Jordan, and Philip and the Eunuch, as they traveled, "came to a certain water," Such is the account, so far as the Lord has seen fit to give it. They found it in its native place where the Lord put it. 4. What did they do just preceding baptizing? Where did they go? Into a chamber? No. Into a house? No. Where then? Philip and the Eunuch "came unto a certain water." What next? They went *down both into the water*, both Philip and the Eunuch." The history says, "and he baptized him." Paul says, "we are buried with him in baptism." When he baptized him, then, *he buried him in baptism*. That is clear enough. 5. What followed immediately after the burying in baptism? The Savior "went up straightway out of the water." Philip and the Eunuch "came *up out of the water*." 6. What followed as a result of baptizing? Their "*bodies were washed with pure water*."

Is there any church in our time and country which has use for all these terms? There is. We, in our practice, have use for every one of them. We cannot baptize in some places because there is not "much water there." We *can*, and *do*, baptize in other places "because there is much water there." A few days since, when we baptized, we "came unto a certain water."—the baptist and the person to be baptized then, "went down into the water." The person then was "buried in baptism." The baptizing was done in the place "because there was much water there. The parties then, as when Jesus was baptized, "went up straightway out of the water." As a result of the baptizing, the *body was washed*. This, an earnest seeker can see for himself.

But in practicing, sprinkling or pouring, you do not baptize any where "because there is much water there," for, "much water" is not needed. The water is usually brought in a cup, bowl or pitcher, and you do not "come unto a certain water," but a little water is brought. The administrator and subject do not "go down into the water," or, at least there is no necessity for going *down into the water*. The subject is not *buried in baptism at all*. The body of the subject *is not washed at all*, and they do not *come up out of the water at all*, and they do not *come up out of the water*. Immersion is clearly the Scriptural practice. Sprinkling and pouring are never used in reference to it.

10/13/63, v.6, #41, pg. 162

Query – If baptism is the door into Jesus Christ, or we are baptized for the remission of our sins—that is, we are never in the kingdom until we have complied with the command of baptism. Does it not, I ask, become necessary for a man, if he apostatizes, fall entirely away, to be baptized again for the remission of those sins which he committed since his former baptism?

Answer–A man who has fully "fallen away," "sinned willfully after receiving the knowledge of the truth," counted the blood of the covenant, wherewith he was sanctified, an unholy thing, and done despite unto the Spirit of grace," and "trodden under foot the Son of God," can never be reclaimed. Such an one will never hear the warnings of God, nor try to return. See Heb 6.4–8, and 10.26–29. But there is a provision for a brother who sins, is surprised into, or overtaken in a fault. See the case of Simon, Acts 8.19–24. He believed, was baptized and became a disciple, the same as others at Samaria. After this he saw the Apostles imparting the gift of the Holy Spirit, and offered them money for the power to impart this gift as the Apostles did. It was a wicked thought, to think of buying the apostolic gift, to impart the gift of the Holy Spirit with money. For this the Apostle reproves him in the following words: "Thou hast neither part nor lot in this matter, for thy heart is not right in the sight of God. Repent, therefore, of this thy wickedness, and *pray God*, if perhaps the thought of thy heart may be forgiven thee." He does not tell him to be baptized again, but "*pray God*" for pardon.

John says, "If any man sin, we have an advocate with the Father, Jesus Christ, the Righteous;" 1 John 2.1 Do you inquire, how we are to approach him? The following shows: "If any man see his brother sin a sin which is not unto death, he *shall ask*, and he shall give him life for them that sin not unto death;" 1 John 5.16. The prayer must be accompanied by confession. See Jas 5.15–16. This accords with the prayer the Lord taught the disciples. See the following words: "Forgive us our trespasses as we forgive those who trespass against us; Matt 6.12 Every child of God should come daily to the mercy-seat, to Jesus our advocate, asking forgiveness.

There is but one initiation of one person into the body of Christ, and consequently but one baptism; but there are many faults in which the children of God are overtaken, and many prayers should be offered. If a baptism was a Christian duty to be performed by a person converted, or in the kingdom, no man could tell why it is not to be repeated. A man is initiated but *once*.

3/23/58, v.1,#12, p.47

Query–What is Christian baptism?

Answer–We take it that this question relates to the *act* to be performed, and shall so answer. If we do not meet the intention of the querist, we have more ink and paper. We shall simply answer the following: In the command to *baptize,* what was the precise thing to be done? Some men when they intend to do as commanded, *sprinkle* water on a person. Was that what was commanded? It was not. How do you know? We know from the following: 1. The command is not given in a word, in the original, the common or any other version, that means *sprinkle.* It is not the word in the original used in the New Testament where sprinkle is meant. We have the word in the New Testament, in the original that means sprinkle, and it is so translated. This is not the word used in the command to *baptize.* If the Lord had intended by the command, *"baptizing* them," *sprinkling* them, he would have used the original word, found elsewhere and rightly translated, *sprinkling.* 2. We find no account of sprinkling for baptism in the first two centuries, in a single instance, in all history. 3. No translator has ever translated the original word in the command, sprinkle, for the simple, that it does not mean sprinkle. 4. No Lexicon in use defines the word used in the command, in the original, sprinkle. 5. No man of any learning and responsibility, will affirm, that the command to baptize, means sprinkle. If any man will, we have room for his arguments.

These reasons put sprinkling, for baptism, entirely out of the question. It has no place in the controversy. Each one of these reasons apply to pouring, in precisely the same way. To see this you, you only have to insert the word pouring, where we have the word sprinkling. No other acts are contended for, or practiced, but immersion. What reason then have we for saying the command is to immerse? 1. The word used by our Lord, in giving this command, means *immerse,* and is so defined in every Lexicon in use. 2. Calvin and Luther both said, that the word used by the Lord in the command, means immerse. 3. Luther, Calvin, Wesley, and a hundred others of the greatest Pedobaptists that have lived in the past three hundred years, say that immersion was the ancient practice. 4. Luther, Calvin, and Dr. Wall, admitted the change from immersion to sprinkling and that it never became general in any country in the world, till the thirteenth century, in France. 5. All history confirms the fact, that immersion was the original practice, and, not only that the change from immersion to sprinkling was made, but that the change never became the general practice till in the thirteenth century in France. 6. Numerous translators have translated the original word in the command, immerse, and numerous others have admitted that it should be so translated though they have not done it. 7. The advocates of sprinkling or pouring, for baptism, till very recently, have almost unanimously admitted that immersion is valid baptism. The only doubt has been about sprinkling or pouring. 8. But few instances have been found of persons having renounced immersion, while numerous instances are constantly occurring of persons renouncing sprinkling or pouring, and utterly refusing any longer to recognize it at all as baptism. 9. The Lord certainly did not require sprinkling, pouring and immersion, in the command to baptize, or all three would have to be performed. The word certainly does not mean sprinkle, pour, or immerse. No authority so defines it. If it means sprinkle, then pour and immerse have nothing to do with it. If it means pour, then, sprinkle and immerse have nothing to do with it. If it means immerse, then, sprinkle and pour have nothing to do with it. This latter is the true state of the case. It means immerse, as is admitted by all the authorities, and does not mean or pour at all. 10. The thing the apostles and the first preachers did, in obeying the command to baptize, was to *bury in baptism*, to *plant* the subjects together in the likeness of his death and they were *born of the water*. These were simply not sprinkling nor pouring, but figurative allusions to immersion, the precise thing commanded to be done.

2/5/67, v.x,#6,pg.45

Query–Can a penitent receive remission of sins without baptism?

Answer–We do not approve this question. The question is not whether a penitent *can* receive remission without immersion, nor whether the Lord *can* pardon a penitent without baptism. It is simple for us to spend our time in arguing about what *can* be, or what the Lord *can* do. The matter is, *does* the Lord promise the penitent pardon *without* baptism? If so where is that promise? There is no such promise. But the proper question is, does the Lord promise pardon to the penitent when immersed? "He who believes and is immersed shall be saved," or pardoned. According to the gospel, are penitents who are immersed pardoned? "Repent and be immersed every one of you in the name of Jesus Christ, for the remission of sins and you shall receive the gift of the Holy Spirit." The Lord, in the commission, unites faith and immersion, and Peter unites repentance and immersion in order to remission. We must not omit an item in either passage, but unite all contained in both passages. Have nothing to do with any questions about whether you can be saved *without* any of the items here included, but lean on the promise of salvation *in doing them.* If any man is determined on salvation *without* any one of those items, let the responsibility rest on *him,* not on us.

2/5/67, v.x, #6, pg.45.

Query– Please give some light on the Baptismal formula, or a part of it, as used by the Christian Brotherhood, beginning "By the authority of Jesus Christ, etc., I baptize you into the name of the Father, Son, and the Holy Spirit." Where do we get the authority from Christ?

Answer– "Where do we get the authority from Christ?" The Father put all things into the hands of the Son. Hence our Lord says, "All authority in heaven and on earth is given to me." In the commission he gave the authority to the apostles. Paul, and the other apostles, gave authority to Timothy, Titus, Barnabus and Silas, and through them to all evangelists, to commit the things they had learned of the Apostles, to faithful men who should be able to teach others also. In the first church the disciples went every where preaching the word. This is mentioned approvingly by the sacred historian. The first disciples, under the Apostles' direction, preached, baptized, and administered the affairs of the kingdom. The Lord committed the whole matter into the hands of the Apostles, and the Apostles committed the administration of the gospel and the kingdom, into the hands of the disciples. Since then the administration has been in the hands of the disciples. In the entire code of the New Institution there is not a prohibitory clause forbidding any disciple to preach the gospel or teach the law of the Lord to the extent of his ability. By virtue of being a disciple, any one has authority to preach and baptize. There are questions of propriety to be consulted, such as relate to ability, suitableness etc., but so far as relates simply to the right and authority, all have it.

2/5/67, v.x, #6, pg. 45.

Query– Would it be right according to the teachings of Christ and his Apostles, to baptize in the name of Jesus, without either the Father or Holy Spirit?

Answer–It would not be right to baptize in the name of the Lord Jesus, without either the Father or the Holy Spirit. It is all done by the authority of Jesus, for he said, "All authority in heaven and on earth is given to me," but the transfer by the authority of Jesus the Christ, the great Head of the church, is into a new revelation, or state—in Christ— into one body—the Church. There is no such thing as being in the new relation to the Father without being in the new relation to the Son—to the Holy Spirit, nor is there any such thing as being in the new relation to the Son, without being in the new relation to the Father.

Whether the administrator in repeating the formula, says, "By the authority of Jesus the Christ," or not, it is by his authority it is done, and the immersion is "into the name of the Father, and of the Son and of the Holy Spirit." These words should be uttered slowly, distinctly, and with profound awe. Nothing appears more absurd and ridiculous than the hasty and irreverent manner in which some men run over those awful words; nor does anything show more clearly that a man has no proper appreciation of what he is doing. It is the initiation into the New Institution; the transfer into the kingdom of God, the body of Christ.

2/5/67, v.x, #6, pg. 45.

Query–Do all persons baptized by the Disciples receive remission of their sins? If so, how do they know it?

Answer–All persons having the faith, the repentance and confession required in the gospel, who are immersed into the name of the Father, and of the Son, and of the Holy Spirit, have the promise of the remission of sins, and the man who does not believe the promise of God, is not a fit subject for baptism. He has not the *faith*. Baptism is of no use to a man who does not believe the promise— "He that believeth and is baptized, *shall be saved*;" "He that believes not the Son, shall not see life."

6/4/67, v.x, #23, p.180

Query–Please give me all the information you can on Matthew 3.11. "I indeed baptize you with water." The Methodists contend that the water is applied to the subject, and not the subject to the water.

Answer–There is nothing in this, only a little trick, such as might be practiced by a very low pettifogger at law, before a very ignorant magistrate. The Greek preposition is translated "with," is the text alluded to, is translated "in," the first six times it occurs in the New Testament, then, once "among," then "in," nine times, then "within," once, then twice "with," then seven times "in," then once "among," and thus continues at about the same rate. It occurs in such passages as the following: Matt. 1.20: "that which is conceived *in* her," not *with* her. Matt 2.1. "Born in Bethlehem of Judea *in* the days of Herod," and not "born *with* Bethlehem of Judea with the days of Herod." Matt 2.16: "Children that were in Bethlehem and *in* all the coasts thereof" and not "*with* Bethlehem and with all the coasts thereof." Matt 2.18: "In Rama there was a voice," and not "with Rama," etc. Matt 3.1 "In those days," and not "with those days" "came John the Baptist preaching in the wilderness," and not "preaching with the wilderness." Matt 3.6: "Baptized of him in Jordan," and not "with Jordan." So ought it to be translated, "he shall baptize you in the Spirit and in fire." The meaning is the same as in all the following places: "fan in his hand," Matt 3.12: "in the borders of Zebulon," Matt 4.16: "in the region," Matt 4.16: "in a ship," Matt 4.21: "in their synagogues," Matt 4.23: "rewarded in heaven," Matt 5.12: "least in the kingdom," Matt 5.19: "in his heart," Matt 5.28: "in heaven," Matt 5.45. There is not a reason for translating en "with" in the passage in question, only to keep it from favoring immersion. John did not baptize "with" Jordan, but in Jordan. He did not preach "with" the wilderness but in the wilderness. Our father is not "with" heaven, but in heaven. Men of sense can but pity the silly attempts of those men who try to justify their modern ceremony, of sprinkling, by scripture. Such men as Luther, Calvin, Wall, Mosheim, Neander etc. etc. never tried to prove sprinkling for baptism, by scripture, but admitted that the original rite was immersion.

9/3/67, v.x, #36, p.284

Query—Please answer through the Review how the thief on the cross got to heaven, if baptism is the saving ordinance; and if all sinners since Adam, and no one can come to Christ without faith, what saves infants?

Answer—When men, in the present state of public sentiment, speak of baptism as "a saving ordinance," those of "the contrary part" immediately think of baptism *saving us*, as a medicine saves us from disease, or of its saving us in some *meritorious* or *efficacious* sense. No one, with even a small degree of intelligence, thinks that baptism saves us in any such sense. We think, the Lord selected immersion in water, as the last, or consummating act, in turning to God, so that all men might know that there was no natural efficacy in the thing done, as in a medicine to remove disease, nor merit or power in the thing done to merit salvation, or take away sin, in itself. There is no merit, efficacy, or power in immersion, to cleanse a person from sin, in itself. The merit, efficacy, or power to take away sins is in Christ. The only reason we know why the Lord connected salvation, or remission of sins, with immersion, was simply because *so it pleased Him.* That He could have taken away sins without it, had it pleased Him to so do, we entertain no doubt. That he does the entire work, by His own merit, efficacy or power, of taking away sins, even when the penitent sinner, the only Scriptural subject, is immersed, we have no doubt. The reason then, why the penitent sinner is required to be immersed is, not because there is any merit, efficacy, or power in immersion to take away sins, nor because the Lord could not take away sins without immersion, but simply because it pleased the Lord, to promise remission of sins to the penitent believer, who is immersed into the name of the Father, and of the Son, and of the Holy Spirit. It is not that *immersion shall save him* who believes and is immersed, but the *Lord shall save him.* It is not a saving ordinance, in the sense that it saves us, or does any part, in itself, toward saving us, but in the sense that it pleases the Lord, by His own merit and grace, to save us *in immersion*, when we come in the proper spirit—believing penitents. We give the glory to Him who saves us, and not to *immersion.* The transaction with the thief was before the inauguration of the new institution, before the keys of the kingdom had been used, and before the general law of pardon was published to the world. Whether he was immersed or not, no man of our time knows, nor is it a matter of any importance to know, as his was a special case, and whatever was done for him, was by a *special act*, and not in the *general law for all.* The case was, therefore, no example for us. When we find a man who is a thief, hanging on a cross, dying, and before the proclamation of the general law of pardon, we may refer him to the case of the thief on the cross as an example, and encourage him to expect a special act, extending mercy to him, without any act of obedience. But this is not the condition of those to whom we now preach the gospel. They are not nailed to the cross, have the clear and general law of pardon printed in their own language, and can obey and come to the promise of God. If they will not come and yield to the commandment of the everlasting God, they will be lost.

Infants are simply not gospel subjects. They need no pardon. The pardon, or justification, proposed in the gospel, "by grace through faith," is from our own sins, and not the Adamic sin. Infants have no personal sins, or sins of their own. They never sinned in their own persons, and need no justification from personal sins. In this respect, they stand precisely on the same footing with those to the years of accountability, who have been pardoned. They need precisely the same as saints to prepare them for heaven. They need to be raised from the dead, changed, immortalized and glorified. The saints need this. Infants are as well prepared for heaven without the gospel, the church, and all that is in the church, as saints are with all these. In view of this, the Lord said, "of such are the kingdom of God," and to those of more advanced years, "Except you be converted and become as little children, you can not enter into the kingdom of God."

10/1/67, v.x, #40, p.316

Query – Does our Savior allude strictly to baptism in water, when he says to Nicodemus: "Except a man be born of water and of the Spirit, he can not enter into the kingdom of God?" If he does not, I have labored under a mistake. And if he does, my neighbors are being led astray, or, at least, are being instructed wrong.

Answer – No expression of Scripture, we presume, has been more tortured to try to make it mean what it does not, or, rather, to make it *not mean* what it *does mean*, than this self-same one, John 3.5. There it stands, boldly and plainly, declaring that, "Except a man be born of water and of the Spirit, he can not enter into the kingdom of God." There stands the word "Spirit" for itself, and that it means *Spirit* no one doubts. There, in the same sentence, joined with it by the conjunction "and" we have the word "water!" This water is connected with the Spirit. In the *one birth* here spoken of, and the one entrance into the kingdom of God, and, for any thing we can see to the contrary, the language makes its presence as essential to the entering into the kingdom as the presence of the Spirit. If this *water* is the water of baptism, then the Lord declares that a man can not enter the kingdom of God without it. Or, to express it differently, if the figurative expression, "born of water," means baptism, then a man can not get into the kingdom without baptism. The kingdom means the Church, and is by the Lord himself used synonymously with it. Matt 16.18–19: "On this rock I will build my *church*," "and I will give you the keys of the kingdom." When the

Lord gave Peter the keys of the kingdom, he gave him power to open it. This he did by declaring the terms of admission, and when this was done the whole was ratified in heaven. Nor is any thing hard as this, or uncharitable. There is not a Church of any note in the world that will receive into its communion a person without what it calls baptism. The Lord's Church, in this respect, is like others: it receives none without baptism. Nay, more; it receives none without conversion in *full*, not only being *born of water* but *of the Spirit*.

But we are not reaching the main matter of inquiry in the letter, calling our attention to this matter. What reason have we, then, for thinking that "born of water means baptism"? We have the following: 1. Not a man in the last fifty years, among all who have tried to make it mean something else, has been able to do so, and make sense of the passage. 2. Baptism harmonizes with all the other Scriptures that treat on the same subject. 3. The fathers, so called, applied it to baptism, we think, without an exception. 4. The first Church, applied it to baptism. 5. The Romish Church has applied it to baptism all the time. 6. The Greek Church has applied it to baptism from the commencement. 7. The Episcopal Church, in her creed and standard works has applied it to baptism, and does still. 8. In the Presbyterian Confession of Faith, the writings of John Calvin, and other standard works of that Church, it is applied to baptism. 9. In the Methodist Discipline, the writings of John Wesley, and all the principle standard works of the M.E. Church, it is applied to baptism. 10. In numerous instances, in the principle authorities in the Baptist Church, it is applied to baptism. 11. No authority of any note gives it any other application. This is sufficient. No matter who a man is, where he is, he is not in the kingdom, or Church of Christ, without baptism. This is enough.

7/18/71, v.14, #29, p.228

Query—Will you please tell the numerous readers of the REVIEW where Paul was baptized?

Answer—He was baptized *in* or *near* Damascus. As to the precise spot in or near Damascus, where he was baptized, I can not tell, nor is it a matter of any importance if I could tell.

7/25/71, v.14, #30, p.236

Query—Did Peter require the same of Cornelius and of his house that he required of the Jews at Pentecost?

Answer—The apostle, in the clearest manner, says, "making no difference between them and us"—the Gentiles and Jews. The circumstance that the apostle did not proceed to state the design of immersion at the house of Cornelius, is no ground for supposing it had a different design there from that on Pentecost or any other occasion. When the Lord states the design of immersion, or in any other item in the plan of redemption, in one place, we ought to remember that design, and not conclude, when we find it mentioned in some places without the design being mentioned, that it there has another design not ascribed to it anywhere in Scripture, or no design it all. It has the one design wherever we find it, no matter how many places we may find it mentioned where nothing is said about the design.

There are several expressions that amount to the same, though they are different in form of expression. "Immersing them into the name of the Father, and of the Son, and of the Holy Spirit," is not the same as "be immersed every one of you in the name of Jesus Christ for the remission of sins;" yet every one "immersed into the name of the Father, and of the Son, and of the Holy Spirit," is "immersed for the remission of sins." "Into the name of the Father, and of the Son, and of the Holy Spirit," is the same, in substance, as "immersed into one body," or "immersed into Christ," or the same as to "enter into the kingdom of God." "Into the kingdom," "into Christ," "into one body," "into the name of the Father, and of the Son, and of the Holy Spirit," "for," or "into the remission of sins," are the same in amount. Every man who has entered "into the kingdom," has been "immersed into the name of the Father, and of the Son, and of the Holy Spirit," "immersed into one body," "immersed into Christ," "immersed for," or "into the remission of sins."

There is but one kingdom of God for all nations, one door into that one kingdom by which for all to enter whether for or against. There is but one Lord, one faith and one immersion for all. The same Lord, with the same love, opened the same door of the same kingdom to the same salvation for all that call upon the name of the Lord, or that come to God through Christ. The Lord has appointed no different Kingdom for Gentiles, different faith, different repentance, different confession, different immersion, different remission of sins, or different impartation of the Holy Spirit, from that appointed for the Jews. The design of the kingdom, the faith, repentance, confession, immersion, remission of sins, and gift of the Holy Spirit, is the same to all, whether Jew or Gentile. The kingdom, the gospel, the faith, repentance, confession, immersion, remission of sins, and impartation of the Spirit, are the same to all of all nations and peoples.

Did Peter present any different kingdom to the Gentiles from that which he had presented to the Jews, any different gospel, any different faith, repentance, confession, immersion, remission of sins, or gift of the Holy Spirit? Certainly not; but came to them with the same Lord, the same gospel, the same kingdom, the same faith, repentance, confession, immersion, remission of sins, and gift of the Holy Spirit, thus "making no difference between them and us," the Gentiles and Jews, but, through Christ, made both one—"one new man, so making peace."

There is but one way to the Father for all of the nations, and that is by Christ. "No man," says he, "comes to the Father but by me." To come by him is to come according to his gospel. There is not a man in the world that has a promise, or one particle of evidence of any kind, that he will be received by our heavenly Father, unless he comes by Christ, or according to his gospel. The great work is to teach men how to come and live according to the gospel.

10/19/71, v.14, #43, p.332

Query–When performing the act of baptism, ministers universally say, "I baptize thee in the name," etc. Now, by consulting Matt 28.19, and Mark 16.16, we find that baptism is the thing to be performed, and we are left to learn from the apostles' teaching and practice the manner in which it is to be performed. Paul, Rom 6.4, tells us precisely how it is to be performed. Now, would it not be more scriptural, more apostolic, and convey much more force of sentiment for our ministers to say, "I bury thee by baptism into the name," etc.?

Answer–We, of course, could not accept the proposed formula. It would be absurd and bungling on several accounts. 1. We are not tenacious about the choice between *baptize* and *immerse* in the formula. The original word *baptizo*, in the time of the Lord and the apostles, expressed an *action* as clearly as our word *immerse*, and was used numerous times before the ordinance in controversy existed, and without any dispute as to its meaning. When we read of a man being *baptized* up to his waist, no one doubts the meaning of the word "baptized." The original word *baptizo*, for hundreds of years before the Christian era, and at the time the New Institution was given, was used in the sense of *overwhelm*, or *dip*. It has this meaning in every place where it occurs in the New Testament. This word has been *transferred*, and not *translated*, in the common version of the New Testament and adopted in the English language, and is now canonized, and as ours is a *living* language, and consequently *changing*, as many other words, this word has changed its meaning. As it is now adopted into our language and defined in the English lexicons, it has *modern* definitions corresponding to the *use* of that word *now*, and not the use of it in the time of the apostles. *Immerse* is derived from the Latin language and has retained its meaning the same as it was hundreds of years ago, and the same as the meaning of *baptizo* was in the time of the apostles. This is only reason we prefer immerse and not baptize now. *Immerse* now has the same meaning *baptizo* had in the time of the apostles, and we use it generally not only in the formula, but in an English translation, in preaching and in conversion. The command to *baptize* did express precisely what was commanded to be done at the time the commission was given as clearly as the command to *immerse* does now.

We are not, however, tenacious for using the word immerse in the formula, though we generally do use it in the formula, in preaching and in talking.

The proposed amendment is wholly unnecessary and without any authority. A formula is not designed to be an explanation, comment or argument. It is not necessary that it should contain the whole gospel, or that it should settle the controversies about the *action* to be performed. We like the simple words, "By the authority of Jesus Christ you are immersed into the name of the Father, and of the Son, and of the Holy Spirit."

1/21/73, vol.16, #3, pg. 20.

Query– In Matt 28.19 are three immersions taught? If there are three immersions taught in this instance, why is it not so taught elsewhere in the Scriptures? Will you please give us light on this subject? If trine immersion is right we want to know it.

Answer– Certainly not, but one immersion "Into the name of the Father and of the Son and of the Holy Spirit." There is but one immersion commanded in the Scripture; that one is in water, and "into the name of the Father, and of the Son, and of the Holy Spirit." Peter said; "Can any man forbid water, that these should not be baptized, who have received the Holy Spirit as well as we?" Here the water is mentioned as the element in which they were to be immersed, and they had already been immersed in the Holy Spirit; and in the next verse we are informed that "he commanded them to be immersed in the name of the Lord." The immersion in water, then is the one commanded, and the only one.

The immersion in Spirit is not commanded; and the command, if it existed, to be immersed in Spirit could not be obeyed. Suppose the Lord would command any one to be immersed in the Spirit, how would he obey? No man ever was commanded to be immersed in the Spirit, nor was any man ever commanded to immerse anyone in the Spirit. Man can not immerse in the Spirit. The immersion in water is commanded, and is the immersion "into the name of the Father, and of the Son, and of the Holy Spirit," "into Christ," "into one body," the initiatory rite into the New Institution. Immersion in the Holy Spirit never initiated any one into any institution, or anything. It was never commanded. No man ever administered it. The Lord was the only administrator of the baptism of the Spirit. It was a promise. It was a miracle. It imparted miraculous power. It never occurred except on Pentecost, and at the house of Cornelius. On Pentecost the subjects of it were in Christ before it occurred, and at the house of Cornelius they were not in Christ after it occurred till they were immersed in water. In both instances they spoke with tongues and prophesied.

When, Paul wrote his letter to the church in Ephesus there remained but "one immersion," the one of the last commission, connected with salvation the remission of sins, or induction "into the name of the Father, and of the Son, and of the Holy Spirit." This is Paul's "one immersion." It is not "pouring," "one sprinkling," or "three immersions," but "one immersion." The three immersions have not one scrap of authority in the commission or anywhere else. In the same sentence where Apostle has "one body, one spirit, one hope, one faith," he has "one immersion," and it would be in no more direct violation of his language to talk of three bodies, three spirits, three hopes, three faiths, than of "three immersions." There is no method by which the language can be so tortured as to get three immersions out of the words, "immersing them into the name of the Father, and of the Son, and of the Holy Spirit." Such a thing was never thought of till the dispute about Trinity sprung up. This dispute originated it. There is not a trace of trine immersion till more than a hundred years after the apostles were gone; till the shallow nonsense of infant sin, infant regeneration, infant immersion and infant damnation were introduced. Here, and not in the Bible, the friends of trine immersion go to find it, and here they find it among those who taught that infants were guilty of original sin and liable to eternal damnation; that infants must be regenerated; that the stain of Adam's sin must be washed away; that this can not be done except in baptism to prepare them for heaven. They practiced no infant sprinkling, but infant immersion, or immersed, and, in time, trine immersion, or immersed them three times. We think some of the Greeks do this to the present day.

9/23/73, v.16, #38, p.300

Query–Please explain the following remarks through your column: "As believers are saved only through the word of God, how are infants saved without it, since they are born in sin?"

Answer–The salvation of believers through the word is *pardon*, or salvation from *past sin*, or what the school men call *actual* sin. Infants have no actual sin and need no pardon, or salvation from actual sin. The salvation of the last commission is pardon, or remission of sins. The commission has nothing to do with infants. The gospel is not for infants. They can not receive the gospel, believe or obey it. They simply have nothing to do with it. The salvation promised in the commission and the condemnation threatened have nothing to do with infants. They are simply not gospel subjects; they need not the salvation, pardon or remission, and are not liable to the condemnation. They have never sinned, and need no salvation from their *own sin*, for they have none.

Are we told that they are under the Adamic, or the original sin? True, they are, but the commission has no provision to save men from original sin, or the Adamic sin. Those who believe and obey the gospel, who become Christians, are still under the Adamic sin, and suffer the penalty consequent on that sin the same as those who are not Christians. There is no remission of the Adamic sin. The sentence is upon all, and will come upon all. The second Adam, the Lord from heaven, comes to our relief after we have suffered the penalty, and delivers us from the penalty in a resurrection from the dead, and adds more to it—changes, immortalizes and glorifies the saints. This saves them from the Adamic sin, or from the consequences of it. We are not under the *guilt* of the Adamic sin, but simply the *consequences*, and when the consequences are removed from us by a resurrection from the dead, we are entirely freed from that sin.

The consequences of the Adamic sin came upon us without our own personal agency or volition, and brought death as a consequence; and the resurrection also comes without our own personal agency or volition, and delivers us from the consequence of the Adamic sin. The condemnation, by one man's disobedience, came upon all men, and the justification from that condemnation, or from death to life, by the resurrection, also came upon all. The justification from the Adamic sin by the resurrection from the dead is just as broad as the condemnation. The condemnation was to death, and the justification is to life. This counteracts and takes away the Adamic sin. This accounts for the circumstance that no man is threatened with punishment in the world to come on account of the Adamic sin. The punishment in the world to come is on account of *personal* or *actual* sin. "Every man shall receive according to *what he has done.*"

Infants have no personal sin, are under no guilt and need no pardon. The salvation of the commission is pardon, the remission of sins, which infants do not need. Common intelligence ought to enable every man to see that the commission can not apply to infants. They can not receive the gospel, can not believe it, can not repent and are not threatened with the damnation of the commission. They simply are not subjects of the gospel commanded to be preached in the commission, and have nothing to do with it, either the salvation or the damnation. But as they have no personal or actual sin, they are as well prepared for heaven as a saint. The Lord said of an infant: "Of such is the kingdom of God." Infants need to be raised from the dead, changed, glorified, to prepare them for heaven. The saint needs precisely the same. The saint has been freed from sin, or purified his soul in obeying the truth, and the infant never had any sin, and both are prepared for heaven alike. The one never had any personal sin, and the other has been saved from sin by submitting to the gospel, or has been cleansed from sin by the blood of Jesus.

10/28/73, v.16, #43, p. 340

Query–Will you give your reasons why Paul had the twelve baptized again that had been baptized unto John's baptism? Second—Why they had not so much as heard whether there be any Holy Ghost?

Answer–1. Some think that all immersed by John were required to be immersed over again, when the new institution was fully established and in operation. We do not, however, receive this. Those immersed by John were "a people prepared for the Lord." By doing his work John prepared the way before the Lord as the Prophet Malachi said he should do. Those people who heard the preaching of John and were "immersed into repentance for the remission of sins," and followed out the instruction given by John and the Savior, after he entered on his public mission some six months later than John, and remained under their directions in all things during our Lord's ministry and till Pentecost, were the nucleus of which the Church was formed, and were not immersed again.

We do not know that any clear and decisive evidence can be given to that effect, but the probability is that the twelve in question had been immersed by Apollos into John's immersion, after it had become obsolete and was no longer of divine authority, or after the kingdom was established. It must be admitted, however, that Paul's instruction looks beyond this, or to something more. When they said they had been immersed into John's immersion. Paul explained to them that "John truly immersed in the immersion of repentance, saying to the people that they should believe on him who should come after him, that is, on Christ Jesus." "When they heard this they were immersed into the name of the Lord Jesus." It is clear, at any rate, that they had not been "immersed into the name of the Lord Jesus." 2. They had not "heard that there was any Holy Spirit," or, as some versions have it, that the Holy Spirit was given simply because Apollos, or whoever had preached to them, "knew nothing only the immersion of John," and did not know or teach that the Holy Spirit had been given.

6/1/75, v.18, #22, pg. 172

Query 1.—Can a man be saved in this country without being baptized?

Answer–No, the Lord said, "Except a man be born of water and the Spirit, he can not enter into the kingdom of God."

Query 2. Is baptism to be understood in John 3.5?

Answer–We must understand baptism to be meant in the passage.

Query 3. Why must we so understand it?

Answer–Because Paul says: "He (God) saved us by the washing of regeneration, and renewing of the Holy Spirit." And Peter says: "The like figure whereunto baptism doth now save us."

Query 4. Why did Peter lay so much stress on baptism?

Answer—And because the Savior told him that he should teach and baptize the people. That he should preach the gospel, assuring him that "he that believeth and is baptized shall be saved; but he that believeth not shall be damned." Mark 16.16.

Query 5. Is baptism as much *essential* to salvation as faith?

Answer—Just the same. Just as *essential*. There can be no degrees in that which is essential. "The like figure whereunto baptism doth now save us" means what it says.

Query 6. How can one outward ordinance save?

Answer—How can faith alone save? Is it not dead being alone? Did not God couple baptism with faith? Who dares to separate them? Dare any one but a skeptic do it?

Query 7. Is it not unreasonable to lay so much stress on an outward ordinance?

Answer—No. We must have ordinances. In God's wisdom he has given them and as we have no inward ones, we trust have what you call "outward ones."

Query 8. Is there not more merit in faith than in baptism

Answer—No, two things that are equal to the same thing are equal to one another. There is no merit in either faith or baptism. The merit is in the death of Christ. "He died to save sinners." "His blood cleanseth from all sin." As the *meritorious* cause.

Query 9. But doesn't *faith* accept Christ as the only Savior, and is it not that which alone appropriates the salvation which he has purchased with his own precious blood?

Answer—No: to be benefited by the power of faith in the Son of God, the believer must be baptized. "He that believeth and is baptized shall be saved but he that believeth not shall be damned."

Query 10. Were not the primitive constituted disciples of Christ, Christian by faith *alone*?

Answer–No, "Ye are all the children of faith in Christ Jesus? (Now, stop! Don't quote another verse. It makes good sense, and answer my last question in the affirmative) "For as many of you as have been baptized into Christ, have put on Christ." Gal 3.27

Query 11. Do you regard baptism as a *condition* of salvation?

Answer–Not unless the Savior has so made it. We are not as a party to a contract, that has a right to specify the conditions upon which we are willing to be saved, or the other party specifying them; we accept or reject at will. No sir! Not at all, we were not consulted as to *conditions*. Suppose a bankrupt, in a legal point of view, has failed to an enormous amount, one man alone being his creditor. Not a cent has he to pay. Does the creditor ask the bankrupt to state the conditions upon which he wills to accept *forgiveness* of the debt? Nothing as an equivalent can be given in the matter of forgiveness. Yet unmeritorious conditions may be submitted by the creditor. Those who talk so much of faith being the only *condition* of pardon, and who so often speak of others "placing too much stress on baptism," I apprehend, in many instances, have but shallow conceptions of the question. God alone has the right to submit conditions, and bankrupt creditors the *privilege* of accepting or rejecting. To accept the conditions is to believe and be damned.

Query 12. Then, if baptism is a condition as well as faith, you condemn all the good people who have lived or died in faith without having been baptized—is it not so?

Answer–No. We have neither the right nor privilege to condemn nor justify. The prerogative belongs to him alone who has power to forgive. We have no privilege to make excuses and apologies for either the living or the dead, the good or the bad. We are wholly unfitted for the task of accommodating the conditions that God has submitted to suit the ignorant or the learned, the captious or capricious, or the willful. Christ is King of kings, and Lord of all. He sent his ambassadors to proclaim the good news of the forgiveness of sins, and to announce the conditions of enjoyment of pardon. The conditions were the same from Jerusalem to Samaria, and all over the Roman Empire. They still remain on the undying pages of the New Covenant Scriptures.

Query 13. Inasmuch, sir, as there are a great many who are full of faith and good works, who do not regard baptism as anything but a *non-*

essential outward ordinance, do you not indorse the benevolent movement of those who propose a union on the principle of faith alone as the
condition of pardon?

Answer–No, It is a radical error for any man, or any set of men, to
propose such a union. Why does any one think that baptism is a *non-
essential*? This is a serious question, and the true answer falls as a mill-
stone on the heads of the teachers of Christianity in modern times. The
teachers cause the people to err, and the people love to have it so. The
only authoritative teachers of the religion of Jesus are the apostles of
Christ. Not an unbaptized disciple, saint, Christian, believer, brother,
sister is found under their personal ministry. The proposition to form a
union of believers, who may accept or reject baptism, is simply treason
and rebellion against the King of kings and Lord of lords.

9/6/75, v.18, #36, pg.282

Query–Will you please be so kind to me as to answer a few questions?
Can it be proved that Jesus was baptized by immersion? I belong to the
Church. I was buried with my Lord in baptism. Myself and wife are all
the members there are here. We live in the midst of Methodists. They
say Jesus went into the water about knee deep and John the Baptist
poured water on him, taken from a well, they suppose. Now, the fact is,
the way Jesus was baptized is the right way.

Answer–We have but one thing to do, and that is follow the book. In
the book there is simply not one word about the Savior going "into the
water about the Savior going "into the water knee deep," nor "pouring
water on him." That is simply talk. It is said in the book that "Jesus was
baptized of John in Jordan." Any one can see that Jesus was not *poured*,
or *sprinkled* of John in Jordan. Your Methodist friends do not express
it in that way themselves. They do not say, *Jesus was poured*, but "*water
was poured on him.*" It says, furthermore, of the Lord, that "he went up
straightway out of the water." He could not have *gone up* out of the water
without having been *in it*. There was no reason for going into the water
to have it *sprinkled* or *poured on* him.

The word baptize means immerse, and when it is said "Jesus was baptized of John in the Jordan," it is simply that he was "*immersed* of John
in Jordan." When men sprinkle for baptism, they do not, according to
the plain reading of Scripture, go "unto a certain water," to where there

is "much water," go "down into the water," do not "bury in baptism," do not "bury by baptism," do not "plant together in likeness of his death;" persons are not "born of the water," do not come "up out of the water," and their bodies are not washed in water. But where we immerse, we go "unto a certain water," where there is "much water," "go down into the water," "bury in baptism," "bury by baptism," "plant together in the likeness of his death," are "born of water," "come up out of the water," and the body is "washed in water."

If your neighbors say, water was poured on the Savior, tell them to produce the Scripture that says so, or anything like it. Tell them to produce any Scripture that has the least appearance of it. They will never find it. Sprinkling or pouring for baptism has not a shadow in its favor in the Bible. We do not say, Jesus was "baptized by immersion," for baptism is immersion, and to say baptized by immersion is the same in sense as *baptized by baptism*, or *immersed by immersion*.

8/31/75, v.18, #36, pg. 27

QUESTIONS RELATING TO CHURCH POLICY

Query–When an offending brother is brought to trial and the case is heard, should the whole congregation vote for or against exclusion, or should the elders, after hearing the case, cast the deciding votes?

Answer–The officers of the church should hear the case with all the evidence, make a decision and come to an agreement if possible. Then, when the church is assembled for the regular worship on the Lord's Day, a clear statement of the case should be made to the church, with the conclusion to which the officers have come. They should then inquire for any objections, requesting parties who may desire to make any to do so to some of the officers against a specified time, with the explanation that if there is no objection by that time the decision of the officers is sanctioned by the church and final, but if objections are made they will be duly considered and satisfaction given before the action will be considered final.

June 25, 1872, vol.15, #26, page 204.

Query –Is it right for any Christian congregation to grant any member the privilege of withdrawing membership without desiring to unite with another congregation, but simply wishing a withdrawal from the church? Should such a request be granted(?) Or should such a one be excluded for making such a request?

Answer –We are of the opinion that after due time for reflection is given, with proper reasoning and expostulations, that a letter of dismissal should be given to every person that demands one; but let these letters always be genuine exponents of the case. A Christian church can not, in good faith, give a letter recommending a person as in *good standing and full fellowship*, when it is known that the letter is demanded on account of disaffection. These letters should be of different grades, some recommending persons in full fellowship and good standing; some recommending the moral character, but on account of dislike to the church or some of its members, or some of its obligations; the lukewarm-ness of the person demanding the letter, his lack of interest in the cause, love to the brethren; his inattention to prayer and reading the Bible—he had been dismissed, at his own request, from the church. Or, a letter might be given in a case where a member can not be reclaimed from sinful practices, setting forth the objections to him, with his dismissal, and the desire that he would return to his duty; and in all these cases, let the causes of separation be clearly stated in the letter, and upon the church record, and we shall soon be excused from applications for letters, where the ground of the application is disaffection. In all cases of disaffection or immoral conduct, it would amount virtually to an exclusion, and so set it forth in the letter, and upon the church record.

There can not be anything more preposterous, than for a person who has objections to a church, does not love it, fellowship it, nor desire to remain in it, to request that church to grant him a letter, recommending him as a member in good standing and full fellowship. If a person has no fellowship for the church, is not of the same spirit as the church, and is alienated from it, let this be stated in his letter as the cause of his dismissal, and upon the church record; or if he wishes to leave the country, or whatever the cause may be, let it be stated in the letter. If a man is in good standing and full fellowship, has good feelings to the whole church, has done nothing wrong, desires to do his duty, and intends to remain where he is, there can be no reason for a letter, and no one would demand one.

1857, vol.2, pg.249

Query—Will you give us your view on sisters taking part in public worship(?)

Answer—It depends upon what part in the public worship is meant. They are not allowed to *teach*, or to *usurp authority over the man*, but that they may not sing, pray, commune and exhort, we think no man can prove. The words "suffer not a woman to *speak*," we think, is of the same import as "suffer not a woman to *teach*," in another place. It is clear that women prayed in the primitive church, or Paul's speaking of their "praying with the *head uncovered*." Would have been without meaning. They could not have prayed without *speaking*, but could without *teaching*.

1/60, vol.3, #5, page 18.

Query– In the Feb. number of "the Review", under the head, "The Church and its Creed," it says: "The first public business of the church, after our Lord's ascension, was the election of a brother to fill up the place of Judas."

Had the disciples any authority or command, to elect one of their number to fill up the place of Judas before they were endued with the Holy Spirit? And where was Matthias ever numbered as one of the twelve Apostles of the Lamb after Paul's conversion and call to be one? Acts 26.16

Answer– Undoubtedly, the election of Matthias was authorized, or he would have been set aside before the supernatural power came upon them, and the cloven tongues *"sat upon each one of them,"* and he would not have assisted in making the *eleven* with whom Peter stood up. See Acts 2.3–14.

3/2/58, vol.3, #5

Query– You are earnestly solicited to publish in the REVIEW whether the law of God or Christ will justify a body of Christians retaining a member who has married a divorced person; or, in other words, is a Christian at liberty to marry one who has a living husband or wife though by law divorced.

Answer– "Moses, because of the hardness of your hearts, suffered you to put away your wives; but from the beginning it was not so. And I say unto you, whosoever shall put away his wife, except it be for fornication, and shall marry another, committeth adultery and whosoever marrieth her that is put away, doth commit adultery."–Jesus. Matt 19.8–9. "But I say unto you, that whosoever shall put away his wife, saving for the cause of fornication, causeth her to commit adultery; and whosoever shall marry her that is divorced committed adultery."–Jesus. Matt 5.32

1/6/1858, vol.1,#11 page 42

Query– You will confer a favor by answering this query in the RE-VIEW. Does the office of elder or bishop which are synonymous terms in the New Testament, remain with those officers after they take a letter of dismissal from one point where they hold their membership until they attach themselves to the church at another point.

Can they act under the authority of their office cease when they take a letter of dismissal and have to be received again at the point where they identify their membership.

Answer–Most certainly no man can be a bishop, or overseer, over any people who did not choose him to be their overseer. When, therefore, a man leaves the community, where he was chosen bishop, he is certainly not bishop over another people who did not choose him to be their bishop. This appears to us too plain a matter to be a query in the mind of anyone.

7/31/60, vol.3, #31, page 123

Query–There is a question agitated somewhat in this section of the country, relative to elders—whether or not they have full power to grant letters to the brethren and sisters, independent of the congregation, when they desire to leave? Your views on the subject are desired very much.

Answers–Letters should be called for in the open congregation, in the presence of all, before granted, as a general view; and we think, this is the practice generally among the brethren. It would be better still, to state to the congregation assembled that application was made for a letter; that if any one had any objection, or knew any, that in the course of a week they would make it known privately to one or more of the bishops, and if no objection was made in the specified time, the letter would be granted. This will give a fuller opportunity to make objections, to speak of them and adjust the matter without giving offense or producing unpleasantness in the public assemblies.

Charges against brethren should be preferred in the same way, privately to the bishops. They, in conjunction with the deacons, or other experienced brethren they might call to their aid, should examine the matter, adjust it, and come to a conclusion before they bring it before the congregation. They make a brief statement of the case to the whole congregation, and allow a specified time for any who are not satisfied to make objections to the bishops, where they can be considered and adjusted. If no objections are made in the specified time, the voice is unanimous, and obtained without formal voting, and yet so as to give all the fullest satisfaction.

6/12/60 , vol.3, #24, page 95

Query–Who has the authority to give a preacher license to preach?

Answer–We know of nothing about "giving license to preach." A congregation of Christ may recommend a preacher of good character and ability, not to give *license* or *authority* to preach, but to show that he is a preacher in good standing and acceptable.

6/12/60, vol.3, #24, page 95

Query–Is a preacher's "license" null and void when his conduct is such as to demand his excommunication from the church of Christ?

Answer–Recommendations given before a man's exclusion, as a matter of course, is no value after he has been excluded.

6/12/60, vol.3, #24, page 95.

Query–Why do we keep the first day of the week holy instead of the one that God sanctified and commanded that it should be kept holy? If he has given no authority for changing it, is it not wrong for us to change, or to keep any other day than the one he has sanctified? Please let me have an answer in your excellent paper.

Answer–There is not one scrap of authority for changing one day for the other. The Sabbath was typical of heaven, or the true rest. The Christian Sabbath has not come, and we have yet entered our Sabbath, or rest. The Christian was never under the old Sabbath, and does not, therefore, change it for the Lord's day. The Christian Lord's day, or the first day of the week, is not in the place of the Sabbath, nor is it a Sabbath itself. It is more to a Christian than a mere Sabbath. It has clustering round it more than ever surrounded the old Sabbath. It is in memory of our Lord's resurrection from the dead, and the worship on that day points to the suffering of the Savior. The objects are not the same, nor like those of the old Sabbath. No truly intelligent Christian calls "the Lord's day" *the Sabbath* day, nor does he argue that it came in the place of the Sabbath. The Christian worship all points to Christ as its great center, and not to the creation, nor the rest from it.

We are truly sorry to find a new figment being agitated, resuscitating the Sabbath as an obligation binding on Christians. This is a sprout of Adventism, nothing-arianism, being advocated by a few carnal and apostatizing men, traversing the country and subverting the faith of some. The Lord grant that they may find mercy

10/60, vol.3, #40, page 161

Query–If the word bishop is properly translated when rendered overseer, why is it that the versions published by Alex Campbell and H.T. Anderson retain the word bishop, which certainly brings to the mind of the common people a very different of the word overseer?

The Bible Union has given us the New Testament without bishops, simply overseer, looking after the fold of Christ. No pontifical robes or gorgeous apparel accompanies the idea of overseer, but certainly does that of bishop. Common English scholars do not consider the words synonymous. Let us have the Word of God in our own language, that we may grow thereby.

Answer–We do not know why the word bishop is retained in the versions mentioned. We are perfectly satisfied that overseer is a better rendering—that it gives a clearer representation of the original. We think the Bible Union has done right in this. The common version does not invariably stick to the word bishop. There are some queer things connected with this matter that we may develop when we have time to look them up and put them in shape.

10/71, vol.14, #41, page 324

Query–Some brethren think it inexpedient or impolitic for Christian congregations, in the country, who are surrounded by the different denominations, as Baptists, Methodists, Presbyterians, etc., to meet *every* Lord's day. What says our Bro. Franklin on this subject? Will he please let us hear from him on this?

Answer–When we are speaking of the weekly meeting of the saints and the celebration of the Lord's death and sufferings, we have no use for the words "expedient" and "politic". The Lord has ordained the regular week meeting and worship, it is always *expedient* and *politic* to attend to any thing the Lord has appointed, and never *expedient* and *politic* to omit what the Lord has appointed. We have nothing to do with the denominations around us. They are of another category, have another work and belong to another kingdom from us. When the Lord's day comes, the Lord's people meet; and his house is opened, his table is set and his people must be in their places. There can be no apology for the disciples failing to meet and keep the established appointments of God. If the worship of the Lord's day were some human expedient we might omit it, or set it aside to attend other meetings, but it is not. It is a divine appointment, as much so as the Lord's day, prayer, baptism, or any thing else mentioned in the oracles of the living God. How can brethren, who have been redeemed by the precious blood of the Lamb and elevated to the position of sons and daughters of the Lord Almighty, fall into a cold and indifferent state and allow the established worship to be neglected? Let no brethren think they shall remain guiltless if they shall do such a thing.

1/60, vol.3, #5, page 18.

Query – Suppose a congregation at a certain place has chosen her elders, but she can not conceive of fasting, prayer and the imposition of hands to be Heaven's order of ordination, and from this cause fails to practice it; and, in the course of time, a member walks disorderly, an effort is made to " restore such an one in the spirit of meekness," without success. Now, under these circumstances, can they, in accordance with the law of Christ, withdraw from the disorderly member?

Answer – We have never found any church that could not conceive *fasting* and *prayer* right, in ordaining officers. We have found some few, who believed in fasting and prayer, but objected to the *laying on of hands*. Why should not a church be able to exclude a disorderly person, whether they used fasting, prayer and imposition of hands or not, in ordination of officers? If they think they can have no officers without fasting, prayer, and the imposition of hands, they had better fast, pray, and impose hands than have no officers. The idea of a church that can not conceive fasting, prayer and the imposition to be right, in ordination, is like a man that can not conceive meeting, singing, the Lord's Supper and baptism right. A church can exclude disorderly persons, even if she has no officers.

10/58 vol.1, #31, page 123.

Query – A Bishop fails to discharge his duty in the congregation; afterwards is guilty of immoral conduct, and afterwards comes to at the congregation, and makes acknowledgment, is he still to be retained in the Bishop's office?

Answer – By no means, a bishop must be *blameless*, of good report, able to rebuke those out of the way. No brother of right feelings would certainly think of such a thing as exercising the bishop's office, who had been accused and confessed himself guilty of immoral conduct, at least till he had given several years faithful devotion to the Lord and to the cause, as an assurance to the brethren in time to come.

8/11/58, vol.1, #32, page 127

Query—I wish to ask you or any of the brethren who see proper to answer, a question, viz—Had the apostles all the same commission? If they, had, why did Paul say that he was not sent to baptize, but to preach the gospel? If you see proper, and think this worthy of notice, I would thank you for your views on the subject.

Answer—The passage alluded to in the above is 1 Cor 1.17. It is very evident that Paul's commission was not the same as the commission of the rest of the apostles, for it was given at a different time for a different purpose, and differs in itself. The only difference however, was in the duties he was to perform and the territory upon which he was to operate, and not *in the doctrine* he was to promulgate; for the gospel was the grand theme which dwelt upon all their inspired tongues. Why it was that Paul was not sent to baptize, while all the other apostles were sent for that purpose, as well as to preach, I am unable to tell, unless the Lord exempted him from that part of the labor of an ancient missionary, on account of his weak and diminutive bodily powers. But of one thing we are assured, and that is that he did baptize some of the Corinthians, and the fact that he did it, proves that it was admissible for him, though not sent for that purpose, to baptize; and if Paul had a right to baptize, though not sent for that purpose, who can give a good reason why any other man may not if necessity shall demand it?

Western Reformer June 1848 vol.6 #8 page508

Query—It is contended by some that there are no evangelists now days(?)

Answer—The dispute about evangelists and no evangelists in our day, we look upon as a mere distinction without any difference. Both the parties believe that we should have preachers, and I cannot see that it is of much importance whether we call them evangelists, elders or preachers, any of which titles or appellations apply properly to our preachers of age and experience. Evangelist, means a proclaimer.

Western Reformer June 1848 vol.6 #8 page509

Query–If two brethren address a congregation, is the second speaker justifiable in correcting a false idea, presented by the first?

Answer–As a general thing, it would not answer at all, for a second speaker to undertake to correct any errors into which he might suppose the first to have fallen. This would throw the church into a debating school, and in ten instances result in confusion, to where it would do good in one instance. I should feel greatly out of my place, to attempt a correction, in the public congregation, of any remark made by an accredited teacher. Not only so, but such a course would encourage a set of little hypocrisies, whose spirits feast more on a supposed or real error, upon which they can carp, than any interesting truth they might be able to advance. Therefore, as a general thing, such differences should be discussed in the private circle. It is true, an old, experienced Elder of a congregation, or Evangelist, might on some occasions, profitably correct some young, fiery and erratic preacher, who occasionally flies off his orbit before the congregation. In this case, it might do the preacher good, and show to the world that we will not suffer error to escape correction. Men of age and experience, ought not to be received unless they preach nothing but truth, and new beginners ought to be corrected. Such is my opinion.

Western Reformer vol.6, #3 page 121

Query–Can a man be scripturally, an elder in a Christian congregation who takes and holds the office unwillingly?

Answer–A man who is the choice of the proper authorities, and chosen an elder, and is not willing to serve those who choose him, is not in subordination to the body, and therefore disqualified.

Western Reformer, Oct. 1849, vol.7, #9, page 649

Query–An individual member or members do wrong, and they are visited by some of the rest of the members, and they acknowledge their guilt, but say to the visitors: "You are in a wrong as well as we, and we will not confess our wrong unless you confess too." Now, the question is, have they a right to make a charge and bring the visitors to trial?

Answer–Surely not. If one man has no right to bring a charge against any one, while guilty himself. It is not the business of a guilty man to keep others in order, but it is his business to get in order himself.

Western Reformer August 1849, vol. 7, #8, page 501

Query–Is it New Testament doctrine that we should give the one-tenth of our substance for the support of the gospel?

Answer–If it is New Testament doctrine to give one tenth for the support of the gospel, we have very few New Testament men in this money loving age, and if no man can be saved without giving one tenth, we might ask an ancient question, viz. "Who then, can be saved?"

We do not know of any scripture which specifies any special amount, but this we are well satisfied of, that there are two classes that are not New Testament folks. One of the classes consist of preachers, and the other class consists of private members. The preachers are constantly coveting the goods of this world, and contriving to get all they possibly can, and ever threatening to "leave the field" if they do not get the desired amount. They pray as little as they can pass along with, preach as little as they can get off with, and hardly ever visit the sick, and are always complaining of their hard times. These are not in any way related to New Testament preachers. The class of private members alluded to, always contrive to give as little for the support of the gospel and every other good object as they can possibly get along with, and do as little of every thing else that is good as will pass at all in the eyes of the world, and talk of an "ABUNDANT ENTRANCE into the everlasting kingdom of our Lord and Savior Jesus Christ." These are not in any way related to the ancient New Testament Christians.

Western Reformer, February 1849, vol7, #3, page 246

Query–I wish to enquire how much our modern evangelists prove themselves to be such. The reason why I make this inquiry is thus: Paul says, the "He gave some apostles, some prophets, some evangelists, some pastors and some teachers for the perfecting of the saints." etc. From these verses I have concluded that if the gifts of the Apostles and prophets have ceased, as is argued by many, some have the other gifts of evangelists, pastors and teachers, for they all rest upon the same foundation. Let us inquire for what purpose these gifts were given. Paul answers, "for the perfecting of the saints for the work of the ministry, for the edifying of the body of Christ." These are noble purposes truly. Let us next inquire, how long these gifts were to continue. The apostle again answers, "Till we all come in the unity of the faith, and of the knowledge of the Son of God, unto a perfect man, unto the measure of the stature of the fullness of Christ, that we be no more children, tossed to and fro, and carried about with every wind of doctrine, by the slight of men, and cunning craftiness whereby they lie in wait to deceive." Now it is argued that the saints had arrived to this state of perfection before the death of the apostles and prophets, and therefore these extraordinary gifts ceased with them, having accomplished all the purposes they were designed to accomplish. But were not evangelists, pastors and teachers designed to accomplish the same thing? Why then, may we not fairly conclude that these gifts ceased also, when the work was perfected?

Answer–The apostles of Christ were given as instruments through which to deliver the gospel to the world ; and when this work was finished, and their testimony was sealed with their blood, this gift and the need of it ceased. The first evangelists, pastors and teachers, were spiritual gifts, bestowed on the church to perfect it for the work of the ministry." This was done before the apostle's death. At their death, all spiritual gifts terminated, and all need of them ceased.

Well the church was then perfected for the work of the ministry. But she has no spiritual gifts and no use for them. What has she remaining? She has no inspired apostles, but in their writings she has all their teachings, and she also has the same mission vested in her that Jesus had, viz. the salvation of the world. He qualified and sent out his apostles. She also qualified and sent out her apostles, not inspired, but pre-prepared to re-teach or teach for the first time to those who have not heard the inspired teachings of the first apostles. These are apostles of the churches. Hence several persons are called apostles in the scriptures, besides the original called and sent witnesses. But if it required evangelists to perfect the saints for the work of the ministry during the short period that intervened before miracles ceased, they cannot be perfected for that work now without them. The first evangelists were supernaturally qualified, there being no ordinary means established and having existed long enough to have qualified any. But in the place of inferring that God intended the church to do without these different officers after the termination of spiritual gifts, we only infer, that they were to be raised up and qualified by ordinary and established means, and not by extraordinary means after that period.

We have seen churches enough without evangelists, pastors and teachers, and have heard the best things that have been said against the existence of such offices; but as God never designed the church to be without them, every church must die without them, and make an utter failure in converting the world.

We allege, and let him show to the contrary who can, that when spiritual gifts ceased no office ceased with them, but the means of raising up and qualifying officers was changed.

Western Reformer April 1849, vol.7, # 4, 249.

Query–Will you please be so kind as to answer the following query? When a member or members of the church become unruly, and act wickedly, and the church does not exclude them, but allows them to remain in the bosom of the church, and fellowship with them just as though they were devoted Christians, does not the whole church become corrupted?

Answer–Certainly it does, but if there is but one man, or a very small minority who thinks the man corrupts, and the whole church thinks he is not corrupt, it is fully as probable that the one man, or the small minority, should be mistaken, as that the whole church should be mistaken. It is a ruinous affair to keep corrupt men in the church, and should be looked to with the utmost vigilance. "A little leaven leavens the whole lump. The leaven must be cast out.

December 1858, vol.1, #49, page 195

Query–How are the elders to "'teach"—feed the flock of God taking oversight thereof; when in reality there are some healthy young brethren and sisters of whom they do not get a *sight* once in a month or perhaps a year? And how are these delinquents submitting themselves to the elders? Answers to the above from you would probably be of use in these regions.

Answer–Those churches and elders where such a state of things is suffered as alluded to above, are in a fearful condition and must repent or their candlestick will be moved out of its place. In such cases the elders are not teaching the flock at all, nor is the flock submitting to the elders. Entire insubordination prevails. Do such ever think of giving an account to God?

Query–We have a case in our church that we do not know exactly how to dispose of, never having had a case of the kind before. It is briefly this: There is a Seventh Day Adventist preaching here who has "turned" one of our brethren to be his brother. He does not claim to be with us now, and wished to withdraw, but not having an example of that kind, we chose to withdraw from him, and we ask of you, on what grounds, Scripturally, can we do so?

Answer–It is too late to be of any service to the brethren in the case in hand for us to notice it. But the case may be of service in other instances and we therefore call attention to it. We think that in all such cases the disaffected party should be saved from all trouble of withdrawing from said party. Adventists set aside the Lord's day, or the first day, and run back to the Sabbath, or seventh day, and in doing so they depart from the divinely appointed day of meeting to break bread, or commemorate the Savior's sufferings. But this one item, though it subverts the Lord's day and worship, is only an item among many errors in the Adventist, Soul-sleeping, Materialistic or Christadelphian teaching. The main things they are now teaching are most degrading errors. They are simply a set of religious adventurers, experimenting on the gullibility of mankind. We would simply charge one of them with perverting and setting aside the Lord's day and withdraw from him for so doing. A more graceless and unscrupulous set of men have not made their appearance among us than the so-called Adventists. They create factions, lead off unsuspecting people, pull down churches, build up nothing. When they gather a little party they do not hold them but a short time. They go to nothing. They are ruined and never amount to anything any more.

3/19/72 vol.15, #12, page 92.

Query–I have seen a great deal written about inviting the different sects to commune with us. I wish to know your opinion about Christians partaking of the emblems with them.(the sects)

Answer–There are many among the sects that have become acquainted with the Savior, love him, have confessed him, been baptized into the name of the Father, and of the Son, and of the Holy Spirit, to whom we stand in readiness to unite at any moment, because they are the children of God. These are *Christians*, and have the same privilege at the Lord's table as we have. The Lord's table is evidently for his people, and I have no scruple in communing with any man who is a Christian, or uniting with him in the same church. Nor do I know that I am injured, if some man thinks himself a converted man, who has never been converted according to the gospel, and comes to the Lord's table with me. There might be a hypocrite there also, without my knowledge, who was once converted. There is not much danger of harm from either. It is not our duty to invite or debar any, but to state that it is the Lord's table and for his people, and if any partake who are not his people, the matter is between them and the Lord. The main matter, if we would be benefited in coming unto the Lord's table, is for the disciples to examine *themselves*, and so eat, and not give themselves much trouble about *others*. The Lord will examine us all.

Query–Is it right for Disciples, under any circumstances short of absolute necessity, to attend the meetings of denominational Christians on Lord's day, to the neglect of their own meetings? Please give an answer as extended as your convenience will permit.

Answer–There can be no "absolute necessity" in the case. It is never right to forsake or neglect the established worship on the Lord's day. It is divine obligation that requires us to meet for the established worship to bear them who condemn our holy profession, and cause a bad state of heart.

5/8/60,v3,#19,pg. 75

Query–An elder of a church in West Virginia on the Lord's day loaded and removed from the neighborhood the household furniture of P., a member of the same congregation. P. is a man who can neither read nor write. What should be the course of procedure in the case of a church officer who has thus willfully led astray one of his brethren?

Answer–1. The term "elder" is used here, we doubt not, in the sense of *overseer*, and not *senior*. We take it he is an *overseer* in a congregation, or has been appointed to fill the place of one. 2. His place, according to the Scripture, was with the Disciples, "when they come together on the first day of the week to break bread," and *seeing over them* and participating in the worship. He ought to be called to account for not being *in his place*, when he was perfectly able to be there. It was a voluntary and willful departure from the right way, and what *he knew to be the right way*. 3. He clearly set aside the example of the first Christians and did that for which he had no example. This was setting aside divine authority and doing that for which he had no authority. 4. In doing this he disobeyed the civil law, in doing which he disobeyed the law of God. 5. In doing this he not only turned aside from the example of faithful Christians, but the example of good citizens, moral and orderly men, who are not Christians. What should be done? The church *chooses* the men for overseers and deacons, and if a man chosen by the church and made overseer *disqualifies himself* for the work and *renders himself unworthy* of the trust assigned him, the church that gave him the trust can take it from him. This the church should do at once. She should further call on him to confess his wrong and promise reformation. Should he do this the brethren should confirm their love to him and encourage him to live a pious life. Should he, after due entreaty, refuse to do this the church should withdraw from him as a brother that walks disorderly.

A little prompt action in such cases would open the eyes of many brethren in regard to things they do of questionable, or worse than *questionable*, character; things manifestly immoral and wrong. It requires continual watchfulness on the part of the friends of order, morality and piety to restrain members under bad influences. We need close and strict attention to a higher order of morality, better order of morality, better order in our churches and greater purity. We can have no great power for good with dead weights pulling down on us; men who love the fairs, the races, the theater shows, games of amusement and all kinds of places of folly; filthy men who set out their bottle and show from their bloated faces that their whole bodies are saturated with and steeped in the poisonous drinks. We must study purity, morality, order, piety and devotion, and maintain these in the church by putting away the unclean and disorderly from among us. Instead of an overseer leading a weak and uninformed brother astray and into disorder, he should take care of the flock, remembering that he shall give account.

4/29/73, v.16, #17, pg. 132

Query—I have a query or two to ask you, through the REVIEW, if you prefer to do so, for the benefit of others as well as myself. Previous to my coming here, an idea got into the head of one or more of the brethren, in regard to the Lord's supper, like this: They affirm that because the testimony tells us that "Jesus took bread, and when he had given thanks he broke it," and because Paul *broke bread* at Troas, etc. that the primitive custom and hence the proper mode, is for the administrator to break the bread into little pieces, ready to be eaten. That because the word of Christ, or the Apostles, does not say that each one broke it for himself, therefore, from all we can gather, it is not for him to do. A portion of the church adopt this idea, and even practice it, and it has created some feeling, though not an anti-Christian feeling. Will you give us your conclusions and grounds of proof, either briefly or in extenso.

Answer–The above is certain a small matter, but still matters of no more importance have caused much trouble. The desire to have something new, troubles a great many brethren. The above is certainly a mere matter of propriety. We can not endure the idea of going into all the reasons now; but, to us, the idea of a brother breaking the bread into small morsels, savors of the Romish custom of putting the wafer upon the tongue, and is ridiculous. It is certainly much more becoming, simply to break the loaf in two, or if there be four deacons, as in some large churches, break it into four pieces.

I presume that when we get a new version of the English Scriptures, that the Greek word *arlos*, translated "bread" in the common version, will be translated *loaf*, and gave it to the disciples. The idea of breaking it into small pieces, is as ridiculous as if, in eating at a friend's table, he would break the bread into small bits. The idea of having more than one loaf, as we have seen in a few instances, is equally absurd. We have one loaf to represent one body.

8/10/58, vol.1, #32

Query–Where will I find the best exposition of the second chapter of Genesis, or must I take it literally that a serpent did speak to Eve? And here is another thing that looks dark—Mark 16.15–19; the command is to "preach to every creature," and then the 17th and 18th verses tells what signs will follow. In Matthew 28.20, he says "I am with you all ways, *even* unto the end of the world." You, to explain the gospel commission, take the four accounts of the evangelists to make one continued whole. Now, I have the same right to do the same. Now, then, why do not those signs follow at the present time?

Answer–1. We are afraid of those speculators who figurize everything. We are inclined to think that Moses wrote to people of common sense and that he did not use terms in a different sense from that in which they had generally been used. We would prefer saying that we do not understand Gen 2 at all, to some of the modern twisting expositions. It is just as likely that the devil appeared in the form of a serpent as that he appeared in any form. We have read expositions of this chapter from several learned Jews and examined many commentators, and still think that a man of intelligence can do no better than read the account given by Moses and make the best he can out of it. 2. Respecting the signs that were to follow the Apostles, we have a short method with all that follows: 1. The signs did follow the Apostles. 2. They could not have followed but by the immediate interposition of the Lord. 3. They could not have ceased but by the will of God. 4. It is an indisputable fact that they did cease with the Apostles. 5. Those who now contend for them, simply contend *for* them, but can not *do* them.

11/29/59,v2., #48,pg. 191

Query – Where is it recorded that the church made evangelists?

Answer – Evangelists, pastors and teachers, at first, were direct gifts, as there was a demand for them before they could be qualified and brought forth by the church. But no evangelists, pastors or teachers are now directly given and qualified by miracle. Timothy, it appears, was made at least in part, by his mother and grandmother having taught him the Holy Scriptures. Paul afterwards taught him more fully and preached to him the gospel of Christ. Men are still taught the Scriptures, by pious mothers, grandmothers and others, and thus made evangelists. The work of making evangelists, both in their education, qualifications and setting apart to do the work, in all its parts, is of the church. No man can show one scrap of authority from any other source for acting as an evangelist, besides the church. The authority of the Lord is now in the Bible and put forth by the church, and can be put forth in no other way. We have no use for evangelists of any professed functionaries, of a religious character, not made by the church.

5/1/60,vol.3,#18,pg.71

Query – If it is necessary for the churches to engage in things that God has told us any thing about, who has he left to give the directions, and where is it made of record? Philip, one of the seven deacons, is called an evangelist, and acted under the direct influence of the Holy Spirit; and consequently was a spiritual man, and his acts and deeds made of record and for our instruction. Timothy was told to do the work of evangelist and was one of the helps of the church, and had received some gift by the laying on of hands. Bro. Franklin, what was that gift? In asking these questions and making these remarks, I have not done it for controversy, but for information upon the subject; which I hope you will give, if you think them worthy of a place in your paper.

Answer–The gifts were in the Apostles, and imparted by the imposition of their hands, when evangelists were made by extraordinary means.

5/1/60,vol.3,#18,pg.71

Query–1.If belief in Christ, as the Son of God, and baptism (by immersion) are all that is necessary to salvation, or to church-membership, may not those who believe in erroneous points of doctrine, or doctrines of *demoralizing* tendency (as, for instance, Universalists, Unitarians, etc.), become members of the reformed; and may not occasion, thereby, be given for all sorts of men to preach and teach all sorts of doctrine, destructive to *unity of faith*—one pulling down what another may build up? 2. Is not the doctrine of the Reformers, in respect to baptism—that it is solely by *immersion,* and essential to salvation—a part of a *creed* (unwritten, it is true, but none the less a creed), to which all must *subscribe* in order to admission into the church?

Answer–1. We never speak of "baptism *by immersion*," because it is precisely equivalent to baptism by baptism. That immersion is baptism, is admitted by all authorities worth note. There is no baptism by sprinkling, because sprinkling is not baptism. 2. That belief in Christ, as the Son of God, was the faith required in order to admittance anciently, is one of the plainest and simplest truths ever uttered. This was the great oracle revealed for our belief for our belief at his baptism, at his transfiguration, and which the Lord says "flesh and blood hath not revealed," but his Father in heaven. This was the great oracle in the mind of the Apostle, when he said, "These things are written that you might believe that Jesus is the Christ, the Son of God." This is now the foundation truth of all revelation. The whole revelation from God to man pivots on this. The Apostles preached Christ, made known nothing but Christ, gloried in nothing but the cross of Christ. To know him, and the power of his resurrection, was the matter for the new convert. When a man inquired, "What doth hinder me to be baptized?" the preacher of Jesus said, "If thou believest with all thy heart, thou mayest." The man said, "I believest that Jesus Christ is the Son of God." Paul says, "If thou shalt confess the Lord Jesus with thy mouth, and believe in thine heart that God hath raised him from the dead, thou shalt be saved; for with the heart man believeth unto righteousness, and with the mouth confession is made unto salvation." In conformity with this, when the Philippian Jailor said, "Sirs, what must I do to be saved?" Was answered by the holy Apostle, "Believe on the Lord Jesus Christ, and thou shalt be saved and thy house." Peter also, at the house of Cornelius, centered the testimony of all the prophets upon Jesus. "All the prophets bear witness *of him*, that through *his name*, whoever believeth *on him* shall receive forgiveness of sins." He was "God manifest in the flesh." "In him dwelt the fullness of the Godhead bodily." He who saw him, saw the Father in him. He who receives him, receives the Father in him.

The whole system centers in him. He is the embodiment of the will of God to man; the personification and embodiment of the whole will of God to man. The issue is over him. We are not to defend Christianity by defending a piece at a time; nor are men to receive it by receiving a piece at a time. But we defend it in its embodiment, or personification, in defending him in whom it centers, and upon whom it rests—the Lord Messiah. In the same way we receive Christianity, in receiving him who is the embodiment of it. The ancient enemies of Jesus never made their attack upon him in whom it centered or embodied itself. They never persecuted a man for his Unitarianism or Trinitarianism, for his Calvinism or Arminianism. They never demanded of any man to repudiate any of these. Nor did they ever demand of any Christian to repudiate the details of Christianity; but they compelled them to blaspheme Christ, deny and *repudiate him*. They knew that if they could induce a man to reject the foundation of Christianity, that all the details were rejected with it. In the same way, in receiving the foundation, they receive all the details in the foundation. Religion never did—the Christian religion—and never can embody itself in, and be personified by, any person but Jesus. He is the soul of the Bible, the personification of the whole will of God to man. He who confesses him, and does not intend to obey him, is a mere pretender, or entirely ignorant of the whole structure of the scheme.

To receive Jesus in the confession and baptism, is to receive all the faith there is. All that is divine is in him, and received by them who receive him, and what is not divine, we do not want. Our friend sees nothing in this to exclude Universalists, Unitarians, etc. He might as well say, that there is nothing in preaching this simple faith to exclude Methodists, Presbyterians, Episcopalians, etc. But in this he is under a grand mistake. Preaching Christ, and nothing but Christ, ignores all these isms of men, and the who intends holding on to any of these modern pets, will not confess Christ unless you will enlarge the confession so as to take his hobby in. The truth is, that a man who is properly a Universalist, does not make Christ the center of his thoughts, and cannot be induced to confess him. The center of his thoughts is the figment, that *all will be saved*. There is no danger of his confessing Christ. The same is true of the Unitarian. He knows that confessing Christ, while it endorses all that is divine, does not endorse Unitarianism. Indeed, there is nothing that has ever been thought of, or that could be thought of, so well calculated to exclude all error, and include all truth, as simple confession, that Jesus is the Christ, the Son of God. That confession embraces all that is divine, and excludes all that is human. It includes all Christianity. In that confession, there is not one particle of Universalism, Unitarianism, Methodism, Presbyterianism, Episcopalianism or any other humanism. Hence those determined to hold on to their humanisms, will not make the confession, but hate and oppose it. The trouble with them is not that it does exclude enough, but that it excludes too much.

But what is there to hinder Universalists, Unitarians, etc., from getting into the Methodist or Presbyterian churches? Nothing under the sun; only that they do not wish to enter. If they desire to enter, they could answer all the questions, pass the scrutiny and gain admittance without any difficulty. But they do not desire to get into their churches; nor do they desire to get into the Christian church. They do not desire to confess Christ, and be baptized, knowing that this is making a profession at war with their daring hobbies. Reasoning on this point, however, is unnecessary. Infinite wisdom cannot be improved upon. That which God requires, is safer and better than all the inventions of men. The only plea that can be made for something more stringent, to prevent the admission of unworthy persons, must eternally rest upon the presumption, that man can and should improve upon the wisdom of God. Because that the ancient church received their converts by the confession with the mouth, of the belief of the heart, and baptism, is incontrovertible.

Touching the sophistries of some blind guides, who make, or try to make, a distinction between *faith* and *belief*, we have a word to say. The Lord says, "He that believeth, and is baptized, shall be saved, and he that believeth not shall be damned;" Mark 16.15–16. Here we have *believe*. Paul told the Jailor to "believe on the Lord Jesus Christ." Both these passages relate to justification or pardon. Paul says, "Therefore, being justified by faith, we have peace with God through our Lord Jesus Christ." Here, it cannot be denied, *faith* is used as precisely synonymous with *believe*. Romans 10, the Apostle commences with *faith*, and then uses *believe* as equivalent to faith, and a few words below uses the word *faith* again in the same sense. From these examples, any person will see that faith and belief are used as equivalents. The same can be shown from many other passages, beyond all dispute. 3. "Is not the doctrine of the Reformers, in respect to baptism—that it is solely by immersion, and essential—a part of a *creed* (unwritten, it is true, but none the less a creed), to which all must *subscribe*, in order to admission into the church?" As to immersion, we only need an English translation to give us immersion in every place where *baptizo* occurs in the Bible. It is not making a creed to translate the Bible correctly, and it is not binding a creed upon a man to require him to receive the requirements of the Bible. Baptizo means *immerse* when correctly translated. The requirement to be immersed, is as much from God as the requirement to repent. As to its being essential, we need no creed but the express command of the Lord to Paul. He said, "Go to Damascus, and there it shall be told thee what thou *must do*." When Ananias came to tell him what he *must do*, he commanded him to arise, and be baptized and wash away his sins, calling upon the name of the Lord. This is precisely equivalent to the language of Jesus: "Except a man be born of water, and of the Spirit, he cannot enter into the kingdom of God." It requires no creed, written or unwritten, but the New Testament, to find baptism or which is the same thing, immersion, and that it "must be," or in the language above, that it is essential to scriptural induction or adoption.

The question, however, whether it is essential or not, is not the question for a man who wishes to be a sincere follower of Christ. The simple matter with him is, does God command it? All parties admit that he does. Then, is it right to obey the commandment of God? All admit that it is. The whole spirit of this dispute, as to its being essential, grows out of disobedience. What would we think of a man who would inquire whether men could be saved without prayer? The man who would argue that we could be saved without prayer, or that prayer is not essential, we certainly would think did not love to pray very well. The true spirit is to submit to God in prayer, without inquiring whether it is essential, or whether men can be saved without prayer. In the same way, let us do whatever God commands, as we know it is infallibly right to do his commandments, even if it were possible for a man to be saved who might omit some commandment. It is a spirit of disobedience that inquires into the possibility of being saved without doing the commandments of God. They who do his commandments shall enter by the gates of the city, and have a right to the tree of life. I know of no Scripture that teaches that he who does not keep His commandments shall enter in through the gates into the city, and have a right to the tree of life. "Not every one who says Lord, Lord, shall enter the kingdom, but he that *doeth the will* of my Father in heaven." "The Lord Jesus shall be revealed from heaven in flaming fire, taking vengeance on them who know not God, and *obey not the gospel* of our Lord Jesus Christ, who shall be punished with and everlasting destruction from the presence of the Lord, and from the glory of his power." "He who hears these sayings of mine, and doeth them, I will liken him to a wise man;" but "he who hears these sayings of mine, and doeth them not, I will liken him to a foolish man," says the Great Teacher. The angels of God in heaven *cavil* not when he commands, but bow to his authority.

3/15/59, v.2, #11, pg.52

Query–Being a firm believer in the New Testament, having one year ago read a work styled "The Christian Baptist" which confirmed in me the faith of the restoration of primitive Christianity, I am now induced to make the following inquiry: Is it right for me to go to the Lord's table with what we consider unbaptized members and with those that we know to be unworthy, belonging to the different sectarian denominations? Some twenty years ago I was immersed and united with the Baptist Church. Now is it requisite for me to be immersed again, in understanding more fully what is meant by immersion and what it is for? They hold it as the door into the church. We hold it as being a positive command and for the remission of sins. Having confidence that you will answer this inquiry, I await with anxiety for your reply.

Answer–It is not, so far as we can learn from the Scriptures, the duty of any Christian, when going to the Lord's table, to examine *another one*, as to the unworthiness or baptism. It is the duty of a disciple of

Christ to examine himself and so eat. The New Testament recognizes no person as in Christ, in the body or church till baptized. Men not in the body or church of Christ can not set *the Lord's table*, and we would go to no table of their setting. They have no right to officiate or do any thing in the Lord's name. We do not think that you ought to be immersed again. While it is certainly desirable to understand as far as we can any appointment we submit to, the want of a full understanding does not invalidate the ordinance. The Jews on Pentecost certainly had very little understanding of the design of baptism. They understood Jesus was the Savior, as well as that what he commanded was right, and submitted to it in obedience to him. You certainly understood as much as they did. You believed in the Lord, loved him and aimed to obey, and understood sufficiently to do what he commanded. As a matter of course, in reading and practicing for years, you will understand more clearly and fully. We presume this is the case generally; but this does not prove, the necessity of taking incipient steps again that have long since been honestly taken.

2/60, vol.#3, pg. 26

Query–Can a bishop of a congregation give a letter of commendation without the consent of the congregation?

Answer–We think not, *for the congregation.* Nothing can be clearer in the very nature of the case, than that, in order to give general satisfaction, persons can neither be received nor dismissed, by letter or otherwise, without the consent of the congregation. It is equally evident, in our mind, that no man can give satisfaction, as a bishop, who is indifferent to the voice of the church and takes too much responsibility upon *himself.*

9/4/60, v.3, #34, p.144

Query–We have another query in reference to ordaining a bishop. It is said that a bishop was ordained in a congregation by *prayer,* but no *fasting* or *imposition* of hands:

Answer–Why select prayer and leave fasting and imposition of hands out, when all three stand together in the Book? This is like selecting *faith* in the justification of the sinner, and leaving out repentance and baptism. It would have been more consistent to have left out prayer also.

We are for taking all or none. The straight forward and manifest way of it evidently is, to ordain by *fasting, prayer* and the *imposition of hands.*

8/16/59, v.2, #33, pg. 131.

Query – Bro. Franklin: At one point where I spend a portion of my time, I often met with the Tunkers, or Dunkards, as some call them. They are very zealous and peculiar—it being Trine Immersion. The candidate kneels down to be baptized, and continues in that position till prayer has been made and hands have been laid on. They dip the person forward instead of backward, and quote the commission, as recorded by Matthew, as their authority for so doing. To our vision, this evidence does not authorize them so to practice. Neither Jesus nor the Apostles so understood the commission. Our Tunker friends are practicing Trine Immersion without authority. I was informed that a Baptist lady wished to join them and was willing to be baptized twice more, having been once baptized by the Baptists, but they refused, unless she would submit to their rule. She declined. Will you, Bro. Franklin, favor the readers of the REVIEW with an article on Trine Baptism? Many brethren have wished to be so favored.

Answer – We have many times, during the past eighteen years, referred to the people mentioned above, and can not now occupy but a small space in that way. That there is not one scrap of authority for Trine Immersion, either in the commission or any other place in the Scriptures, or anything written in the first and second centuries of the Christian era, or even a mention of such a thing, is as clearly settled with men of reading, as that there was no infant baptism, or sprinkling for baptism, during the same period. Still, men wedded to a mere invention of men care nothing for that. They can find persons who can be turned aside from the commandments of God, or from the faith, to mere fables, or to the most stupid inventions men have ever introduced. Where is there one word of authority for all the mere farce of kneeling in the water; laying hands on them before they are baptized, or immersing three times? Suppose the Lord were to appear before these men and inquire of them, "Who hath required this at your hands?" what answer could they give? None under the shining sun; they would stand speechless, or say something of which instructed men would feel ashamed, as we have seen them do, when called on for authority.

They admit that *baptizo* means *immerse*; and this being granted, when the apostle says, "One Lord, one faith, one baptism," the "one baptism," is *one* immersion—not *three*. It is as likely that "one faith," means *three* faiths, as that one immersion means three. It would not be more perverse and schismatical in tendency, to preach three bodies, three spirits, three hopes, three Lords or three faiths, than three immersions.

It is most wonderful thing that men can not be content to let the simple appointment of the Lord stand; but they must be tampering with it in some way, either adding to it, or detracting from it, in every variety of form and degree, from the laying moistened fingers on the forehead in the name of the Trinity, to immersing three times, with the accompaniments described above. In this way, the pure and holy religion of the Savior and the Bible are disgraced in the eyes of sensible men and the power of the gospel destroyed. There will one day be a reckoning for all of this. The Lord and his gospel may not be thus trifled with and disgraced before the world.

Never was there such a demand for good, sound, sensible and well educated men, to preach the simple gospel of the Son of God and set aside the dreadful follies of this generation. The authority of the Scriptures must be established in the hearts of the people of our times.

Western Reformer 10/1849, v.7, #3, pg.509

Query–Is it more proper to attend to the Lord's Supper in the afternoon or evening, than in the forenoon? Is the time material or set in the Testament?

Answer–We esteem it a matter of no consequence, except as a mere question of convenience, whether we break the loaf in the morning or evening. Where the members are conveniently situated so that they can meet in the morning and afternoon, as we do in the city, it is more suitable to break the loaf in the afternoon. We make that the principal object of our coming together in the afternoon.

4/29/62, v.5,#17, pg.2.

Query–Has a Christian a right to neglect his daily business to attend public worship? Does he commit a sin in no doing?

Answer–These are amusing questions. They can not have reference to the worship on the Lord's day, for a Christian lays aside "his daily business on that day." The question then, must relate to meetings for public worship on other days. If this is the meaning, the question amounts to about this: Has a Christian a right to neglect making money, speculating, trading and working, for a few days, and make an effort to turn men to the Lord? In this case, the question must be asked in irony and not seriously, to show how ridiculous and absurd it is for men to excuse themselves from a noble effort to save men and women from ruin by referring to their "daily business." Some, professing to be Christians, and to believe their neighbors are in their sins, in their blood, and rapidly rushing down to ruin, and yet would think it cruel to ask them to stop business for a week, or only to stop it, for this is all that is generally necessary, make an effort to save men from bottomless perdition. Such men only show that they do not appreciate the religion which they profess. They frequently quote, the "he who provides not for his own and especially they of his own house has denied the faith and is worse than an infidel." And is that what they are "attending to their own business" for? Is it merely to provide for their own, especially they of their own house? or are they not striving to lay up money to buy out all their neighbors whose land joins them? Many men are deceiving themselves. The Lord is not mocked. Let us attend to his work while we have time and opportunity.

9/2/62, V.5, #35, p.2

Query–Suppose that a brother is guilty of an offense of the most flagrant character, which, substantially proven, and according to gospel order disowned, would it be in accordance with the usage of the Church of Christ and the gospel for another congregation of the disciples, who were acquainted with all of the facts in the case, to take such person in as a member of their congregation where there were no manifestations of reformation by such person; and should such person visit the congregation from which he was expelled be entitled to a place at the Lord's Table?

Answer–We do not insert the above to give an answer to the question proposed, for as stated, there can be but one answer, viz: that is, for any congregation to receive a person as described would be an outrage on all order and respect to the authority of the Scripture. We insert it for the purpose of saying, that it is no part of an editor's office to act as a kind of general referee to decide little difficulties that may arise among brethren, or in the management of congregations, and we prefer greatly not to be a party to any such matters.

The preachers and officers of churches, who live in the immediate locality of little troubles and are acquainted with the parties concerned, are much better judges and safer arbiters than editors, and have much more time to bestow upon cases of the kind. Many of these cases are of no general interest, and should never occupy a line in any paper. Any preacher, officer in a congregation, or private member, can answer the question; if fairly stated, as well as all editors in the brotherhood. Any doubtful matter, involving general principles, and at the same time of importance, might appropriately find way into our publications, to elicit from editors or others the best opinions and most prudent judgment that can be elicited. In like manner, also queries may be presented concerning the salutation of intricate matters in Scripture, for the purpose of eliciting the best light from any of the abler brethren. But, as we said before, we prefer not to be called on to give opinions in reference to all in any way to become parties to them, as it opens the way to incur prejudice, without doing any good, and introduces things into the paper of no general interest or utility. Not only so, but frequently the statement is one-sided and gives no chance for a correct opinion in the case. The above case may be stated very correctly, for anything we know, but we are not always certain of a correct statement; and then it is not our business to decide all these little matters. Our position is sufficiently perplexing when to confine our self to our legitimate work.

9/9/62,v.5, #36, pg.2

Query – I wish to state a case and would like a few remarks from you on the subject. It is a matter of vital importance and should be understood by the brethren. A minister among us labors for a Church some two years, during which time many reports are in circulation relative to his character, caused by manifest improprieties with a female member of the congregation. Another minister is obtained to preach a few months, the first one still living in town, but *not allowed by the Church to enter the pulpit with the officiating minister.* He (the accused) now determines to leave the place to soak some other field of labor. The Church, which is large and influential, refuse to give him a letter of *fellowship* as a Christian—much less as a worthy minister. He then appeals to individual friends in the Church and *out*, and gets some 6 letters from Church members and 10 out of the Church, from citizens of the place. He likewise obtains a letter from the minister who preached for the brethren—although not allowed to officiate with him. He goes with these letters and is hired by another Church in the State, having no letter of fellowship from a Church of 200 members, and only some six individual letters from personal friends, and one from a preacher who was only temporarily hired. 1st. Now, Bro. Franklin, what should be done with individuals, members of Churches, who give letters—when the Church as a body, refuses for good reasons? 2nd. What should we think of ministers who will so far disregard the necessity of Christian discipline as to treat with contempt the decision of a large and influential Church, and give an individual letter? 3rd. What course should be taken with a Church that knows all these facts and still hires such an irresponsible man to preach among them—a cause of sorrow to men of a different stamp? Many intelligent and godly brethren will await your reply.

Answer–The difficulty is one from which the cause has suffered much, ever since our first acquaintance with it. Good men, who desire to preserve order, have grieved much on account of this evil. From our experience and observation, we are satisfied that the following, as a general rule, will hold good: 1. It is an unfavorable indication for a man to have *too many letters* of recommendation. 2. It is an unfavorable indication for these numerous letters of recommendation to be *too good-to overdo the thing*. 3. It is a clear ground of suspicion for these letters to come from *individuals*, and not from a Church. 4. It is unfavorable for these letters to be of too ancient date. 5. It is a very suspicious circumstance to see a preacher forward to show and read his numerous letters. If a church will practice on the following rules she will not fall into many troubles from the source alluded to: 1. If a stranger comes along, with his pockets filled with letters *of different sorts*, of various dates, etc. tell him that you know nothing against him; that he may be all right, but that you do not receive a man as a preacher, and become responsible for him, before the public, *till satisfied that he will be profitable*. Tell him that you do not refuse to receive him because *you know anything against* him, but because you do not know *his character to be good*. It is no reason why you should receive a preacher, that you know nothing against him. There are many bad men that you know nothing 1. The reason for receiving a man and presenting him before the community as a preacher of righteousness, should be that you *know something good* of him—that you *believe him to be true*. 2. Make it a general rule, to receive no man, who has no recommendation but letters from *individuals*. No man carries and presents letters from *individuals* who can procure a good letter from *his Church*. 3. Receive no man who is not in standing in a congregation. It is a most preposterous and absurd to receive a man, as a teacher of the people, and preacher of righteousness, who maintains no standing in any congregation. 4. Be cautious in receiving those whining, croaking and bitter men, who are down on all their preaching brethren, and who suppose the preachers are against them on account of their success, or their superior ability. Take all their simpering as evidence against them. 5. Churches should remember, that they are not bound to receive every man, *as a preacher*, and become responsible for him before the world, unless they would be willing to prefer and undertake to sustain a charge against him. This is not the case. If a man comes before you in a *doubtful* or *suspicious* manner, that is not your fault, and you are under no obligation to be involved with him. Let him pass. His doubtful, or suspicious attitude, is his fault, or misfortune and he has no right to involve you in it. In letting him pass, the Church does not decide *against* him, but simply that she does not know enough about him to think it profitable to receive him, *as a preacher.* 6. We have very little confidence in brethren going from Church to Church, *without invitation*, preaching. No manly preacher will press his services, as a preacher, and compel a Church to *receive* or *reject* him. Men who stand right, generally wait for an *invitation;* and when they do not, it is because they *know themselves to be acceptable.* 7. Touching one Church receiving a man, who is rejected by another, we know of no rule that can be urged invariably. A Church has a reputation, like an individual, and may act unwisely and imprudently, from mere want of information, from prejudice or ambition, in receiving an unworthy man, or rejecting a good man. The actions of Churches are not infallible, and will be taken by neighboring Churches, according to the real weight and character of the Church. If a Church is known to be composed of well informed, judicious, prudent and good men, of long standing, where just and wise counsels have prevailed, the action will be respected. If it is composed largely of ignorant, strongly prejudiced and imprudent men, where unwise counsels prevail, its decisions will not be generally respected. The value of a letter, or the weight of a decision, depends on the character of the Church. 8. Preachers should have their standing in the Church where they reside, and not at a distance, where their real standing is not known at all, from which they have a letter. Such a letter is about as good no letter at all.

In one word, we have never been half strict enough with preachers, and private members, in preserving order. It would be well to turn over a new leaf, and institute more strict order, and see that all, in cases of changing locations, have letters, and present them immediately.

11/18/62, v.5, #46, pg. 2

Query–1. Is it scriptural to receive persons into the Church, who have been cut off without confession? 2. If confession is made to the overseers, is it not their duty to make it known to the Church, before receiving them? 3. If the cause of Jesus Christ is checked by persons holding the office of overseers, and a majority of the Church urge them to resign, is it not their duty to do so? 4. If brethren who stand up for the truth are, by so doing, cut off, have they not the right to organize a body for themselves? 5. Have the Elders a right to cut a brother off from the Church, without the consent of the Church?

Answer–It is generally of but little use to reply to questions of this sort, for they are almost always propounded by a party involved in some difficulty, and so stated as not to involve the real issue. Men, otherwise good and fair men, when involved in some difficulty, become one sided and prejudiced, and frequently make very unfair representations. But we proceed to answer the foregoing questions. Ques. 1st.–Certainly not. Ques. 2nd.–It certainly is. Ques. 3rd.–This question ought to have been stated as follows: If, *in the judgment* of a majority of the members of the Church, the cause is checked by persons holding the office of overseers, and this majority urges them to resign, is it their duty to do so? We then answer, it certainly is. No right thinking man would think of holding the office of overseer contrary to the desire of the majority, or even a respectable minority. Still, there may be another side to the matter, out of which this question has grown. Ques. 4th. We have traveled much in the brotherhood, and the idea of brethren being cut off for "standing up for the truth" strikes us as such a novel thing, that we think there must be some other phase to the matter. There is sometimes a wide difference between "standing up for the truth" and standing up for what some *think* the truth, or *call* the truth. Of course, if any Church has become so corrupt as to cut off good men for "standing for the truth," such good men would do right to embody themselves in a Christian congregation, or unite with one. Ques. 5th. Certainly no one should be cut off without consent of the Church. The overseers should attend to an offense, put it in form, obtain the evidence and bring it before the Church, and the cutting off should be by resolution passed by the congregation assembled on the Lord's day.

We find sometimes very incompetent overseers, and sometimes disagreeable men get into a snarl with overseers, make war upon them, and nothing will satisfy them but to put the overseers out of office. Such brethren would do wisely to heed the apostolic injunction, *to study the things that make for peace.* Getting into a war on the overseers, getting cut off from the Church, and establishing a new Church of excluded members, never amounts to much good.

3/24/63, v.6, #12, p.46

Query–Has an elder any legal right to withdraw the congregation, or the fellowship of the congregation from an individual member without conferring with the congregation.

Answer–Certainly not. The only Scripture to which we shall now refer is the following: I wrote to the church: but Diotrephes, who loves to have the pre-eminence among them, receiveth us not. Wherefore if I come, I will remember his deeds which he has done, prating against us with malicious words ; and not contented therewith, neither doth he himself receive the brethren, and forbids them who would, and *casts them out of the church.*" 3 John verses 9 and 10. The italicized words are the words applicable in the case. Little men assume *great authority*; great men assume *little authority.* Good men do all things in love.

4/28/63, v.6, #17, p.66

Query–The Catholics have followed the building of railroads, and I suppose a few are left on all the lines, at least in the villages. It is so here at any rate, and they propose to build a church, soliciting funds on all hands. Now, Brother Franklin, will it be right for us to aid in this work? Your views on this subject will be thankfully received.

Answer–If the brethren want to build up something for the Lord to destroy at his coming, we do not know where they can invest to better advantage than in building up Romanism. See Rev 18 and 2 Thess 2.1–8.

6/23/63 v.6, #25, pg.98

Query–An individual presents herself to the Church of Christ for membership, who had been taught the first principles of Christianity as taught by the apostles, to wit: faith, repentance, confession and baptism for remission of sins, and who had been immersed by a teacher of Christianity (professedly) of the persuasion called Mormons, but who had renounced all belief in Mormonism, and was satisfied with her baptism, is her baptism valid, and should she be received into the Church?

Answer–There can be nothing more than an opinion given in such a case as the one stated above. If the person concerned had the faith, repentance and confession required in the New Testament, and, from the heart, yielded obedience to Christ, she was certainly very inconsistent in doing so under a Mormon imposter. Still, under such religious training as we have now, it is not strange that a lady of good ordinary intelligence should have involved herself in such an absurd position. Persons are constantly being told in all directions that "it is no difference what Church you join"—that "whatever you think right, that is right *to you*"—that "if the heart is right, that is all," etc., etc., With such teaching constantly afloat, why should any one think strange, that a lady of ordinary intelligence, who honestly believed in the Savior of the world, was truly penitent, and desired to be immersed, according to the Scriptures, for the remission of sins, if such should be the first opportunity, should receive immersion at the hands of a Mormon? We think that the matter may be disposed of as follows. The person in question knows whether her purposes were pure in what she did. She knows whether she believed in Christ, repented and was immersed in obedience to Christ. If she did what the New Testament requires to become a disciple of Christ, she became one. If her aim was simply to become a Christian, and she did what the Scriptures require to that end, she entered the kingdom, though he who administered her immersion was an impostor. Nothing depends on the administrator, so far as the validity of the ordinance is concerned. If the greatest impostor in the world should preach the gospel—"the truth as it is in Jesus"—and nothing else, and a man should receive it, obey it, with an eye single to the glory of God, he would become a Christian. But, the impostor who preached it would receive no reward.

The receiving of the person in question, would be no endorsement of the Mormon or Mormonism. This difficulty is one of the many imposed on us by corruptions of Christianity, and nothing in the way of the practice of the true gospel of the grace of God. It only shows that persons may place themselves in doubtful positions by following the false theories of our times.

7/21/63,v.6, #29, p.114

Query–In our Church's record, I find the following note: "At a meeting of the elders and brethren of the Church, held on 26th of July, Bro _____, who had been admonished from time to time for neglect of Christian duty, and for which he manifested no disposition to make acknowledgment; neither would he promise or fulfill his neglected Christian duty, viz. : that of communing, in which he had not been a participant, for better than a year; he was therefore excluded."

Is the above sentence of the church in strict accordance with apostolic teaching? Be kind enough to favor your readers with an early reply to the above.

Answer–If the proper labors were performed to induce the brother in question, to amend his practice, the action of the church was correct.

11/17/63, v.6, #46, pg. 182

Query–About four months since the Church of Disciples, on York Street, employed an Evangelist, with the understanding that he was to preach a part of the time, in an adjoining neighborhood, where there were some four or six members, and if possible, to organize a church. The immediate success was one addition; but it was not thought prudent by some to organize a church. These four held their membership in the York Street Congregation well. On last Lord's day the Evangelists, with the advice and consent of the four members, proposed to organize a church. This was without the knowledge or consent of the York Street Congregation. In the afternoon, the loaf and wine were brought over; but in the meantime the Elders (both of whom were present in the forenoon) talked the matter over, and came to the conclusion that the Evangelist had no authority to organize a church, without first consulting the mother church—that these members had no right to leave the York Street Church and go into a new organization, without the consent of the Church; and on this ground they opposed the organization. The Evangelist claimed that he had a right to organize, without consulting the York Street Congregation.

One of the Elders lived in the neighborhood of the proposed congregation, and got up in the afternoon and stated his reasons for not wishing to organize at present, that the proper and only prudent way was to get the consent of the Mother Church; and, finally, it was decided that they would not organize. But some are dissatisfied and claim that they had a right to organize a new church, without the knowledge or consent of the church where they had their membership. The Evangelist claimed this. Will you please inform us, through the REVIEW, as to which is or was the proper course to pursue?

Answer – Of course all about the foregoing matter is merely prudential and discretionary. It is a mere matter of propriety or impropriety. The matter is not, to be settled by Scripture authority. If we comprehend the question, it may be stated as follows: Is it prudent, or in accordance with propriety, for an evangelist to organize a few members into a church, in the immediate vicinity, or in a few miles of an old congregation, depending on some members from the old church to compose a part of a new one, without consulting with the old congregation or obtaining her consent? We should certainly not think it proper, or prudent so to do. Members cannot reasonably expect to enter a new congregation, or go out of it without the consent of the congregation—Evangelists should act in co-operation with existing churches, and not without consulting them, specially in reference to matters so intimately relating to the churches, as forming new congregations in their immediate vicinity, to be composed partly of members from the old congregations. There should be co-operation, fellowship, and harmony among churches. This cannot be had unless their action is mutual. Forming new congregations in the immediate vicinity of old ones, and sometimes involves their very existence, and should certainly, as a general rule, take place without the consent of the old churches. The evangelist in question, we think, should consult the old church and come to a mutual understanding what should be done. It is not good to form weak churches not capable of supporting themselves. Many of these only last for a short time, dwindle away and die. It is much better, generally, to strengthen and build up old congregations than to establish new ones, especially when there is no assurance of their ability permanently to sustain themselves.

11/17/63, v.6, #46, pg. 182

Query – Is a Deacon duty bound, and is there any law in God's word that a Deacon should preside in the absence of the Elders of a church? Is it not the duty of any member that is incapable of officiating to administer the Lord's Supper? Suppose that there are members that are more capable of filling the Elder's seat, temporarily, than any of the Deacons are, would it not be more orderly for them to do so?

Answer—There is nothing in the Bible about Deacons presiding in the absence of bishops. Such matters are purely matters of discretion. Any brother may preside at any time, with the consent or approbation of the church. There is nothing in the law of God about Bishops or Deacons administering the Lord's Supper. Any brother of good report, capable and having the approbation of the congregation, can administer the Lord's Supper. These are matters purely of discretion and propriety. Churches, if they have piety of heart and the Lord with them, can meet, break the loaf, exhort, pray, sing and carry out the Lord's work, officers or no officers, preachers or no preachers. We must abandon all these notions that we cannot do anything without officials. The church has authority to make officials. Strange then, indeed, if she has not power to appoint some one to conduct her worship! When we get back to the simplicity of Christianity, as it was at the beginning, we shall find it a plain matter—that plain people can conduct and enjoy the glory of God.

2/23/58,v.1,#8, p.30

Query—When a brother has been set apart to the office of Deacon by fasting, prayer and imposition of hands, and is afterwards advanced by the voice of the church to the Eldership, must he again be set apart to *that* office by the same solemnities that attended his induction into the deaconship?

Answer—We have no clue to the above, as there is not one word about it in the Bible. So far as reason and analogy go, we cannot see how ordination to Deaconship could be considered an ordination to any other office or station. Whether Deacons were never "advanced" to the bishopric, anciently or why, we cannot tell, but certain it is that there is nothing about the case in the Bible.

2/23/58, v.1, #8, pg.30

Query—As we, in this part of the country, are weak on the subject of church government, a few of us have concluded to solicit, through the REVIEW, your opinion with regard to the action we should take in reference to the following classes of persons: 1. Those who have moved away and their names still on the church book. 2. Colored persons who have been sold and taken away. 3. Those who are in the army, on either side 4. Those whose names are on our church book and they really in fellowship with the world. 5. You will please give your opinion on ordination, and whether or not hands should be laid on in ordaining church officers.

Answer–1. Make a record on the book, of their removal, the time when, and the time when, and whether they took letters. The importance of always taking letters, when members move away, ought everywhere to be impressed on the minds of brethren. 2. Make a record of their being taken away, the manner how, and the time, on the church book. 3. Make a record on the church book, of their leaving, when and what for. 4. Visit them and make a good effort to save them, and, if it cannot be done, withdraw fellowship from them. 5. Church officers were certainly ordained by fasting, prayer and the imposition of hands, in the original church, and should be now.

11/24/63. v.6, #47, p.186

Query–Has an elder power to excommunicate deacons from the church, without any citation, trial or charge against them, only one of his own?

Answer–A Bishop has no authority to exclude any person, no matter whether a deacon or not, without a full and deliberate consultation with the other officers of the church, charges preferred, a fair hearing, faithful attention to the testimony, and the concurrence of the church, assembled on the Lord's day.

12/1/63, v.6, #48, pg.190

Query–Is an elder the absolute power of the whole church?

Answer–He is not. The Lord is the absolute power or *authority*, as we suppose, was intended in the church. The idea, if anyone has it, of a *bishop* claiming absolute authority is preposterous. There should be overseers in every congregation, and they, with the deacons, should *all act in harmony*, and then, their action should receive *the sanction* of the church assembled on the Lord's day.

12/1/63, v.6, #48, pg.190

Query–In the case where there is a rich brother, and he has a difficulty with a sister, has the elder power to refuse to act because she is a sister?

Answer–The law of God knows no difference, in the case of a *rich* brother, nor in the case where the difficulty is with a *sister*. The character of one should be brought into suspicion by charges being preferred, unless there is good ground; but when there is good ground, neither the rich nor sisters are exempt any more than anybody else. Brethren, be careful and do nothing by partiality, or under the influence of mere worldly feeling. These are terrible times, and many thousands will look back to these days, with bitter anguish and regret, from the eternal state, as the time when they lost the love of Christ, commenced their retrograde movement which terminated in utter apostasy. Many overseers who have failed to take care of the flock of God, will render a strict account when the Chief Shepherd appears, and will regret seriously their reckless course. Many deacons, too, and private members will then see their awful folly in being carried away by the frenzy of the world from the holy commandment. In this time of convulsion, when law, authority and government, are called into question, the vilest passions of earth and hell are unchained. Religious, moral, and even civil restraints are thrown off. Wicked men, and the lawless, with the powers of the vast abyss, appear to be making an effort for universal anarchy. But the Lord is still on the throne. The crown is still on his head, and the oath of the Almighty Father of heaven and earth, declaring, that he shall reign till every knee shall bow and every tongue shall confess, has not failed and will not. The Lord God omnipotent reigns. His government will not be overthrown. Hell, with all its vile tenantries, with all who are proper subjects for punishment, will be put down.

Query–I have seen that a brother is preparing some forty or fifty sermons of our most gifted Brethren for publication; this seems a little mixed with sectarianism. The apostle says, "preach the word." Well, then, we have the word published by them, and we can read it in the book. The sects have their sermon-books, and I think if we had them, some of our brethren would study them more than they would the *word*. However, they could study to show themselves approved unto men, yea, workmen that ought to be ashamed when they commence dividing these sermons. I suppose these will be text sermons, and I will suggest a text for one of them to preach from: Genesis, 19th chapter, 26th verse.

Answer–We can see no "sectarianism," or even impropriety, in printing sermons, or volumes of them. True, the requirement is to "preach the word," and we suppose, the intention is to have sermons, in which the word is to be preached, and nothing else. If it is wrong to print the sermons, it is wrong to preach them. If we may not print a sermon, or a volume of sermons, because sectarians print sermons, then, for the same reason, we may not preach sermons, for sectarians preach sermons. The wrong in sectarians is not in the, printing or publishing sermons, which are not good, in which the word is not preached, or something is set forth contrary to the word. We are not now using the word "sermon" in any sense, only as indicating or designating a *religious discourse.* The religion of Christ started through the world, and, indeed, went through it, by talking privately, publicly, and writing. No matter whether the discourses were long or short, public or private, oral or written, provided the true gospel of the grace of God was advocated, all was right. Paul gloried that the gospel was preached, though it was done through envy, to add to his bonds. Let us rejoice that the gospel is preached, whether it be by some obscure and private disciple of the Lord, in the private circle, some able defender of the faith in the public assembly, in our publications, tracts or volumes of sermons. Any means by which sectarianism can be propagated, in teaching orally, or in writing, may successfully be employed in propagating the true gospel. Do the sects teach sectarianism in Sunday schools? Then let Christians preach the gospel in the Sunday school. Do they propagate sectarianism in their publications? Certainly they do. Then let us propagate the true gospel in the same way. All we ask is, that the sermons be good, sound gospel sermons.

8/11/63, v.6, #32, p.126

Query– Is it right to take the Lord's money out of the Lord's treasury, to give it to the poor outside of the church, or in other words, the world's poor.(?)

Answer–It would not only be right, but if the Lord's treasury can afford it, we should delight to do it, thus doing good to all men, especially to the household of faith. The Lord's poor first, and then all men, as far as we have power. We have many poor brethren now that should be attended to.

3/12/67, v.x, #11, pg.84

Query–A good brother says, "Some members are very prompt to meet for worship on the First Day of the week, others can be persuaded to meet on an average of once a month." (?)

Answer–There is nothing new in the circumstances that some are prompt in attending worship, while others are not. This has been the case from the forming of the church. One reason why the Lord gives us time on earth, is that we may prove ourselves, and exhibit to heaven and earth, our love to the Savior, our devotion and integrity. The "good and faithful" must continue good and faithful, true and loyal to our King. If there are others, who have not love enough for the Savior, devotion and integrity to meet according to his will and commemorate his death, and who can not be persuaded to do his will, they can not be saved. The Lord will never say, "Well done, good and faithful," to any one who has not been good and faithful. It is the duty of those who come up regularly and worship, as required in the law of God, to do their utmost to bring others to realize their obligations. This is all they can do. They must then leave them in the hands of the Lord.

3/5/67, v.x, #10, p.76

Query–A part of a congregation contribute regularly to the treasury. Others equally able can not be persuaded to do so.(?)

Answer–It has always been the case, that *part* contributed and *part* did not. The Lord has opened a fine opportunity here for each member of the church to show the *liberality* or *illiberality* of his own heart. If the heart of a man is narrow, hard and illiberal, there is no concealing it when the contribution is called for. How can a man, with ability, can remain in the church, year after year with the fact open to the Lord and to his brethren, that his contributions are insignificant side of those of his brethren, and compared with what they ought to be, is a mystery. One would think such a man would manage in some way to get out of the church, and hide himself from society, so that his littleness and narrowness might not be constantly coming in contrast with the deeds of the noble and liberal. For these too, we must do the best we can, and if we can not save them; they will have to be given up to be lost. Those who have it in their hearts to do right, must not be governed by the narrow, pinch-fisted and stingy, but continue to do their part nobly.

3/5/67, v.x, #10, p.76

Query—A worthy brother, with a small family, has been reduced to want, by circumstances over which he had no control, and the elders, with a part of the congregation, decide that it is their duty to buy him a small home, and other things essentially necessary, and part of the brethren positively refuse to assist in this matter. What is our duty?

Answer—It would certainly be noble in a church to buy an unfortunate brother a small home. Such a thing would be a noble example and commend the religion of the Savior. Those in favor of this beneficent deed, ought by all means to make the unfortunate brother feel the benefit of their liberality, that the Lord, the righteous judge may put it down to their credit. This will bring the unwilling to their feeling that it can be done. Those willing to do charitable deeds ought to do them whether others do them or not.

3/5/67, v.x, #10, p.76

Query—Please say through the REVIEW, that the statement made by yourself and somebody else, that I hold and preach that the use of instruments of music is enjoined by divine authority on the church, is wholly untrue.

Answer—Desiring to do even justice to all men, but specially our querist, the church and the cause at large, we cheerfully insert the article. It will, however, be readily seen, that the statement which he ascribes to as and others, and pronounced wholly untrue, varies considerably from our precise words. Our precise words are as follows: He finds *divine authority* for the use of instrumental music in worship, in the meaning of the word "psalm." These are not the words which he pronounces "wholly untrue." Nor does he pronounce the words of the charge made against him, in the meeting of the messengers, sent up from surrounding churches to investigate the troubles in the church, all wholly untrue. We never made the statement which he ascribes to us and others, and pronounces wholly untrue—that "he holds and preaches that the use of instruments of music is enjoined by divine authority on the church. This is quite a variation from our statement.

Did he never attempt to find divine authority in the meaning of the word "psalm," for instrumental music in worship? If he did not, our information has been incorrect, and we stand corrected, as well as take the pleasure at being thus corrected and being assured that he did not attempt this.

4/2/67,V.X, #14, P.108

Query–Does faith, repentance, confession and baptism induct one into the kingdom, and *also bring that one under the eldership in the vicinity where that one is baptized?*

Answer–The simple process of induction into Christ, the body or kingdom does not make a person or a member of one local congregation than another. It does not constitute a person a member of the general body. After becoming a member of the general body, or which is the same thing, entering the covenant with the Lord, it is a step additional to take membership in a local or a particular congregation.

4/16/67, v.x, #16, p.125

Query–Is it good order for a preacher to remain out of the congregation, keeping his letter of recommendation (if he has one), in his pocket for months and years, meeting with them, however, and voting on questions brought before them? Ought he not to put the letter into the hands of the brethren, and thereby give his influence fully on the side of the congregation where he resides? Does he not, by remaining out, say by his example that there is no necessity for an organization, and encourage others to do likewise? To whom is he amenable for misconduct? I ask for information on this subject not to create disturbance.

Answer–Suppose all would follow the example of a preacher who carries his letter in his pocket, where would the church be? There would be no church. Such a course would forever abolish the church. Shall a preacher be at the head of a course of disorder that would destroy the church, if all would follow his example? If a man is not willing to identify himself with the body, there must be a reason for it. Nor can we see any consistency in his acting with the body, or voting in its business meetings, when not a member of the body. We have known several preachers, of fair character, living in the same disorderly manner. They must be indifferent to good order, or anticipate trouble. We have known some instances, when trouble would come and the brethren would be proceeding to call them to account, they would inform the brethren that they had no jurisdiction over them, as they did not belong to the church. The brethren should hold such preachers responsible wherever they are, the same as members.

4/16/67, v.x, #16, p.125

Query–Is it essential to the Scriptural performance of ministerial duty that he who is getting into the work as preacher be previously "ordained by fasting, prayer, and laying on of hands?" You doubtless have answered this question before, but as I have not been a constant reader of the REVIEW, I have never seen the answer given. Please answer immediately, as I desire to practice as the Scriptures require, in this and all other respects.

Answer–Ordaining men simply to *make preachers of them,* or to *authorize them to preach,* is entirely unknown to the New Testament. The way to "get into the work," is to find an opportunity to preach and go at it and preach. There is not a man in the whole kingdom who has not *a right* to publish the good news by virtue of his discipleship. The way of getting into the work is to go at it and prove to the brethren that a man has ability—that he can and will preach to edification. When the brethren are satisfied of this, and desire to send him to any certain work, or mission, they should ordain him to that *certain work or mission,* by fasting, prayer and imposition of hands. The man should be a preacher first, and then, *because he is a preacher,* an acceptable preacher of ability and integrity, the Disciples recognize him as such and ordain him to the work. They thus endorse, commend, and send him with their own hands.

Young men should first prove themselves well, that they be considered *tried men,* when they have been ordained to any certain work or mission.

4/16/67, v.x, #16, p.125

Query–What difference is there between A. Campbell and John Wesley? I saw in the REVIEW some time since that John Wesley started Methodism at the wrong time and wrong place. Did not A. Campbell do the same?

Answer–What difference is there between A. Campbell and John Wesley? The inquiry, of course, relates to religious difference. There were many differences, some of the chief of which we will mention. Mr. Wesley was a reformer in a much narrower sense than Mr. Campbell. His effort at reformation related mainly to the Episcopalian church, of which he died a member. Even in that church, the aim was not to reform it in teaching so much as in the personal holiness, piety, or, as he frequently expressed it, to attain to a *deeper work of grace.* This narrow and limited work, confined to one body, the Episcopalian, the merely to the deeper work of grace, was an insignificant affair compared with the aim of Alexander Campbell, which was confined to no one religious body, to no one feature of Christianity, and, to no one country; but *was an effort under the blessing of Heaven, for a complete return, in all things, to the original ground of the Lord and the Apostles, in preaching, faith, obedience, teaching and everything.* This latter is as broad as the government of God, on one hand, and as broad as humanity on the other. Who among all the sons can make a valid objection to this undertaking? Mr. Campbell did not start a new cause, but enlisted his soul in a cause that was started eighteen hundred years ago—simply, *the cause of Christ.*

6/4/67, v.x, #23, p.180

Query–How much wages or salary did the Apostles get a year for preaching?

Answer–We are not informed how much wages the Apostles received per annum. They evidently did not receive near as much as they deserved. The pecuniary recompense was small enough to convince all intelligent people, that they were moved by some other consideration to preach, and suffer as they did, besides their wages in *money.*

6/4/67, v.x, #23, p.180

Query–Where in the New Testament does it teach men to build colleges to manufacture preachers?

Answer–Education is entirely left to *human wisdom* and *prudence* and consequently, is not a matter of *divine appointments.* We may invent new plans of education, change plans or improve them, but we may not invent new plans, and substitute them for divine appointment, or the things set forth in the New Testament.

6/4/67, v.x, #23, p.180

Query–How is it that the Disciple preachers use so much Greek in their writings, and addresses or sermons?

Answer–The New Testament Scriptures were originally written in Greek, and references back to the original are necessary on the part of those who follow the Savior. Our Lord spoke in Greek, and we go back to the Greek to get nearer to him, and more fully understand him.

6/4/67, v.x, #23, p.180

Query—Will you give a little on the following: Paul says, "I exhort, therefore, that, first of all, supplications, prayers, intercessions, and giving of thanks, be made for all men; for kings and for all that are in authority." See 1 Tim 2.1–3.

Now, if there is no converting power separate from the word, how are kings and rulers to be affected by prayer?

Answer—There is nothing about conversion in this passage, either of kings and rulers or anybody else. The prayer is not for the conversion of kings, rulers, or anybody else. The prayer is not for the conversion of kings, rulers, or anybody else; but "that we may lead a peaceable and quiet life in all godliness and honesty." There is nothing about "converting power," either "separate from the word," or throughout the word. The prayer is to the Lord, to so overrule kings and, other rulers that the people of God may lead a peaceable and quiet life in all godliness and honesty. Does the querist say, that he does not see how this can be done without an influence of the Spirit separate from the word? If he does, we inquire, can you see how it can be done with the influence of the Spirit, separate from the word? He may answer, "By the influence of the Spirit." But that explains nothing. If he will not pray for the Lord to do anything, till he can see how it is to be done, he will not pray soon. If he can not believe the Lord can do a thing, till he can see *how*, he has not faith enough to pray at all. We have no trouble about all this. We believe that He who made all the worlds, and has upheld them by the word of His power for six thousand years, and has made all angels and men, giving them life and being, can turn the hearts of magistrates as easy as we can move the regulator of a watch, and when we ask Him to do so, we do not stop to inquire into any speculative, skeptical questions, as to *how* He will do it. He *can* and *will* do it, and we *ask Him believing*.

7/9/67, v.x, #27, p.220

Query—I would like to ask your opinion, also that of your many correspondents, upon a subject which as of yet I have not noticed among the various ones which appear weekly in your columns. In partaking of the Lord's supper, should the invitation be extended to all or to the immersed believers only?

Answer—The communion is in Christ, in the body or church, as well as all the other acts of worship, and for those in the body. There is no need of any invitation. In the teaching and preaching we show who are in the kingdom, and how all others may enter into the kingdom. All in the kingdom have a right without any invitation to participate in all the worship. Those not in the kingdom, not citizens, or not in the body of Christ are not worshipers. We hear some people talking of "close communion" and "open communion." The communion is no *closer* than all the other parts of the worship, all the other privileges and immunities of the kingdom, but *just as close*. It is for all the children of God, the saints.

We invite no man who is not in Christ to commune, nor is it necessary to invite those who are in Christ to commune, nor is it necessary to invite those who are in Christ, as they should understand their rights in the kingdom without any invitation. If some person, not in Christ, sits down and communes without any invitation, the church is not injured by it, any more than if such a person should partake in any other part of the worship. There is no reason in making the communion a specialty, arranging any peculiar bar around it. It is precisely as open and close as all the other privileges of the kingdom. There is not a reason for starting any question who shall worship in the communion any more than in any other part of the worship, or to start up the question who are worshipers at the time of communion than at any other time of communion than at any other time. Let these things be fully explained in all our teachings. We have no right to offer any part of the worship to any not in Christ, and we set aside his authority when we do it.

7/30/67, v.x, #31, p.244

Query—1. Is it the practice of our brethren to meet for the purpose of celebrating the Lord's Supper on every first day of the week? 2. Have we any authority for it? 3. How long have our brethren been practicing this thing? 4. Name a few churches that have kept this thing up a great many years. 5. In what light are we to deal with brethren that are not only dissembling themselves, but persuading others by telling them that we are not to meet every Lord's Day and that it is not the practice of the church?

Answer–1. It is the practice of the brethren to celebrate the Lord's sufferings and death every first day of the week. 2. Have we any authority for it? We have the same authority for meeting *every* first day to break bread that we have for meeting on *any* first day. The following is an allusion to an established custom: "And upon the first day of the week, when the disciples came together to break bread, Paul preached to them." It was not an occasional thing for them to come together to break bread, but a regular practice, and when they came together, as the regular custom, Paul preached to them. It was not an occasional thing for them to come together to break bread, but a *regular* practice, and when they came together, as the regular custom, Paul preached to them. It was their usual habit to come together to break bread, but in this instance, they had something as usual, which was that *Paul preached to them.* "They continued steadfastly in the apostles' teaching, and in fellowship, and in breaking bread, and in prayer." See Acts 2.42, and Acts 20.7. There is exactly the same authority for the breaking of bread that there is for attending to the apostles' teaching, the contribution and prayers, besides that, the Lord gives it the prominence of being the object of meeting, in the words, "when the disciples came together to break bread." He does not say they came to hear preaching, to contribute, or pray, but *to break bread.* This was the prominent object in their coming together. It is an unfavorable symptom, when a disciple needs to be urged, persuaded and pressed to meet with the saints, or to commemorate the Savior's love as shown in his sufferings for us. "Do this till I come"— "Do this in remembrance of me," says the Lord. The disciple who does not love to commemorate his Lord's death, is not in love with him. The communion is the standing test of our love to Jesus. 3. "How long have our brethren been practicing this thing?" Ever since the Lord delivered it to them, in the founding of the New Institution. There have been some, at times, who neglect the assembling of themselves together, as in the case alluded to, Heb 10.25, in violation of the law of the Lord, and in the expostulations and persuasions of the true and faithful. But the true and faithful continue to come together to break bread. 4. We are called upon to name the church that has kept this thing up for years. The churches in Jerusalem, Antioch, Galatia, Corinth, Ephesus, Rome, and everywhere else in the time of the apostles, the churches in Cincinnati, St. Louis, Louisville, Chicago, Cleveland, Philadelphia, New York, Baltimore, Washington City, and a thousand other places—in one word, everywhere among the people over whom Jesus fully reigns.

5. Brethren such as alluded to under this head, are disorderly, and violating their covenant with the Lord and, we trust, they will repent. If we love not the Lord Jesus Christ, we shall be accursed. See 1 Cor 16.22.

Query–We have a lady preacher among us at this time, who has preached several sermons in our community. She claims to be a disciple of Jesus, and is called by the world a Campbellite. Now I wish to know if Paul means what he says— "Let your women keep silence in the churches, for it is not permitted unto them to speak, but they are commanded to be under obedience, as also saith the law and if they will learn anything, let them ask their husbands at home, for it is a shame for women to speak in the church." And if he does not mean what he says, please tell us what he does mean. And if it is not right that she should preach, should the disciples encourage it by offering their houses? Please give us your reply through the REVIEW and so encourage a young brother.

Answer–The Apostle John says, 1 John 4.6, "We," the apostles "are of God. He that knows God hears us. He that is not of God, hears not us." If this woman is of the Lord she will hear Paul, 1 Tim 2.11–12: "Let the women learn in silence with all subjection. But I suffer not a woman to teach, nor to usurp authority over the man." If she is not of the Lord, she likely will go on preaching.

10/15/67, v.x, #42, p.333

Query–Regarding Acts 13.2–3.1. Was Barnabas set apart— what some *now* call "ordained"—to the work of an *evangelist?* using the term evangelist in the common meaning attached to it by our brethren. 2. Have we here, or elsewhere in the New Testament, any authority, by *precedent* or precept, for the ordaining of *evangelists?* I am led to make the inquiry from having heard one of our preaching brethren suggest that "a person has no right to perform the duties of an evangelist (preacher) until he has been ordained?

Answer–Acts 13.1, we learn that Barnabas and Saul were "prophets and teachers," before they were "set apart" to the work which the Holy Spirit called them. The following is true: 1. These men were already "prophets and teachers," and had been for years. They were not ordained to make them "prophets and teachers." 2. They had been evangelizing for some fourteen years. The ordaining, or setting apart, was not, therefore, to make them evangelists. They were already authorized evangelists. 3. They were not "set apart" to authorize them to preach, to baptize or administer ordinances. This they had been doing for many years. 4. They had been set apart to "the work to which I have called them;" the work to which the Holy Spirit called them, and "sent forth by the Holy Spirit called them, and "sent forth by the Holy Spirit;" not to the work of evangelizing in *general*, nor of preaching, but "the work," is a *special work*, to which they had not been called before; a special mission and field. 5. We may then ordain, or set apart, evangelists; men who are evangelists, or authorize them to evangelize; but to a *certain field or work*. 6. The practice obtaining in certain quarters, and, which we participated in on two occasions, some years back, we are fully satisfied, is utterly without authority in Scripture. We allude to the practice of ordaining men, either to authorize them to preach, to make them preachers, or evangelists, and we have recently declined to participate in that ceremony where all the parties were unexceptionable.

We must have clear precept or example for all we do. We know of none for the custom in question.

12/3/67, v.x, #49, p.388

Query–Does the expression "to eat" in 1 Cor 5.11, refer to the Lord's Supper or to the ordinary meal?

Answer–The passage is a little dark, and we can not answer with the same degree of confidence as we can in some cases. We incline to the impression that the *eating* is not the communion, nor the incidental eating of a common meal where we might happen at the same table, but to accept an invitation from such an one, or more properly *frequent* invitations from such, visit him, keep company with him, and eat with him. The command verse 9, to "deliver such an one to Satan for the destruction of the flesh," and verse 13, "put away that wicked man from among yourselves," would put him away from the communion, so that the command "not to eat" at the communion *with him*, would be unnecessary. The apostle too, admits that we can not entirely escape the company of such; for then we would have to go out of this world. The full scope, as it appears to us, of the requirement, is not to visit such and receive visits from them; but make them sensible and fully to realize that they have cut themselves off from the repast and association of the pure and the holy.

It would be well for us to look and see how large a class is included in the list. He says, "If any one that is called a brother be a fornicator, or covetous, or an idolater, or a railer, or a drunkard, or an extortioner." This class is to be shunned by the true, the pure, and the holy, and not associated with on equal terms. They must be made to feel their degradation, their wickedness, by being avoided by the saints. Drunken, bloated and swaggering men; the slimy fornicator, close and narrow-hearted who have their thousands and not a liberal and noble deed in their whole history; in every instance where benevolence was demanded, their littleness, narrowness, selfishness and pinching hard-heartedness shown out; the railer and extortioner should all be avoided and shunned by the pure in heart. These characters shall not enjoy God. The Lord does not intend them to be placed on an equal footing in Christian society with the saints.

12/3/67, v.x, #49, p.388

Query—What books would be best to present to a young preacher to the value of fifty dollars, or could I lay that much out in any better way for the cause of Christ? I know of a young man of good promise who has but few books.

Answer—The above was only intended as a private letter, but the example is such, that we take the liberty to lay it before our readers, to excite others to similar deeds of liberality. How many poor young men are now struggling to qualify themselves for usefulness and not able to obtain even fifty dollars worth of books. We remember well when we were in that condition. How welcome too, this rich gift will come to a good young man. If this gift is received and rightly used, it will tell for the good of the cause for many years to come. We can see the use in making money when men perform such deeds as this with it. The Lord bless the donor and recipient.

12/3/67, v.x, #49, p.388

Query—There is a small sect here (only one church) who are called Morrisites, and many of them, whom I know, persist in saying that the Church of Christ or Christians believe in baptismal regeneration, even after they have been taught that it is not so. Why do pious people glory in misrepresenting the Christians and making them appear to the world as ignorant? What reply would you give to those who do so?

Answer–*Pious* people will not misrepresent. If they do not know a thing *to be* so they will not say *it is so*. If they know a thing *not to be so*, they, of course, will not *assert it to be so*. When persons continue to make misrepresentations in matters explained as clearly as the light of the sun in the heavens, and the false view a thousand times contradicted, they show a perverseness of a dark hue and will, most likely, continue to become worse and worse, deceiving and being deceived.

All we have to do in the matter is simply to hold, practice and teach the truth, the whole truth and nothing but the truth. The tongues of men are free, and we can not stop them. We are not responsible for them. To the Lord they will give account. Men represented our Lord, and of course they will misrepresent his friends.

10/19/71, v.14, #43, p.332

Query–Is it right for some twelve or fifteen members to meet, read, sing, pray and exhort, and then, because there are no elders or deacons there, disperse without breaking the loaf?

Answer–We do not like the idea of elders (overseers, we suppose, is meant) and deacons not being present, as much as appears to be implied in the above. But should they be absent from inattention, sickness or any cause, there is no reason why the Disciples who meet should enjoy a part of the established worship and leave off a part. Why, too, should they select the very part for which the first disciples came together—"to break bread," to commemorate the sufferings and death of Jesus—and leave that off? There is no reason for this. If we love the Savior, never omit the commemoration of his sufferings and death. There is not a greater evidence of the lack of piety—of love for the Lord Jesus—than this constant disposition to avoid the nearest contact we can have to his sufferings and death. Come to the Lord's table; sit there with the few who love him and meditate on his sufferings for us. "Do this, " says he, "in memory of me"— "Do this till I come."

If overseers and deacons are simply neglecting their Master's business and not attending to the work to which they have been solemnly appointed, and can not be prevailed as to be in their places, others should be seen as children more faithful.

10/19/71, v.14, #43, p.332

Query–1. Can a person become a member of the Church of Christ without a proper knowledge of the gospel and its commands, as also submission to its requirements?

Answer–No person can become a member of the Church of Christ without believing on Christ and submitting to him. The amount of knowledge necessary to believing on Christ and submitting to him is the amount necessary to become a Christian, or, which is the same amount, to become a member of the church. It must have been a very small amount in many instances in the time of the apostles, where they preached the gospel to them the first time, and took them into the church the same day.

4/2/72, vxv, #14, pg.108

Query–Has a man a right to preach in the church, or for the brethren, that has been ordained by the M.E. church, and has not been ordained by the authority of Christ?

Answer–No man has a right to preach in the church, ordained or not, unless he has the expressed will of the church. But any man, who can, may preach Christ, and we know nothing to hinder. But to be received as a preacher, in the true sense, a man should have standing in the church and be indorsed by the brethren. As to ordaining men to preach, the authority of Christ for it is exceedingly hard to find. We have declined to participate in it for years for the want of authority.

We find clear authority for overseers and deacons, for ordaining men to a certain mission, as in the case of Paul and Barnabus; but simply ordaining a man to preach is not in the New Covenant.

4/2/72, vxv, #14, pg.108

Query–Is there anything wrong or sectarian in making deeds of conveyance for a church lot to Mr. A, B, or C as trustees for the use and benefit of the Christian Church? What I am at is the name "Christian Church"—is it a sectarian name, or is there such a church as the Christian Church?

Answer–We see nothing wrong in it, if sirs A, B, or C is a member of the church. Church property is held by deeds to trustees, in trust for the church. They ought to be members of the church. True, there are other men and honest, who can be trusted who are not members of the church; but it is no commendation to Christians to go out of the church for trustees to hold the property for the church.

We have repeatedly explained in our columns that "Christian Church" is not the style of the New Testament. We find not the words "Christian Church" in the Bible. The phrase is not in Scripture and it is not correct in sense. We find not even the "church of Christ" in Scripture, but in one instance we have "the churches of Christ." The church of Christ is correct in sense. The church is of Christ as it's author. It belongs to him. "On this rock I will build *my* church." But "Christian Church" is not proper in sense. It did originate with Christians, or is not *of* them and does not belong *to them.* They belong *to it.* It is styled in Scripture, if our memory is correct, the "church of God" twelve times. If we have any love and respect for Scripture names, for Scripture things, or Scripture style, there is no reason for continually using designations not in Scripture at all, as "Christian Church," "Disciple Church" or "Disciple preacher," etc. If we desire to talk with intelligence, it is just as easy to do so as to continually use designations not in the Bible. How easy it is to say "the body," "the body of Christ," "the church," "the church of God," "the kingdom," "the kingdom of God," "the kingdom of heaven," when speaking of the whole family; or if speaking of that portion of the body in any given place, speak of it as the body in Dayton, the church in Hamilton, the church in Covington, etc. In nine cases out of ten nothing is needed more than simply "the church."

If you are asked what you are, it is simply proper to say opportunity to enlighten him. Show him that to be a Christian is enough, and to belong to *the body* of Christ is enough. We need nothing more. If a man can not understand what it is to be a Christian, you can explain to him that it is not to be a Mohammedan, a Romanist, a Mormon, Universalist, Shaker or Quaker—that it is simply for a man to be converted to Christ and then follow him. If he can not understand how a man can be a member of the body of Christ, or, which is the same, a member of the church of God, show him how to become a member—that he can be a Christian and nothing else, a member of the body of Christ and nothing else. You can not have a better opportunity to preach to him the gospel. There is an immense work to be done here. The body of Christ, or the kingdom of God, must be kept distinct from everything else. All the grand and significant designations given it in Scripture must be kept, maintained and used in the same sense as we find them used in Scripture. We must revive our great plea, "Bible names for Bible things." There is a power in Bible expressions found in no others. Not only so, but whenever you see a man departing from Bible names for Bible things, there is a reason for it. You will soon find him departing from Bible things. If we love the things of God, we love the words in which God speaks of them. There is no reason for departing from the words in which God speaks of things, unless we desire to depart from the things themselves. Be careful about *new names*. They are not always *new names* for *old things*, but *new* names for *new things*. The word "Pastor," borrowed from sectarianism, has come *slipping* into the church. Some thought it was an *innocent* thing, and that he was only a bishop who labored in word and in teaching. But already we have an elaborate, undertaking to show that he is a superior officer to a bishop, or overseer, and that other officers must obey him. No wonder brethren are rousing up all over the land and alarmed at the tendencies. Bolder and more impudent strides were never made to ride into power than some now manifested among us. But there is somebody in this country called the people, and they have not, with small exception, sold their birthright yet. They do not propose that any class of men shall "ride legitimately by the grace of God" over them.

4/2/72, vxv, #14, pg.108

Query – 1.Can we say of any Christian body or church that it is duly organized till elders and deacons have been set apart? 2. Can such officers transact the official business of the church till after their ordination? 3. Can it be said of "ordaining" or setting apart, that it is done in any other way than by prayer, fasting and the imposition of hands? 4. If no miraculous gift is imparted, why observe prayer, fasting and the imposition of hands?

Answer 1. A church is a congregation, or an assembly, and we do not organize a congregation or an assembly. Where disciples are made, called out from the world and meet together, they are a church, congregation or assembly. To set this assembly or congregation in order there should be overseers and deacons. It is not duly or fully set in order till it has overseers and deacons. 2. Overseers and deacons should be chosen by the church and ordained. When they are chosen they should be proved or tried, to give full proof of their fitness for the place to which they are chosen. There is no necessity for haste in the matter. Due time should be given for them to demonstrate their fitness for the work to which they have been chosen. 3. We know of no Scripture for any other way of ordaining overseers and deacons except by fasting, prayer and the imposition of hands. 4. Fasting, prayer and the imposition of hands took place in the time of miracles where no miraculous gift was imparted. Certainly no one thinks that *fasting* and *praying* have ceased. If this be so, then fasting and prayer should also cease. Miracles followed prayer in some instances, and in some instances no miracles followed. But prayer was not limited to the impartation of miraculous gifts, nor to the age of miracles. The same is true of fasting and the laying on of hands. Fasting, prayer and the imposition of hands were practiced in ordaining officers in the church, and while overseers and deacons are to be ordained, and the original practice observed, they will still be practiced.

6/18/72 vol.15, #25 pg. 196

Query–When persons order their names off the church book because there is an apology demanded for offenses public and private, and in aftertime present themselves for membership, what course should be pursued? Should they be received as common aliens, or as members from another congregation, or should they make the apology before required?

Answer– 1. They can not be received as aliens. They are not *aliens*, but *disorderly* Christians. 2. They can not be received as members from another congregation, for they can have no recommendation. 3. If the "apology," or confession, to give it the right name, required in the first instance, was justly required, they should not be received anywhere without it. It should, too, be made without an evasion or an equivocation. In addition to this, a kind, but firm and plain reproof should be administered before all, that others may take warning and fear, and words of encouragement offered and entreaties to faithfulness, and the whole congregation should be exhorted to confirm their love to such. At the same time a most solemn and devout prayer should be offered for the erring and reclaimed party and for the whole congregation, that they sin not. Such occasions, properly conducted, are of great interest and profit to the church, and the opportunity should never be lost to turn them to a good account.

Transgressions should never be passed over lightly, nor treated as matters of small moment. It is a fearful matter to sin against God; and men who are clearly transgressors should never desire the matter to be blurred over in such a manner as to make the impression that sin is a matter of but little consequence. It was sin that brought death into the world, and it is sin now that fills the land with various miseries. It was sin that nailed Jesus to the cross. It will ruin the souls of men and women if they are not freed from it. Where they have sinned they can not be freed from it without confession. In this way proper order can be maintained and the work of the church be carried on till the day when that work will be complete.

9/10/72, vol.15, #37, pg. 300

Query– Is a man scripturally qualified to hold the office of elder after the death of his wife, if he held an office previous to and at the time of her decease. We have such a case in our congregation, and wish to know if it is expedient and according to "thus saith Lord" to retain him as such. Please answer through the Review.

Answer– If the elder in question was qualified before the death of his wife, we see no reason to doubt his qualification; now. The question of making an elder, or, properly, an overseer, is not before the church. When that question was before the church, and that brother was made an overseer, he was "the husband of one wife." There is no intimation in Scripture that an overseer is disqualified for or loses his position by losing his wife. We see no ground for any question in the case.

6/24/73, vol. 16, #25, pg.196

Query– 1.In a difficulty between an elder and a private member of a church the elder claims that they (the elders) are the *church*, and the members have no power to try his case?

Answer– 1.We do not regard any action of overseers final till they have laid it before the church, and in some way obtained the sanction of the church. Overseers are not "the church," but *servants* of the church. The church must in some way adopt the action of the overseers before it is the action of the church.

Query– 2. In reference to question 1, would it be proper to try the case by a committee from another church before attempting to settle the difficulty in the church where it originated?

Answer– 2. There might be reasons for referring the matter to a committee of good men, owing to his being an overseer, and other considerations. This, however, is discretionary with the church, and she must decide whether she needs a committee, or will refer it to one.

7/8/73, v.16, #27, pg. 212

Query–When an elder becomes obnoxious to the main body of the church have they not the power to displace him?

Answer–Most unquestionably the church that can make an overseer can take the office from him when he shall become obnoxious to the church.

7/8/73 v.16, #27, pg. 212

Query–Is it right for a church-membership that is paying its pastor(?) at the rate of $1,000 per annum to permit a sick and indigent sister to be thrown upon the township in which she lives, and by so doing oblige?

Answer–We do not see that paying the preacher $1,000 per annum has anything to do with the case. It is certainly not right to permit the poor sister to be taken to the poorhouse whether the preacher is paid or not, if the church has the ability to support her. The Lord is represented by the poor here and regards our treatment of the poor as done to himself, and will so regard it in the day of judgment. "Inasmuch as you did it to one of the least of these you did it *to me*," he will say in the great day. See Matt 25.

7/8/73 v.16, #27, pg. 212

Query–In a volume issued from the gov't printing office, styled "Ninth Census of the United States," on page 505, I find the following: "Christian and Disciples of Christ." The members of the latter denomination, much the stronger of the two, are so frequently termed Christians, indeed, call themselves by that name. How is it that they hold to that name yet eschew denominational status. How is this, and do two such separate organizations exist? If two, please state the distinction.

Answer–There are two distinct bodies, as alluded to above, not in union at all. One is styled, and, and we think styles itself frequently, "The Christian Denomination." The other is frequently styled "The Christian Church," by some of its own writers and speakers. The former almost invariably call themselves "Christians." The sects do not like to call them "Christians," and to avoid thus calling them, call them "New Lights." The latter frequently call themselves Christians; but, it may be, more frequently call themselves "Disciples." Of course, in taking the census, confusion arises from finding the two bodies with such similar designations.

It is, then, a fact that two such separate bodies exist. The one called the "Christian Denomination," or sometimes "The Christian Connection," or "The Old Christians," arose in this country about the beginning of this century, from among the Presbyterians. Barton W. Stone and four other men, of Cane Ridge, Kentucky, were immersed, took the Bible alone as their rule of faith and practice, and repudiated all human creeds and sectarian names. They attracted considerable attention, and spread into several of the States.

At a subsequent period, A. Campbell and his father, Thomas Campbell, also from the Presbyterians, were immersed and took their stand, in like manner, on the Bible and the Bible alone. These bodies for some years knew but little of each other. A main plea of both was for the union of all the people of God. A. Campbell was a man of much more power than Barton W. Stone, and attracted much more attention, and enlisted a class of men of much more power, and consequently increased the body in numbers much faster than the other body. In a few years these two bodies became acquainted with each other, and found that in many respects their positions were similar and their aim the same. Their plea for union led them to inquire why they were not united. After much prayerful meditation and consultation large numbers of them united and became one. Specially was this the case in Kentucky; at present there, if not all, very nearly all, are merged into one. In other States extended bodies of them have united. We know of some now that have the matter under advisement, and we think will shortly be one, as Jesus and the Father are one.

The "Old Christians," so called, have changed considerably, and have gone back from their original ground. They have some kind of a Conference or Ministerial Association, unknown to the early men of the body. They have not the zeal, the earnestness or power they had in their early day. They receive sprinkled persons, or persons not claiming to have any, baptism, and under the idea of liberality, are becoming more and more latitudinarian. While they claim to take the Bible and the Bible alone, they do not enforce the Bible, but appear to entertain the idea that liberality requires that every man shall do as seems good in his own eyes. This body is gradually sinking away, and no doubt will soon disappear altogether.

The empty claim to take the Bible and the Bible alone will not save any people, nor build them up. The Bible must be put in force, executed. The best laws ever made are of no value unless enforced. The Bible alone, as an empty theory, is no better than faith alone. The Bible enforced, or carried into practice, will save the world. So faith, followed by the obedience it involves, will save the world. We must have the Bible alone, or faith alone is dead. We must have the Bible and the works which it enjoins; the faith and the obedience of faith.

7/28/73, v.16, #30, pg. 228

Query–When the brethren meet to transact business in connection with the church, is it right and scriptural for the sisters to vote at such a meeting?

Answer–There is simply no authority, or one word about women voting in transacting business in the church, participating in ruling, administering discipline, or anything of the kind, under any dispensation, Patriarchal, Jewish or Christian. There should be precious little voting in the church anyway. Where there is much voting in the church there is generally much trouble. The business of the church should be transacted by the officers of the church, and then presented to the church on the Lord's day, in the presence of all, and an opportunity given for any one, in a given time, say one or two weeks, to call on any one of the officers *privately* for any explanation desired, a fuller understanding of the matter, or to present objections. If any explanations are called for they should receive careful attention, and, if possible, all things made satisfactory, or, if any objections should be made they should be done to bring all to one mind, and to have all harmonious. If women are dissatisfied, or have objections, they have the same privilege to make them, and should receive the same attention as men, when they apply to the officers privately.

The women will be transcendently happier, better, greater and wiser, if they follow the Bible than they can be if they follow the impulses arising from evil revolutions. Read the Bible carefully, and note the part the women took, the greatest and best of them, as well as all classes, in the Patriarchal, Jewish and Christian institutions, and follow what you find there. It is safe to follow that, and for the good of all, both men and women. No improvement can be made upon that.

7/23/73 v.16, #30 pg.228

Query–Do the Scriptures teach that Matthias was one of the apostles?

Answer–Matthias was an apostle. This is certain from the following: 1. Luke wrote the book of acts some thirty years after the resurrection of Christ, and he records the transaction of electing Matthias (Acts 1) not only without the slightest intimation that the procedure was unauthorized, but with approval. Had the transaction been without authority, he could not consistently have recorded it without any intimation of the want of authority, and even giving the Scripture quoted on the occasion of the election of Matthias, as an authority for their procedure, and thus added, as he did, that he was numbered with the eleven. If all this had been unauthorized, Luke could have not omitted the mention of it, after relating the transaction. His recording the transaction, and saying thirty years after, "He was numbered with the eleven," it is an endorsement of it. 2. On the day of Pentecost, after the Spirit had fallen on them, Luke says "And Peter, standing up with the eleven." This included Matthias, as Peter could not have stood up "with the other eleven." without him. He was then with the other apostles, when the Spirit came to guide them into all truth, and was indorsed by the Holy Spirit the same as the other apostles. See Acts 11.14. This fully recognized him, with the other apostles and by the same gift of the Holy Spirit. 3 Paul 15.5, says of our Lord, "that he was soon of Cephas, then of the twelve," and adds, verse 7, "then of all the apostles," included Matthias. There were not twelve without him. Paul, in the same connection, speaks of himself, distinct from these, in the following words: "Last of all he was seen of me also"—that is, "me also," as well as the twelve.

Paul is never included in the twelve. There were twelve without him. Then he did not have the required qualifications of the original twelve. See the following, Acts 1.20, 22: "For it is written in the book of Psalms, Let his habitation be desolate, and let no man dwell therein: and, His bishopric let another take. Wherefore of these men who have companied with us all the time that the Lord Jesus went in and out among us, beginning from the baptism of John, to that same day that he was taken up from us, must one be ordained to be a witness with us of his resurrection? Of whom must one be ordained? "Of these men who have companied with us, all the time the Lord Jesus went in and out among us." Paul did not fill his description. He was not with them all the time that the Lord Jesus went in and out among us, beginning with the baptism of John, to that same day that he was taken up from us. Matthias did fill this description, and for this cause he was chosen, numbered with the eleven, took "part of this ministry and apostleship from which Judas by transgression fell."

10/14/73 v.16,#41p.324

Query–When letters of commendation are granted members of the church are they members of the congregation from which they receive letters until these letters are placed in another congregation? If they are give us your reasons for it.

When members of the church violate the teaching of the Scriptures ought they be required to come forward in the church and make public confession of their wrongs and receive the right hand of fellowship? Please answer and oblige.

Answer–1. Letters should be so worded that persons receiving them are not dismissed till united with another church. This can be done by wording the part of the letter relating to the dismissal as follows: "Dismissed from us, by his own request, when united with another church." The person, then, taking the letter and remaining in the same community without taking membership in another church, or even going away from the community and not uniting with another church, still remains a member and is amenable to the church that gave the letter the same as if the letter had not been given. This prevents persons from becoming entirely isolated from any church and responsible nowhere in the church, or makes it to others and authorized them to state it to the church in the presence of the erring party. It is well for the offender to meet the overseers and agree to a proper confession. 2. Let it be written and signed by the erring party and authorized to be read in the church and receive the sanction of the church as to its being satisfactory. The confession can then be entered on the church-book for reference should there ever be any occasion for reference to it. 3. If the erring party has not been excluded from the church there is no reason for extending the hand. Where fellowship has not been withdrawn the person is not restored to fellowship, but simply in the proper way prevented from expulsion. His relation to the church has not been lost, but he has erred in that relation and been set right without losing his relation. The dealing with him has been *as a member*, and not as an excluded man *who is not a member.*

11/11/73, v.16, #45, pg. 356

Query 1—Why call the communion the Lord's Supper?

Answer–We know of no reason for it except that the apostle, in, his rebuke of the Corinthians for their desecration of the ordinance, says, "When you come together into, one place," in the manner in which they did it, "this is not to eat the *Lord's Supper.*" This indirectly calls it the "Lord's Supper." They come together to *break bread.* The *communion* is proper.

Query 2.— When should the Supper be celebrated?

Answer–This question styles it the "Supper." We do not come together to *celebrate* the Supper, or the communion, or the breaking of bread, but the Lord's death. "Do this in memory of me," says the Lord. "Do this till I come." We break bread to *celebrate* the Lord's death. We celebrate the sufferings of Jesus, and not the institution. The Disciples come together on the *first day of the week* to break bread. The first day of the week is *the time.*

Query 3—Would the officers of the church be doing right to take the loaf and wine to a sick man in the week—say Thursday?

Answer–Certainly not. There is no authority for the institution on any day but the first day of the week.

Query 4—Should a brother refuse to commune because a brother differs from him as to the time of celebrating the Supper?

Answer–Not if the celebration of the Lord's death is on the first day of the week. We would have nothing to do with it on any other day. We have clear authority for coming together to break bread on the first day of the week, but no authority for it on any other day.

Query 5—. Would the church celebrate the Supper properly by doing so on Thursday night?

Answer–By no means. There is no authority for it.

Query–Is it right to have a singing-school a meeting-house, and that, too, accompanied by the violin? Is it right to use a notebook in place of the *Christian Hymn Book* in the worship of the Lord? Is it right to sing the different parts of music in public worship ?

Answer—The Book containing the New Covenant has not one word in it about a singing-school," a "meeting-house" or a "violin." A singing-school is simply school in which to teach singing, whether it shall be held in a meeting-house or not depends on no divine law, but on the *will* of the owners of the meeting-house. If they please to grant the privilege, and the school is conducted in an orderly manner, and the use is not abused, we see no particular objection to it. But the *will* of the owners of the house should be consulted, and not merely *a part of them*; otherwise trouble may arise. Better be no singing-school than to create hardness among brethren. As to the *violin*, it has been in too much bad company to be attended with good. It is found in the vilest places on earth, and the vilest are its most devout admirers. True, it has been found in *good company*. So have gamblers, drunkards, and other vile characters in found in *good company*. But good company is the exception and not the general rule. So the violin in good company is the exception, not the general rule.

We want a *moral man*, at least, to teach a common school, and a man of character too. We want the same—a moral man and a man of character to teach singing; and a teacher that maintains *order*, and knows the meaning of the word order ; and not a lad who goes around with an old fiddle on his back, and who has no respect for either order or religion. We want a man who maintains as good order in his school as there is in a house of worship. In that case, if the members are agreed to it, he might occupy a meeting house. If he is not that kind of a teacher, we do not want him in a meeting house, or out of it, with his violin. We want no rowdies to teach singing nor anything else.

12/9/73, v.16, #49, pg. 388

Query—Will you give your views on the following passage of Scripture: "Let the deacons be the husband of one wife, ruling their children and their own houses well." 1 Tim 3.12 Does it mean they *must* have a wife?

Answer—We do not see how language could be plainer. Whatever else the language may mean in the words, "Let the deacons be husbands of one wife," it can not mean the husbands of *no wife*. No matter which way we take it, the husbands of *only* one wife, or of *one wife*, it does not mean the husband of no wife. This is clear from the language that follows: "ruling their children and their own houses well." It is clearly contemplated that they should be heads of families. We can not reasonably expect the cause to do well or the Lord to be pleased when we regard not the clearest expressions of Scripture.

1/5/75, v.18, #1, pg.4

Query—Should Disciples of Christ, when so elicited, support sectarianism by giving money to build and repair houses, pay preachers etc?

Answer—We have for thirty-five years been preaching against sectarianism and praying for its overthrow. We have been doing this because we most solemnly believed sectarianism to be wrong—to be sinful. The longer we live, the more we see of sectarianism, specially of its opposition to the gospel of Christ, its wicked and antagonistic spirit to the right way of the Lord, the less reason we see for showing it any leniency. It is wrong in spirit, in temper, in all its parts, essentially wrong and opposed to the right way of the Lord; more opposed to the gospel itself and adverse to all for the gospel, and nothing else than to any other thing. There can be no good sense nor propriety in preaching against anything a lifetime, and giving our money to build it up. We have no money nor prayers for the up-building of sectarianism. Every dollar we can spare, every prayer we can offer, every sermon we can preach, and every article we can write, till the last breath, we intend shall be for the overthrow of sectarianism and for the union and up-building of the kingdom of God. Sectarianism is for scattering, tearing and destroying the kingdom of God. The cause of God is in eternal antagonism with all forms of sectarianism, and can never form any kind of compromise with it, or with any part of it. A man can not be in sympathy with sectarianism and a faithful advocate of the cause of Christ.

11/7/71, v.14,#45, pg. 356

Query—Are any of the sectarian churches the "Church of God"?

Answer—No modern sect claims to be "the Church of God," or which is the same, the kingdom of God. The Romish, the Greek and the Episcopalian Churches, each claim to be the true church, or, which is the same, the Church of God. The others do not claim it. If they were to do so, it would be like as it is with the Romish, the Greek, and the Episcopal Churches; the claim would be *without foundation*.

6/25/72, vol.16, #26, p204.

Query—I have seen a great deal written about inviting the different sects to commune with us. I wish to know your opinion about Christians partaking of the emblems with them.(the sects)

Answer—There are many among the sects that have become acquainted with the Savior, love him, have confessed him, been baptized into the name of the Father, and of the Son, and of the Holy Spirit, to whom we stand in readiness to unite at any moment, because they are the children of God. These are *Christians*, and have the same privilege at the Lord's table as we have. The Lord's table is evidently for his people, and I have no scruple in communing with any man who is a Christian, or uniting with him in the same church. Nor do I know that I am injured, if some man thinks himself a converted man, who has never been converted according to the gospel, and comes to the Lord's table with me. There might be a hypocrite there also, without my knowledge, who was once converted. There is not much danger of harm from either. It is not our duty to invite or debar any, but to state that it is the Lord's table and for his people, and if any partake who are not his people, the matter is between them and the Lord. The main matter, if we would be benefited in coming unto the Lord's table, is for the disciples to examine *themselves*, and so eat, and not give themselves much trouble about *others*. The Lord will examine us all.

Query—Is it occasionally the case that members of the M.E. Church become dissatisfied with their sprinkling and want to be immersed, and call on our preachers to immerse them, and let them continue in the M.E. Church? This is practical.

Answer—We think it better to give those Methodists, who desire to obey the command of the Lord, an opportunity to be baptized, even if they do not understand the balance of their duty. Nine out of ten of all who get far enough convinced to be baptized contrary to the will of their preacher and church, will come all right as soon as baptized. At all events, it is one step in the right direction, and it is right for them to take that, if they never take another—Where we find persons in that state of mind, as we have several, we advise them not to look so far ahead—not to decide what they will do. Leave that all open; submit to the Lord in baptism, and afterwards decide all other matters of obedience and do what they then decide to be right.

Query—When was Methodism established? Will you please give us a notice of its origin?

Answer—John and Charles Wesley, two young men in England, from reading the Bible, in 1729, "saw that they could not be saved without holiness; followed after it, and invited others so to do."

Eight years after, or 1737, "they saw, likewise, that men are justified before they are sanctified; but still holiness was their object. God then thrust them out to raise a holy people." "These," we are assured, "are the words of Messrs. Wesleys themselves." It does not appear that any Methodist church was at this time established. The Wesleys were members of the Church of England, and, we believe never belonged to any other. The "Societies" alluded to in the Discipline and other works, existing at that time, were simply praying societies in the Church of England, and no distinct organizations.

In 1766 the first move appears to have been made on this continent. "Philip Embury, a local preacher of our Society, from Ireland, began to preach in the city of New York, and formed a society of his own countrymen and the citizens; and the same year, 1766, Thomas Webb preached in a hired room near the barracks."

Before the year 1729, we are not aware that there was any religious body called *Methodists*, or any religion called *Methodism*. There was, probably, two centuries before this, a very rigid, abstemious and Methodist class of physicians, called *Methodists*, from their strict *methods* of life and practice. We think, also, that the name *Methodist* was first applied to the Wesleys out of derision, or a nickname borrowed from the class of physicians mentioned, on account of their very *methodical* manner of life. There is no religion in the name *Methodist*, however much there being the people called *Methodists*. There are as many *methods* of doing evil as there are of doing good. Indeed, the Greek *methodia*, from which we have our English word *method*, is found twice in the New Testament, Eph 4.14, and 6.11 translated *wiles* in the latter place. The *wiles* of the devil, are simply *methods* of the devil. The notion of making *method* the central idea in a system of religion, is preposterous, when there are just as many *methods* of doing evil as good.

We have just two arguments to prove that Methodism is not Christianity, as follows: 1. Methodists themselves admit persons can be Christians who are not Methodists. Then, unequivocally, Methodism is not Christianity. 2. There were millions of Christians before the year 1729, but no Methodists, and there was Christianity in the world from Jesus to the year 1729, but no Methodism. There can be Christianity now, and no Methodism. Methodism is not, then, Christianity.

Query–Can a man be a Universalist properly speaking, and believe in the *everlasting punishment* of the wicked? Mr. Burriss, of Montgomery, Alabama, a mighty champion and professed Universalist, refuses to deny the following proposition in debate, and gives as his reason that he believes in the *everlasting punishment* of the wicked. The Scriptures teach the everlasting punishment of all persons who live in rebellion against God and die in their sins. He says he believes that punishment will be *everlasting*, but does not believe that it will be of *endless* duration! He says that he is able to show that there is a wide difference between the meaning of the phrases *"everlasting"* and *"endless."* I have always thought, and still think that these phrases are synonymous terms.

Answer–We have no doubt but *everlasting* and *endless* are equivalents in meaning. The literal meaning and full value of these words, as the Greek word *aionion*, is unlimited or perpetual *Aionion*, Matt 25.46, in the same sentence expresses the duration of the life of the righteous and the duration of the punishment of the wicked. It can not in one sentence be used in a limited sense, or in less than its full import, in one place, and at its full import, or in the literal sense, in another.

Even the word *endless* is used in a limited sense, where we read of "endless genealogies," as we have it in the common version. It is liable to all the same sophistry, cavils and quibbles that *eternal* and *everlasting*.

What good does the belief of Mr. Burriss, or any Universalist, in "everlasting punishment" do, so long as he teaches no man that he must repent, or perish—that God commands all men everywhere to repent, because he has appointed a day in which he will judge the world in righteousness—that the Lord commanded us to preach to the people and testify that he is ordained to be the judge of quick and *dead?* Let him look at the fact, staring him and every Universalist preacher in the face, that *their doctrine never does reform any man.* If he is a drunkard before he is a Universalist, he is one after.

Query–Although unknown to you by face, I have been one of your readers for the last two years, during which time I have learned that you are profound at unraveling knotty questions; I therefore take the liberty of presenting the following query, viz: If a man, by evocating primitive Christianity, Universal Liberty, Temperance, Congregational Independence, Christian Union and Education, is a man of *one idea?* What would a man be who advocates only a part of the above-named subjects? Would he be a man of less or more than *one idea?* Please answer this through the REVIEW, as many of your readers would like to be enlightened upon this subject, and oblige your brother in Christ

Answer-1. No one, that we know, says that a man who advocates all the above items, is a man of one idea. 2. The writer of the above appears to think that "primitive Christianity" does not include "universal liberty, temperance, congregational independence, Christian union, and education," hence he adds these to "primitive Christianity." 3. We do not think that the man who advocates all these is a man of one idea, but the man who hitches all these on for a *show*, and at the same advocates *but one*, and shows that he cares for none, only as they will answer for hobbies, is a hobby rider and a man of *one idea, if he has even that.*

1/4/59, vol.2, #1, page 30

QUESTIONS ABOUT THE HOLY SPIRIT

Query—Is there any difference in the meaning of the two expressions, "gift of the Holy Spirit," and "the Holy Spirit," both being used in the New Testament? If any difference, what is that difference? If none, why use the word "gift?" What office does it perform?

Answer—We do not think that the meaning of the writer is fully expressed in the above. Of course "the gift of the Holy Spirit" means more than "the Holy Spirit." We think we see what he aimed at. Is there any difference between "the gift of the Holy Spirit" and "receiving the Holy Spirit?" Does "the gift of the Holy Spirit" mean the impartation of the Holy Spirit, or something imparted by the Holy Spirit? We read of "the gift of God," where it means that which God has given. Does "the gift of the Holy Spirit" mean something given by the Holy Spirit? We think the latter is the meaning. We are certain that we can give an instance of the two expressions, "the gift of the Holy Spirit," "received the Holy Spirit," being applied to the same thing and we are not certain that "the gift of the Holy Spirit," ever means that given by the Holy Spirit. God gave the Gentiles "the like gift" as he did to the Jews, and referring to the same thing, we have the expression they have "received the Holy Spirit." The "like gift," was the gift of the Holy Spirit and that was receiving the Holy Spirit. The gift, or the impartation of the Spirit, manifested itself in miraculous tongues, divided or distributed tongues, visible, in appearance like fire, in prophecy, healing and other miracles. These are styled "spiritual gifts," and by the same Spirit, but none of them, we think, is ever called "the gift of the Holy Spirit."

We have never yielded to the opinion that the promise, "and you shall receive the gift of the Holy Spirit," means *what the Holy Spirit gives,* but that *the Holy Spirit should be given.* We do not *like forced construction.*

6/26/ 72, vol.15, #26, page 204.

Query–Are we authorized by the Holy Scriptures to say that the Holy Spirit is received (personally) since the days of miracles ceased? Will Bro. Franklin let us hear from him at some length on this subject?

Answer–We are not authorized to say any thing about the Holy Spirit being received *personally*, either before or since the days of miracles. Since the age of miracles, no one receives the miraculous or supernatural gifts of the Holy Spirit, so as to speak with tongues, prophecy, or do miracles; but all Christians receive the Holy Spirit. Because they are sons, the Spirit is sent forth into their hearts, crying Abba, Father. He gives the Holy Spirit to them who obey him. We do not desire now to discuss this subject at length.

We would prefer discussing something practical. We do not have to give the Holy Spirit, and there is, therefore, no danger of our giving it wrong. We do not have to do the work of the Holy Spirit, and there is, therefore, no danger of our doing it wrong. The Lord gives the Holy Spirit to all who receive it at all, and there is not the least danger of his giving it too soon, or too late, or of his making a mistake and giving it to the wrong person. We therefore have never attempted to superintend the giving of the Holy Spirit in any way. All may rest assured that there will be no mistake in the giving of the Holy Spirit. It will not be given miraculously, when it should have been the ordinary gift or common comforter; given too soon, too late, nor to a wrong person.

Nor need any man preach to explain how the Spirit will operate, or how he will do his work; for it is the business of no man to direct the influence of the Spirit, or how he shall do his work. All we need is faith in the Son of God, that he will do all work, do it well and at the right time; and confidence that the Holy Spirit will do all his work, do it well, and at the right time. We do not think the Holy Spirit needs any instructions from editors, preachers or any body, either in writing, preaching or prayers, how, when or where his work shall be done. What we are concerned in, is to learn what the Lord requires us to do, how and when to do it; not that it is hard, or difficult, either to learn what the Lord requires, or to do it; but because there is such a disposition to inquire into every work but the *precise work* that we ought to know more about than all others, *the work we have to do*. If a man desires to serve the Lord, let him inquire simply first what he must believe to save him. When he has found out what he must believe, then inquire what he must do, and then do it, and the Lord will do all the balance and do it all right.

1/60, vol.3, #5, page 18.

Query–What are we to understand the *gift* of the Holy Spirit to be, as promised by Peter on the day of Pentecost?

Answer–The gift of the Holy Spirit, promised to those who received Christ, was the common indwelling Comforter, sent forth into the heart, by which we call God Father, enjoyed by all the children of God.

1856, vol.1, pg 159

Query–There is a respectable brother here (one of your subscribers) who finds a difficulty in John 3.8 "The wind blows where it listeth, and thou hearest the sound thereof and canst not tell whence it cometh and whither it goes: so is every one that is born of the Spirit." He thinks it teaches the mysterious operation of the Spirit. This I know it cannot do. It cannot refer to the operation of the Spirit from the construction of the language. Yet it is ambiguous, and we would be thankful to you for an explanation, through the Reformer.

Answer–Many good men of different denominations, have been puzzled with the passage quoted above, nor are we certain that we ever saw its exact meaning set forth by any one; and, of course, we do not feel very sanguine in the opinion that we can explain it. We have generally observed that the more ignorant the preacher, the more frequent use he had for this passage. We shall not hesitate however, to state what appears to us to be as good a view as we can take of it. It will be observed, that the passage occurs in a conversation between our Savior and Nicodemus an honorable ruler among the Jews. This noted personage approaches the Savior acknowledging him to be a teacher from God. The Lord addresses him in words setting forth an entire new doctrine to him. This he does in a very earnest manner, in the following words: "Verily, I say unto thee, except a man be born again, he cannot see the kingdom of God." This astonishes enquiring man and he at once enquires, "How can a man be born when he is old?" The Lord proceeds, "Verily, Verily, I say unto thee, except a man be born of water and of the Spirit, he cannot enter into the kingdom of God." This he uttered in view of the position which Nicodemus occupied. He was a Jew the only way he knew of establishing church-membership, was by tracing up his genealogy, to Abraham, who stood at the head of God's chosen people. Hence his confidence was in the flesh, or in a fleshly relation to the head of what he regarded as the true Israel of God. He is therefore advised the first thing, that he must be born again—that he must "be born of water and of the Spirit" and the reason assigned is that, "that which is born of the flesh is flesh, and that which is born of the Spirit, is spirit." He is startled at the idea of being born of the Spirit, and at once enquires, whence this spiritual birth, or this man born of water and of the Spirit? The Lord perceives that he does not discern whence the spiritual man is, and remarks: "The wind bloweth were it listeth, and thou hearest the sound thereof, but canst not tell whence it cometh, and whither it goeth: so is every one that is born of the Spirit. Here is a comparison—one thing compared to another.— What are the things compared ? Surely not the *Spirit* and the *wind*. What then? The *"wind blows,* and you hear the sound, and cannot tell whence it comes, and whither it goes." Well what is like the wind? The Savior says so is every one that is born of the Spirit." Had the Spirit been compared to the wind, the Savior would have said, *"so is the Spirit"* Nicodemus could see men who had been born of the Spirit, but like the wind that he discovered blowing, he did not perceive whence they came nor whither they tended. If the passage anything more than this we do not perceive it.

Western Reformer. Sept.1848, vol.7, #9, page 569

Query—We read, Acts 2.38, that on obedience depends the promise of the "Gift of the Holy Ghost." In another case they "Received the Holy Ghost," and another, "the Holy Ghost came on them." What may the obedient believer be taught to expect on obedience? Or is this to be consequent on prayer and the imposition of hands?

Answer—The prophets represented the reign of the Messiah as peculiarly distinguished by the communication of the Holy Spirit. This marked an entire change in the Divine administration. The Jewish nation could not receive the Spirit. Lawgivers, Judges, Kings, Priests, Seers and Prophets, as representatives of the great Theocrat, were commissioned and empowered by the Holy Spirit. David prayed the Lord "not to take away his Holy Spirit from him," as he had from Saul. But when Messiah should come, the Spirit was to inhabit the Church and inspire the people, male and female, old and young. Nevertheless, the

Spirit only comes and works as he is needed. "God is a God of order," and does nothing without a reason. "Now there are diversities of gifts, but the same Spirit. And there are differences of administrations, but the same Lord. And there are diversities of operations, but it is the same God which worketh all in all." 1 Cor 12.4–6. Perhaps all the Gentile Churches had the *manifestations* of the Spirit, in some form, diffused throughout the whole body. The manifestation was not such as is claimed now, but such as was a sign to unbelievers, was "given to every man for the profit of all." But when the Church was furnished with sufficient knowledge, and the New Testament books were written out, and the cause was firmly established in the earth, that manifestation like the *manifestation* of Jesus, was withdrawn from the Earth. But Jesus is yet among men, and so is the Spirit, though neither Jesus nor the Spirit are in the manifestation of the first century

The era of the first manifestation of the Spirit, was the time of the coronation of Jesus. It was both visible and audible. It was overwhelming and therefore called a baptism. Among the many objects attained by this manifestation was the public approval of the believing Israelites as the followers of Christ. This manifestation was repeated among the Gentiles in the house of Cornelius. It was thus that God took a people first from among the Jews and then from among the Gentiles, putting his seal upon them. But in addition to this manifestation to legalize the opening of the doors for the Jew and the Gentile, there were frequent impartations of the Spirit, sometimes directly from Heaven and sometimes by the imposition of the Apostle's hands. It was thus that the gift of miracles were imparted, and thus that the mongrel race of Samaritans was welcomed into the Church by the twelve. Acts 8. Nevertheless after withdrawal of these manifestations from among men, there is a "residue of the Spirit," bestowed as a *gift*, in the singular, upon those who obey the Gospel. This gift must not be confounded with the gifts and manifestations spoken of in the Sacred Scriptures.

Proclamation & Reformer 1851

Query–I had a brief controversy the other evening with a young brother, concerning the gift of the Holy Spirit, promised by Peter to the three thousand on the day of Pentecost. My position was, and still is, that the promised gift was the power of miracles, such as speaking with tongues and interpreting.

The gospel, which is the power of God unto salvation, to every one that believes, is the gift of the Holy Spirit. This Gospel Peter had just been preaching to them. They received it; hence, it was not to the gospel that he had reference when he said, "you shall receive the gift of the Holy Spirit." Could Peter have referred to any other gift, save the power of doing miracles, which he and the other apostles would confer upon them by prayer, and the laying on of hands? The brother denies the correctness of my view, and yet is unable to tell me to what other gift Peter referred. Neither his salvation nor mine is involved in the decision of this question. But in the doing of the will of God, if we are both just entering the ministry, each having preached but two or three sermons, I desire that we have a correct view of this matter, and avoid all mysticism and untenable positions concerning the gifts of the Spirit. If you are not overstocked with matters of greater moment, and will favor us with a few remarks on this gift, you will oblige your brethren in Christ.

Answer—We think the gift of the Holy Spirit promised to the three thousand on Pentecost, by Peter, was not the miraculous gift of the Spirit, but the ordinary impartation of the Spirit to all who obey the gospel. The promise is as general as the remission of sins and to the same persons. "Repent and be immersed every one of you, in the name of Jesus Christ for the remission of sins and you shall receive the gift of the Holy Spirit." The promise is unquestionably to them that repent, are immersed and receive remission of sins, and we think amounts to the same as the following: "And we are his witnesses of these things, and so is also the Holy Spirit, whom God hath given to them that obey him."– Acts 5.22.

9/22/63,v.6, #38, pg.150

Query—When does an individual receive the Holy Spirit, and how can he know that he has received it?

Answer–1. The miraculous or supernatural gift of the Holy Spirit, inspiring persons, empowering them to speak foreign languages, and perform other miracles, is not now conferred at all on any person. But the Holy Spirit, imparted and common to all Christians—the Spirit of adoption, by which they are enabled to cry Abba, Father—is conferred at the time when the person enters into Christ, or into the kingdom. It is promised with pardon, in Peter's reply to the three thousand on

Pentecost. 2. How does a person *know* that he has received the Holy Spirit? We must take a little space first in telling how *it is not known.* It is not known by *feeling.* The presence or indwelling of the Spirit is not known by an *impression on the flesh.* The sense of feeling is in the flesh. We, therefore, never read of feeling the Spirit, of knowing the Spirit to be present by feeling or knowing that we have the Spirit by feeling, or knowing that we have the Spirit by feeling. Not an instance is mentioned, in Scripture, of any divinely authorized teacher ever directing any one to look to his feelings to determine that he was a child of God, a Christian, or pardoned. Nor is there an account there of any one ever looking to any peculiar class of feelings as an evidence of having the Spirit. Thousands have been deluded, and are still being deluded, into the idea that some strange sensation in the flesh, or convulsion of animal feeling—some mere shock of feeling, sudden sensation in the flesh and blood— is an evidence of the reception of the Spirit. This is utterly without foundation in Scripture. Sudden changes of feeling, in some instances, arise from something unwholesome received into the stomach, breathing impure air, or enduring sudden changes of temperature; from sudden alarm, a shower-bath, or a shock from an electric battery. But these changes are mere results of adequate causes, and no evidence of spiritual influence. There is not, in our humble opinion, a more mischievous, dangerous and destructive delusion, in our time, than that which turns the mind of the people away from the divine testimonies of the Spirit of all light, and truth and revelation, recorded in the Bible, to the changeable, uncertain, and unreliable *feelings* in the flesh. The devil never desired a greater delusion than this. Joy arises from knowing that we are pardoned; but we do not know that we are pardoned by the joy that we have. All the joy, peace, comfort of love the saints have, arise from their knowing that they are in Christ; but they do not know that they are in Christ by the joy, peace and comfort that they have. The knowledge gives the joy; the joy does not give the knowledge. How, then, does a man know that he has the Spirit? He knows it by the following means: 1. *By the promise of God.* To him who believes in the Savior, repents and is immersed, the promise is, "and you *shall receive the gift of the Holy Spirit.*" This promise has the veracity of God in it. The man who does not believe it, and will not rely on it, is a skeptic. Such a man cannot even come to God, because he who comes to God must believe. Without faith, it is impossible to please him. 2. He knows that he has the Spirit of God by the wonderful change wrought in him. A man *knows* whether he loves the teaching of the Spirit of God in the Bible. He *knows* whether he loves the children of God. He *knows* whether he loves God. He *knows* whether he delights in the law of God and doing the commandments of God. He knows whether he is in harmony with God, and his main purpose of life is to do the will of God. These are all matters which a man can know as certainly as he can know any thing. A man can know that he is at heart with God and that the great aim of his life is to walk with God and please him. This, too, others can know who are acquainted with him, by his visible life he lives. A man can know that the love of God is in him, that he is not under the power of the Spirit once controlling him, but under the power of a better Spirit, whether we can tell all about how he knows it or not. There are many things that we know well, but cannot tell *how* we know them. We know the face of the writer of the query at the head of these remarks from any other face, at a glance, but we could not readily tell how we know it. We saw a man once, running over a lot of Bank Bills, throw out one. We inquired what was the matter with that bill. He said, "It is a counterfeit." We inquired how he knew. He said he could not so readily answer that, but remarked that it was a *strange face*—that *it did not look like the genuine.* So a man can know that the Spirit dwelling in him *is not the same*—that *it is different* from the Spirit formerly dwelling in him, as well as he can know fresh from impure atmosphere, pure from filthy water, though it may be a little difficult to tell clearly *how* he knows it. 3. Many persons are misled and troubled by the erroneous views advocated round them, and persons are troubled by listening to marvelous experiences told to them by others. Some persons receive the truth gradually, and consequently never realize any sudden and wonderful change, though they are as really changed, and the change as great, when properly considered as in any other case. Others have the truth brought to their understanding suddenly and in an overwhelming manner, producing a change so impressive that the realization of it has a more vividly marked period than in the more gradual change, though the change in itself, is no greater nor better. But the change, in either case, is produced by the Gospel, and is of no value if it does not result in turning the person from the power of Satan to God. When it does result in turning the sinner to the Lord, by his taking the steps laid down in the Gospel, and the person loves the Savior, walks in the commandments, delighting in them, that person has the Spirit, no matter whether he at any particular time experienced any wonderful change of feeling, or not, or any sudden or *striking* change of any kind. Persons may have sudden and striking changes of feeling and not have the Spirit at all, and they may have the Spirit and not have any sudden and striking change of feeling at all. Yet, when the entire change in this latter case is considered in all its extent, though it has been very gradual, it may be greater than in the former case. It is no evidence that any one did not receive the Spirit, that did not feel some wonderful and sudden sensation; but it is an evidence that any one has not the Spirit, if he does not love God and keep his commandments. 4. Granting pardon and imparting the Spirit are the work of God, and never fail when we come to him according to the Gospel. If we have confidence in him, and in his gracious promise, we cannot doubt when we come to him according to his will, that he has graciously pardoned us and imparted to us His Holy Spirit. If we do those things that are pleasing in His sight, He will give us meekly all things to enjoy. "He who hears these sayings of mine," says the Lord, and *does them,* I will liken him to a wise man." They who do his commandments, shall enter by the gates into the city and have a right to the tree of life.

12/1/63, v.6, #48, pg.190.

Query–In St. Luke 12.10, what is blasphemy against the Holy Spirit?

Answer–The sin of ascribing the power of the Spirit of God, by which our Lord cast out demons, to the devil. They said, "He has an unclean spirit." This was their offense; they alleged that he cast out demons by Beelzebub, the Prince of the demons. He who shall blaspheme, even against the Son, may be forgiven; but he who shall blaspheme against the Holy Spirit, by ascribing the works done by him to Beelzebub, shall never be forgiven. Why does our brother use the Romish prefix "St." to the name of Luke? Luke was a saint, but no more so than any other Christian. The Romish idea of *saint* is one that has been canonized by their infallible Church, generally after he was dead, and about the worst man they had. The apostles frequently spoke of the whole Church of the whole Church as saints or *holy ones*, but never addressed "St. Paul," "St. John," or "St. Peter," etc. We do not admire, rounded up, and pretty phrases without regard to the *sense.*

10/19/71, v.14, #43, p.332

Query–It is said there is no subject or position without difficulties, as there is no rose without a thorn, and I am inclined to believe there is truth in the adage. Well, to my difficulty, which, perhaps, you or some of your correspondents will at once explain. It is the difficulty in the position of "plenary inspiration," or the infallibility of the sacred pen men. I do not know that it is necessary for us to believe in their infallibility, nor do I know that you will so contend; but it is so taught by some. Now, we know the sacred writings are both authentic and genuine; moreover, we know that the writers and guides spoken of must have been more or less under the influence of the inspiring Spirit, that "holy men of old spake as they were moved by the Holy Spirit." But whether the Prophets and Apostles *were at all times under this influence,* is another question. Well, to mention some of the difficulties, if all were equally and plenary inspired, how is it said Jacob *saw God,* that Moses and others saw him, when John 1.18 says, "No man hath at any time seen God;" and again, "Ye have neither heard his voice nor seen his shape." And even Moses declares that no man can see his face and live. Did Jacob think he saw God and was he mistaken, or is it an interpolation, or further is it an erroneous translation?

Again, was Peter under inspiration when he denied his Master? And were not Moses, David, Solomon and others fallible men like ourselves? And how was it with Peter after the day of Pentecost—did he not erroneously teach the necessity of circumcision for several years, and did not Paul reprove him for dissimulation? We do not wish to speak lightly of these holy men, but we state simply what the Bible records concerning them. That they are credible historians, we have no doubt; but we do not know of any man infallible and without sin except Jesus of Nazareth. Nor could the Apostles work miracles at all times, under all circumstances. Jesus himself refused to work because of unbelief, and Paul left a brother sick without healing him. What we want to know is the truth, and we fear not the consequences. "Let's know the worst and provide for it" is always the motto. If these be difficulties and require a reply, you will confer a favor upon others beside myself if you will but add your comments in the REVIEW. We have been much pleased heretofore in reading over your explanations of difficult texts; now can't you say something on the above?

Answer–Many such difficulties, and, we presume *all such* as alluded to above, if we had sufficient information, could be explained satisfactorily, without affecting the inspiration of the sacred writers. We do not profess to be able to explain all of them, nor do we think it probable that any man now living can. But we have found explanations of many things of the sort, that we once thought difficult, entirely satisfactory. This shows the high probability that other things of seeming difficulty might easily be explained, and shown to be no difficulty at all, if we had more information. It is a shocking mistake to imagine that our want of information, or, in simple terms, that *our ignorance is a difficulty in the Bible*. When we read that the Lord appeared to Moses in a flame of fire at the bush, it is easy to catch the conclusion that the Lord himself appeared there; but when you read in another place that the appearance was by an angel, we readily conclude that the Almighty Father, in person, was not there. How easy it could be true, as John says that "no man hath seen God at any time;" meaning the person of the Almighty Father, and it could have been equally true that he appeared, *by an angel* in the bush. We know but little about the Almighty, and not as much about his manifestations as we ought to know. It has been common at different times, when the most glorious and grand manifestations of God were seen, for the sacred writer to speak of seeing God. But his assuming some visible form, or embodiment, to manifest himself, as he has repeatedly done, and manifesting himself in that form, so that man may properly say he has seen him, is one thing and to see his face, in the sense in which John speaks, is another and a very different thing. To speak of seeing directly and personally the great Eternal, the Infinite Spirit, who fills heaven with his glory, is one thing, but it is a very different thing to speak of seeing him in some of the divine manifestations, as in the bush, in winds, in flames, or in some personification, in the form of a man, an angel, or his Son. "He who sees me, " says Jesus, "sees the Father." The Father is manifested in the Son, seen in the Son, and approached through him.

The Prophets and Apostles were fallible *as men*, but *infallible in the revelations*. The revelations that God gave through them were infallible, but the men were not infallible-. God, who could cause a dumb beast to speak with man's voice and forbid the madness of the Prophet, could easily deliver an infallible revelation through a fallible and imperfect man. We are not, then, to assume that the revelations are imperfect, and thereby account for what we can not reconcile, or probably what we cannot comprehend, on the ground that the revelations are imperfect or contradictory. The shorter, simpler and more rational solution is, that our information and understandings are imperfect. This is safe, for we know this to be the case. Man would sooner account for a difficulty in almost any way, as a general thing, than honestly to admit that its foundation is simply in his own ignorance. But our ignorance of the government of God, his dealings with men, and the wonderful displays of his divine and miraculous powers, is no evidence of difficulty in the procedure of the Infinite One. Men of sense find difficulties all around them, not only in things that they can not understand, but things that appear irrational and inconsistent. Why should God create one set of insects to kill, eat and live on another set? Why create one tribe of animals to live by making a prey of another tribe equally good? Why create thousands of acres of desert, producing nothing for man or beast? Why create polar regions of interminable ice and snow? Why the disagreeable changes of heat and cold, wet and dry? Why shoot forth vegetation, and then send a freeze and kill it? Why give birth to thousands of infants, and send pestilence to destroy them? Why raise up cities and thickly populated countries, and swallow them up of earthquakes? Why raise up a splendid young man, and in the very morning of life cut him down with consumption? Why send the devouring worm to kill the peach tree, or the rot upon the apple and potato? Why create a cockle and cheat, thistle and thorn? Why destroy our crops with rain one year, and with drought the next?

Who can explain all these difficulties? No man. What, then, shall we do with them? Know what we can, and leave the balance with the all-wise God, who can, when he sees fit, reconcile all these matters, and show a good reason for everything he has done. We are not to think his works are not wise and good, because we can not understand them. The reason is entirely different; it is that we are not wise—that we are weak and ignorant. All these difficulties are humiliating to us, not evincing imperfection in the works of God, but imperfection in the works of God. But imperfection, weakness and imbecility in us—in our knowledge, in our understanding, in our reason. "The wisdom of man is foolishness with God." Here has been the grand blunder of skeptics, they have supposed that things which they could not understand were inconsistent. The Pope thought the daily revolution of the earth was inconsistent, because he could not understand it and reconcile it with some of his superstitious notions; but as more light was developed, and the proof became more conclusive, his infallibility had to yield. There was no inconsistency in the revolution of the earth; the whole difficulty was in the ignorance of the Pope. In precisely the same way, the difficulties are supposed to be in the Bible. Every thing is consistent in the Bible, so far as understood, which of itself is pretty strong evidence that the whole is consistent when understood.

The Lord had to take fallible and imperfect men as the instruments through which to communicate his revelation to men, and he never claimed infallibility for *the men*, but on the contrary, made them with their own lips tell their foibles, publish their weaknesses and follies; but the revelations he communicated through them are infallible. Still, we must discriminate between that which is purely revelation and that which is not; that which is truly and properly from God, and that which is not. Errors in translating, or transcribing, interpolations and corruptions of every sort, as a matter of course, are no part of revelation. Then there are two distinct classes of revelation as follows: 1. Direct or plenary inspiration, in which an inspired man speaks under the power of the Holy Spirit without even himself comprehending the import of what he says. In this case, the man is not inspired *understand or practice* what he says, but to speak the mind of the Spirit of all wisdom and revelation. Every other man of the same common sense, has the same opportunity to understand and practice what he says as himself. 2. An inspired man, writing a history of things that have occurred, many of which are not a part of revelation, but many of them things said and done not only by men that are not good men, but the opponents of Christ and the Apostles, as well as demons, and even the devil himself. Giving a faithful record of these things, is very different from speaking under the direct and infallible influence of the Spirit, as Peter did on Pentecost.

We may find apparent discrepancies in these narratives, and even what some have thought inaccuracies; but when properly considered and appreciated they amount to nothing, only a conclusive evidence to a sound mind that there was no collusion, no concerted story, and no learned and studied argument. The books of Matthew, Mark, Luke and John, are simply records of the testimony of four of the witnesses of Christ. When we reason deliberately upon the matter, we are not to look upon the *Bible* and *Christianity* as synonymous. Strictly speaking, the saying of Chillingworth, that "the Bible is the religion of Protestants," is not true. The Bible contains the religion of Christians, in word, but it is not the religion of Christians; or rather, it is more than that. Nor is the New Testament, strictly speaking, the religion of Christians, or more properly, the religion of Christ, in word, but it *contains the religion of Christ, in word.* The testimonies of Matthew, Mark, Luke and John are not the religion of Christ, but the divine testimonies that prove it. Infidels, therefore, who try to find discrepancies in these testimonies are not affecting Christianity or the truth of it, unless they can destroy this testimony so as to render it unworthy of confidence. This they do not attempt to do; but simply look upon their testimony as a system of religion, which they try to show could not have come from God, because they think they find incongruities in it. That which is truly and properly Christianity, or the religion of Christ, is perfect, consistent, and invulnerable, and can be true, divinely and infallibly true, and there be thousands of things in the Bible, or things even in the New Testament, that we can never explain or understand. Christianity is a belief in Christ, a full and confiding belief from the heart in Christ, so as to trust in him, and obey him. If that is not from heaven, then our religion is not true. Our skeptical opponents must make their attack directly upon Christ and take him from us, or our religion remains unshaken.

5/29/59, vol.2, #21, page 82

QUESTIONS RELATING TO THE CHRISTIAN LIFE

Query— If those under the law received a just recompense of reward for every transgression and disobedience in this world, will they be punished in the world to come for the same transgressions?

Answer— The subject introduced by a brother in the above question, is one that can not be satisfactorily discussed and answered in a few words; yet we have but a small space for its elucidation now. We, therefore, can not promise full satisfaction. The law of Moses neither could give eternal life, nor punish with eternal punishment. Its rewards and punishments were not spiritual, but worldly; not eternal but temporal; not in the future, but in the present world. The law could not purge the conscience. By the deeds of the law no flesh could be justified in the sight of God. The law offered no heaven, and threatened no hell. A man could conform to the letter of the law all his life, so as to escape all its punishments; or as in the case of Saul of Tarsus, as touching the law be blameless, and yet have no piety towards God, no purification of conscience, or not at all justified in the sight of God. A mere conformity to the law of Moses prepared no person for heaven, or guarantied to no person any thing in the world to come. A man receiving all its rewards— all its promises, its Canaan, its milk and honey, etc. etc.—in this world, was no reason why he should not enjoy heaven. On the other hand, the penalty of that law failing upon its transgressor, was no reason why he should not be punished in the world to come, any more than the penalty of the civil government falling upon a transgressor is a reason why God should not punish him.

The truth is, Abraham was justified by faith, in the sight of God, four hundred and thirty years before the law, even while yet in uncircumcision. His faith looked not to the law, its rewards or its promises, but to Him who was the end of the law, who is the resurrection and the life—the Lord from heaven. In receiving the promise, Abraham received Christ, was justified by him, and through him gained heaven. All the justification, from Abraham to the giving of the law, and from them to Christ, was through faith in the promise, or in Christ, the substance of the promise, and not through the law. Abraham, by faith, saw the day of the Redeemer; and through that faith reached beyond the law, beyond all its rewards and punishments, and above them, to a spiritual life, and spiritual world. Upon this promise, and faith in it, rested the piety of Abraham, and all his descendants, to Christ; in it was their hope of heaven and the world to come; through it was justification, and without that faith there was no justification. Without this faith there was no purification of conscience, no purification of the heart, and union with God, though a man had kept the law all his life. But if a man lived without this faith, and died in his disobedience to the law, he certainly died without justification, without his soul being purified, and consequently without any preparation to enjoy God.

The mere circumstance of a man being punished for his sins in this life, has nothing in it to purify his soul, purge his conscience, or prepare him for the enjoyment of God. The Egyptians, the antediluvians, the Sodomites and the Jews, had a just recompense of reward sent upon them in this world, but this only sent them down to *tartarus*, to be reserved, with the angels that sinned, to the judgment of the great day, where, we are assured, Sodom and Gomorrah shall appear. Some men appear to think, that if men are punished, to use their own style, as much as their sins deserve, they must necessarily be happy then. But men can not be happy—can not enjoy God, without justification, purification of heart and conscience, and, unless thus prepared for the enjoyment of God, they can not enjoy the world to come. This is a work that punishment can not do. The hurling of angels that sinned, down to hell, the drowning of antediluvians and Egyptians, the burning of Sodomites and slaying of the Jews, did not purify one of them; nor can we see that any punishment will ever purify, or justify one of them. If men live in unbelief, commit some capital offence and are executed for it, though this may be a just recompense of reward, it will not purify their souls, and prepare them to enjoy God. When men pass the boundary line of life, they pass all the means, in the economy of God, for preparing them for heaven, and no punishment will ever do what the grace of God could not do.

1857, vol.2, #2, pg.59

Query—When Paul said, "Let a man examine himself, and so let him eat," etc., did he teach that every man must be his own judge as to whether or not he has a *right to partake of the supper;* or, did he not teach that the members of the church of God, when partaking of the supper, should be their own judge as to whether *they were eating to gluttony, or drinking to drunkenness?* To my mind, the latter is unquestionably the teaching of the Apostle. But what say you?

Answer—We accord with the good brother. The Corinthians ate and drank to drunkenness and gluttony, "not discerning the Lord's body." The examination was not to decide the question, whether persons should commence or not, but to examine himself, and *so eat,* to eat *unworthily,* is to eat discerning the Lord's body. The caution is not to prevent *unworthy persons* from communing, but to prevent all from communing *unworthily,* not discerning the Lord's body and blood. We are not aware that it would make the case any worse for one much out of the way to commune, nor any better for such a one not to commune. We are certain that the meaning of the passage is not that persons should refuse to commune simply because they feel a little gloomy, as is the case with some of the most conscientious persons in the world. The unworthiness consisted in the abuses alluded to in the passage, and certainly not in something not mentioned in the passage.

1/4/59, vol.1, #1, page #3.

Query—Notwithstanding being requested to send you the following query, it is with a blush of shame that I propose such a question, seeing that those of us who should be teachers "have need that one should teach us which are the first principles of the doctrine of Christ." 1 Tim. 2.1, "I exhort, therefore, that first of all supplications, prayers, intercessions and giving of thanks be made for all men, etc." Is this the only proper arrangement of the worship of God in his house? And if so, in what order does the remaining items of worship of God come?

I am truly sorry that such questions should be permitted to vex the church of Christ. Will you be so kind as to reply and oblige yours in the Lord?

Answer—The passage in question has nothing to do with the order of worship, nor saying one word about it. But as an item to be observed in our Christian practice, first in importance, let prayers, intercessions, and giving of thanks be made for all men, for kings and all that are in authority, that we may lead a peaceable and quiet life, in all godliness and honesty.

12/18/60, vol.3, #51, page 206

Query–There is a report going the rounds in the southeastern portion of Iowa, that you admitted to Bro. Shortridge that "while you did not believe the soul sleeping doctrine, you could not disprove it." Now, my dear Brother, the advocates of that dogma are not few, and some of them are talented, and they are making a capital out of the above alleged admission from you. I hope it is wholly untrue. I have been requested to write you on the subject. To be understood, does the human spirit sleep in the grave with the body, from the death of the body, in a state of unconsciousness? Now, Brother, when you admit in your paper that you can not disprove the above figment, I will believe it, and not before. I have ventured for you to pronounce it a slander on you. Please insert the foregoing, with your reply *in extenso.*

Answer–We never admitted to any human being that we could not disprove the doctrine of soul sleeping. On the contrary, we certainly have long since disproved it many times, both in the pulpit and prints, as many thousands with testing. We regard the doctrine of soul sleeping, or *no soul* doctrine, as death to the cause of Christ wherever preached.

10/21/58, vol.1 #40, page 158

Query–In the tenth and last chapters of the gospel by Matthew are found the two commissions. When did the Apostles commence acting under the second of these commissions?

Answer–The Apostles commenced acting under the second and last commission on the day of Pentecost. (Acts chapter 2)

6/19/60, vol.3, #25, page 99

Query–On the day of Pentecost, spoken of in the 2nd of Acts, were any persons present except Jews and proselytes to the Jewish religion?

Answer–None were present, that we know of, but Jews and proselytes. At all events, none but Jews were converted.

6/19/60, vol.3, #25, page 99

Query–If we are subject to errors, interpolations, etc. in translating or transcribing, either intentionally or accidentally; and if "language is unstable," as Bro. Walter Scott says, "and liable to change and corruption;" and if words are constantly losing their primitive meaning, and by the refining and discriminating processes by which they multiply themselves, are constantly losing their original significance and distinctiveness; I say, if all this be true, then is human language, oral or written, a perfect medium through which for God to reveal his will to man?

Answer–Human language, perfect or imperfect, is the only medium through which is a revelation to man ever was or ever can be made. We do not claim for the *medium* that it is perfect, but the *revelation itself* is perfect. The imperfection of language and instability form the occasion for new translations and revisions. Revelation, when first given to man, was perfect, and the language employed to convey it to the mind of man answered the purpose. In the providence of God, the original languages through which revelation was made died, and consequently ceased to change. But, in the very nature of things, a living language is always changing. The circumstance, however, that language is an imperfect vehicle through which to convey divine things, is no objection to the divine things thus conveyed to us. It may be a reason why our knowledge of revelation will never be perfect in this life; but certainly no reason why revelation itself shall be considered imperfect. It may be alleged that revelation to man is more difficult on account of the imperfection and instability of language; but the same difficulty lies in the way of every kind of communications to men.

The true state of the case is, that the medium of language is sufficiently perfect and entirely adequate for all the purposes of a revelation to mankind. The communication from God to man found in the Bible is sufficiently clear and intelligible for all the purposes of its original design. The man who will make an honest effort, can understand the will of God concerning him—can discriminate between good and evil, right and wrong, the way to hell and the way to heaven. But the man who will not make an honest effort, would not be a Christian if one would rise from the dead before his eyes. If he had seen the Lord in person, he would have found occasion for caviling. The seed of the kingdom must fall into a *good* and *honest* heart. It is useless to fall out with the medium through which revelation has come to man. The best medium in existence was employed, the very one through which we communicate man with man, and the one with which man is more familiar than any one or—the medium of *language*.

8/9/59, vol.2, #32, page 126

Query– What are we to understand from Rom 2.13: "For not the hearers of the law are just before God, but the doers of the law shall be justified." Rom 3.20: "Therefore by the deeds of the law shall no flesh be justified in his sight." What law has the Apostle reference to?

Answer–The law of Moses, unquestionably. The good works or the deeds, of the gospel, are ordained that we should walk in them. See Eph 2.10. "He that is the doer of the work,"—not the law of Moses, but of the law of Christ—"this man shall be blessed in his deed." James 1.2–5. "For if you do these things"—the deeds, not of the law of Moses, but of the law of Christ—"ye shall never fall." 2 Pet 1.10.

3/16/1858, vol1, #11, page 42.

Query– What *promise* did Peter allude to on the day of Pentecost?

Answer –That which Peter called "the promise," on Pentecost, and which is emphatically called *"the promise"* in the Bible generally, if not always, is the promise made to Abraham—"In thee and in thy seed shall all nations be blessed." This is the gospel in promise.

1856, vol.1, page 159

Query–When is an individual born of the Spirit?

Answer–An individual is born of the Spirit when he is converted, or when he obeys from the heart the form of doctrine delivered to him.

1856, vol. 1, page 159.

Query–Bro Franklin; I am young, and would be glad of formation on several questions, some of which I here present: Under the former dispensation there was a high priest, and there was a yearly sacrifice, and there were daily offerings, besides peace and trespass offerings I wish to know whether the high priest, who offered sacrifice every year, also offered daily offerings, or were there daily priests whose business it was to offer the daily sacrifice together with peace and other offerings.

Answer—We have not time now to examine, but, if memory serves us, all the priests participated in the daily offering, but the high priest went alone into the most holy place. *Western Reformer*

April 1849, vol.7, #4, page 252.

Query—Can any person creep into the church hypocritically, be immersed, and afterwards become awakened to a deep sense of the awful danger impending him, forsake his sins and become a true exemplary Christian, without being re-baptized?

Answer—We know not whether a person, who would hypocritically be baptized, and creep into the church, never could repent, be baptized or come into the church in such a manner as to be acceptable to the Lord. It is a fearful thing to tamper with the appointments of the Lord; and he who does it, does it at the peril of his soul. One thing is evident, we think, to every reflecting person, and that is, that nothing that a man could do, under a hypocritical pretense, in the name of religion, could be of any value. Neither the faith, repentance, confession, prayers, joining in the church or anything else, done under a hypocritical pretense, could be of any value. If such a person ever comes to the Lord at all, he must evidently come as one that had never started. The best thing that such an one can do, is to repent solemnly, and pray God if peradventure pardon may be found.

1858, vol.1, #32, page 127.

Query—Why could not the man under the law of whom we read Romans 7th, "do what he would?"

Answer—Because he "sees another law in his members warring against the law of his mind, and bringing him into captivity to the law of sin which is in his members," (see verse 23,) and "when he would do good, evil is present with him." v 21. This, however, is only the reason why he *did not* do what he would, and not the reason why he *could not.*" It does not say he *could not* but simply that he *did not.* It is simply what the Jew *was* and not what he *could* have been.

Western Reformer August 1849, vol.7, #8, page 501.

Query—What relation does an individual occupy after he or she is out of the body of Christ, and how does he or she get back into that relation again, seeing that we become Christians by being buried with Christ by baptism? See Paul to Gal 3.27.

Now, if we have been adopted into the family of God by faith, repentance and baptism, thus becoming members of his body, heirs of God and joint heirs with Christ, and then get out of the body of Christ, do we not occupy the same position the world does?

Answer–We could not give the letter in full, for the want of room, but we have given enough to give the questions, but we have no room for any argument, but simply state, that if a Christian gets out of the body of Christ, he is gone forever. "There is no more sacrifice for sin." Such an one does not occupy the place of the man of the world. An individual, however may be suspended from the privileges of a congregation for disorderly conduct, and not be yet out of the body of Christ, or finally fallen away, and even be reclaimed by confessing his sins.

Western Reformer August 1848, vol.6, #10, page 634.

Query–What death did Adam die, in consequence of eating the forbidden fruit? If spiritual, show that he was a spiritual man—if temporal, show that he died *that day*.

Answer–Just as certain, as the expression, "in Christ all shall be made alive," means a literal resurrection from the dead, the expression "as in Adam all die," means a natural death or just as certain as the expression, "by man come also the resurrection of the dead," means a literal resurrection from the dead, the expression "by man came death," means a literal death. And just as certain as the Lord meant a literal death by the words, "unto dust shalt thou return," he meant a literal death when he said, "in the day thou eatest thereof, thou shalt surely die."

We are compelled to admit, that he died that day, or that the divine threat was not executed. Some contend that the Lord granted Adam a respite beyond the limits prescribed in the threatening. Others say he was immediately driven out of the garden, and separated from the tree of life, and commenced dying that day. Others explain "day" in such a way as to include *an age*, as when we say a certain transaction transpired in Washington's day.

We are inclined to the opinion, that from the time the ground was cursed for man's sake, and the seeds of death were sown in it, that he was dead in the eye of the law. That he did not enjoy the same spiritual union with the divine Father, after the transgression as before, we think very clear.

Western Reformer December 1847 vol. 6, #2, page 122

Query – Please say to us, in the next Reformer whether the slavery that now exists in these United States, taking into consideration all the circumstances that surround the case and are attendant thereto, is authorized by the gospel of the son of God, or not in your judgment. I mean the black population. Can't you visit our country soon?

Answer – I do not believe that any slavery is authorized by the gospel of the Son of God, not even such as I find in this state in some places. But it is not the *power* a civil relation gives any man that condemns him before God, but the *abuse* of that power. I do hope to visit your country soon.

Western Reformer August 1848, vol.6, #10, page 635.

Query – Please give us a strong and weighty lecture on church members tippling and drinking, and show them that they are exerting a very bad influence before their children and their neighbors' children, and we will lend it to some of them to read.

Answer – This is a bad report of your part of Indiana. I have noticed, however, that members of all churches indulge in drinking, and that membership in no society, not even the "Sons" is a guaranty of abstinence. Indeed "moderate" drinking, sometimes called "temperate" drinking, is not disreputable in many places. This reputable indulgence is the entering wedge that rives asunder the moral power of Church membership, family and social connection, saps the foundation of conscientiousness, and finally drowns conscience, reason and sense in one long oblivious debauch, which is uninterrupted but by death. The unhappy victim by the influence of pride and of character, during the stouter period of life keeps his appetite under measurable control, but as the powers of life decay by age and by the corrosion of the liquid fire swallowed every day, for a term of years, the shattered nerves make such a vociferous demand for something to steady them, as the dictates of judgment and the reproaches of conscience, cannot withstand, and the man, the Church member, perhaps the Church member, perhaps the Church officer, falls a victim to an insidious foe that he had, a few years before disdained and despised. These persons never get drunk, but in after life they are seldom sober.

Take another view. They are temperate drinkers, perhaps without an example of intemperance in their households, generally their lives are prematurely consumed by their fiery appetites. But what shall we say of their sons, whose appetites are whetted by the fumes of the sweetened, scented and flavored poison, and the drinking of which is legalized by parental precept and example. If the father is a temperate drinker, the son is frequently a sot which reads as follows: "*It is* not for kings, O Lemuel, *it is* not for kings to drink wine, nor for princes strong drink." "Lest they drink, and forget the law, and pervert the judgment of any of the afflicted." Prov 31.4–5. "Do not drink wine nor strong drink, thou, nor thy sons with thee, when ye go into the tabernacle of the congregation, lest ye die: *it shall be* a statute for ever throughout your generations." Lev 10.9 "Awake ye drunkards, and weep; and howl, all ye drinkers of wine, because of the new wine; for it is cut off from your mouth." Joel 1.5. "Woe unto him that giveth his neighbor drink, that puttest thy bottle to *him*, and makest *him* drunken also, that thou mayest look on their nakedness." "Thou art filled with shame for glory; drink thou also, and let thy foreskin be uncovered; the cup of the Lord's right hand shall be turned unto thee, and shameful spewing *shall be* on thy glory." "For the violence of Lebanon shall cover thee, and the spoil of beasts, *which* made them afraid, because of men's blood, and for the violence of the land, of the city, and of all that dwell therein." Hab 2.15–17. " "That the aged men be sober, grave, temperate, sound in faith, in charity, in patience." "The aged women likewise, that they be in behavior as becometh holiness, not false accusers, not given to much wine, teachers of good things." "Young men likewise exhort to be sober minded." "Teaching us, that denying ungodliness and worldly lusts, we should live soberly, righteously and godly in this present world." Titus 2.2–3, 6, 12. "It is good neither to eat flesh, nor drink wine, nor anything whereby thy brother stumbleth, or is, or is offended, or is made weak." Rom 14.21. "Abstain from all appearance of evil." 1 Thes 5.22.

If a man is responsible for the harm he does, fearful will be the account to be rendered by the maker, vender and drinker. The Lord preserve any one called a brother from such a doom.

Query–There is a question on which the brethren(both preachers and common folk) are divided. The question alluded to is the ordinance of washing the saint's feet. Some think it a command and necessary to be attended to. Others say it has had its day and ceased. Those who believe and practice this ordinance disagree, some putting it in the church, and some in the household.

Answer–There is no such *ordinance* in the New Testament as *washing the saint's feet*. The Lord, in the family capacity, after a common supper, gave the apostles a practical lesson of humility, to counteract that kind of spirit which led to dispute who should be the greatest. He commenced washing their feet. Peter objected through shame. The Lord commanded him to yield, or he should have no part with him. The Apostle then cheerfully yielded. The Lord then proceeded to make the practical deduction: "If I, your Lord and master, wash your feet, you ought to wash one another's feet." " If He, though greater than all, humbled Himself to the most lowly service, we should humble ourselves to any service for the most humble and lowly of the human family.

Such a thing as a ceremony called "the ordinance of feet washing," practiced in the congregation, met to worship among the primitive Disciples, is unknown to all history. Owing to their wearing sandals, and their sandy country, it was an important item to bathe the feet before retiring, both to cleanse them and prevent soreness. It was consequently an important item in hospitality, to furnish water and bathe the feet of a friend in entertaining him. In this sense Paul looks at it, in the only mention of it in the apostolic writings. It is mentioned in a catalog of good works, such as lodging or entertaining strangers, bringing up children, guiding the house, etc.

1857, vol.2, page 249

Query–Please give us your views of Luke 16.16. Does our Savior mean to say that His kingdom, or church was established when He uttered these words? Also, your views of Luke 17.20–21.

Answer–The passage, Luke 16.16 is: "The law and the prophets were until John: since that time the kingdom of God is preached, and every man passeth into it." The Lord did not *mean* to say, and certainly *did not say*, in this passage or any other, that His kingdom was established when he uttered these words. If the translators had been as free with their supplements here as in other places, we should read: "The law and prophets *were preached* until John: since that time the kingdom of God is preached," etc. The law and the prophets were in full force, when these words were uttered, and never died till the Lord expired on the cross—the "handwriting of ordinances" was never taken away, till this wonderful event.

The other passage, Luke 17.20–21, is: "And when he was demanded of the Pharisees, when the kingdom of God should come, he answered them and said: The kingdom of God cometh not with observation : neither shall they say, Lo, here! Or Lo there! for, behold, the kingdom of God is within you." The kingdom of God was within or *among* them, not established, fully developed and progressing in full glory, but in its inefficient or embryo state embodied in the Lord, and its approach announced by John the Baptist, the Lord, the Twelve and the Seventy, in all its fullness and glory.

1/7/57, vol.2, page 249.

Query–As the Levites were given to the priests for the service of the tabernacle, I wish to know what part of the worship they performed.(?)

Answer–The Levites were appointed over the tabernacle of testimony, and over the vessels thereof, and over all things that belong to it: they shall bear the tabernacle, and all the vessels thereof; and they shall minister unto it, and shall camp round about the tabernacle. Num 1.50. They were to "execute the service of the Lord," "lay their hands on the heads of the bullocks" and "wait upon the service of the tabernacle of the congregation." See Numbers 1.11, 14, also 22, 26.

Query–Will you please give us through the columns of the REVIEW, your opinion upon the propriety or impropriety of a Christian engaging in the sale or traffic of intoxicating liquors, either by wholesale or retail? Do you think the plea a good one to say, that we merely proffer to sell it as a medicine, when we lay in stock or four to eight barrels at a time? What should a church do with a member that does so engage?

Answer–There can be but one opinion on the propriety or impropriety of a Christian selling intoxicating drinks as a beverage. The impropriety of the thing is hardly is hardly equaled in any way; and if done under a pretense of selling for *medical purposes*, it is adding *hypocrisy* to the very grave and obvious impropriety. If this can all be clearly established in any case, the subject should be subjected to church discipline. No man can have a Christian influence, or be worth any thing to the cause of Christ, who engages in the unworthy, low and shameful traffic of selling out five cents worth of liquor to some poor, degraded rum sucker, who has not money to buy bread for his children. What a low and degraded moral feeling a man must have to turn to such a calling!

7/12/59, vol.2, #28, page

Query–Should Christian parents direct their children to pray? I mean before the child is a Christian from his youth up. If he ought *not* to pray in private daily, why require him to join in *family* worship? If *it is* his duty and privilege to pray, can he—*an* alien—ask and receive the forgiveness of sins? Why encourage children to *sing* the praises of God, if they are not permitted to approach him in supplication with thanksgiving?

Answer–All persons must begin at the beginning. Is prayer the first thing? Is prayer the beginning of serving God? Is prayer in the church, or out of it? Is prayer a Christian practice, or an institution for sinners to convert them? What is the first thing to teach children, or any body? Is it to *become* Christians, or to *practice* Christianity? Did the Lord teach his disciples how to pray? Or persons before they were disciples? -It is rational at least, to teach the easier and simpler lessons first. The first great lesson for our children, and for all, is to know the Lord, or to believe on him, for "without faith, it is impossible to please him." "He that cometh to God must believe." When our children have been taught to know the Lord, or to believe on him, the next lesson is to teach them to become his disciples. There is a much easier lesson than prayer, and certainly goes before it. Teach our children first to become disciples of Christ, and then to pray and do everything else the Lord commands.

8/14/60, vol3, #33, page 132

Queries–If a sinner believes with all his heart that Jesus is the Christ, the Son of the living God, will he (the sinner) receive pardon without ever asking God to forgive him of all sins committed?

Answer–We see no particular point in the above. The very circumstance of a sinner coming by faith and inquiring what to do to be saved, and proceeding honestly forthwith to carry out the instructions, is substantially *seeking, asking,* "calling on the name of the Lord," and has annexed to it the promise of the Lord.

10/71, vol.14, #41, page 324

Query–I wish a few questions for your solution. Had Paul, when he wrote to Timothy (2nd letter 3.16–17) on the all sufficiency of the Holy Scriptures, references to the Holy Scriptures as now compiled, or to Jewish scriptures only? I would like something on this question in the form of an essay; for I consider it of immense importance. For many that say, to take the Holy Scriptures as all sufficient; but in practice they too often substitute the inventions of men, which our Lord intimates is in vain. For in this is involved the credibility of the apostles, and the validity of the Sacred Scriptures. If we take the license to cull any part out, we may upon the same principle cull any, or even all.

Although, as you will see in the sequel, I ask the question, I take the stand on their all-sufficiency and say if they are sufficient it is to be read therein. The Apostle Peter says, "But holy men of God spake *as they were* moved by the Holy Ghost." So we have the Holy Scriptures through that medium; which Paul says is sufficient for all purposes. One further reason for my wanting an essay from you is that we have here, not only Atheists, Deists and Infidels, but Licenciates; (I call them by the right name,) for they assume the license to throw away any part of the sacred scriptures that does not suit their notion. I have heard such language as this used, they did not think much of Paul, or his writings. He did not allow women their rights, and it has, I am informed, been held forth in this county, that the apostle Paul was a slave-catcher. This would, with them, defame the character of Paul, and per consequence, invalidate the Holy Scriptures.

Answer–The apostle certainly had the Old Testament Scriptures in view when he wrote to Timothy. Such of the New Testament books as had come into circulation, would come under his general rule, but much of the later revelations were not then committed to writing and no such volume as the New Testament was collected. But if the apostolic commendation of the Old Testament was of authority with the Christians, the apostolic authorship of the New Testament would certainly be an equal passport to the confidence of the discerning then, as it should be to us now. These skeptics of whom you complain, whether they follow some erratic woman or some weaker sister of the sturdier race, have sense enough to know that Paul's endorsement of the Jewish Scriptures is as valueless as anything else he may write. They have no use for any part of the Bible, only in so far as it may be distorted into an excuse of some of their aberrations, intellectual and moral. They have weighed anchor and dislike to hear the old Apostle's speaking trumpet, calling out, "Cease to be children. Be not tossed to and fro in your little vessel, and carried over all seas theological, by every wind of doctrine, by whomsoever blown, by the slight of men and cunning craftiness, whereby they lie in wait to deceive." Children often upset and drowned, but as long as their boat is not bottom up, they think all such sober advice the tamest conservatism. But Paul knew more than they do. He had seen both the deceivers and the deceived, more than they do. He had seen both the deceivers and the deceived, and those who are not blind, have often beheld the same humiliating spectacle, in every age. These persons are correct enough when they style such caution tame, for relative to themselves and in comparison with them, it certainly could not be called wild. Nor is it presumable that their present selves will be called wild in comparison with their future selves, for to be sure they are people of progress. Half the Scriptures is already obsolete. The other half will shortly be pronounced absurd, and some spiritual knocker will be invoked to settle its fate forever, by consigning to destruction all that has survived the assaults of Pharaoh, Antiochus Epiphanies, Herod, Dioclesian, Julian, the Pope, Voltaire and Thomas Paine. Poor Bible, thou hast a bad chance! Howbeit, there is yet some hope as it is now being read in more languages than were created at the confusion of tongues and by more people than constituted the Roman Empire. The Bible is truly an old-fashioned conservative book, that is desperately out of place in this world of ours, for it stands by some old customs, such as that women should not wear men's clothes, Deut 22.5, that public teachers had better be men, that there should be wives and husbands and many other arrangements which comported with staid notions of primeval simplicity, concerning conjugal and other domestic relations.

Self-will is at the bottom of all this strange farce. In a free country it can only cure itself. With a little latitude, it generally manages to bring the matter to a close, by the summary process of suicide. Public taste is a more sovereign antidote than argument. When men are sane and make it a matter of conscience to be sane, rather than self-willed, even their errors should be sufficiently respected to allow of their examination and refutation; but some things cannot be argued down. Mormonism, like the Crusades will have its day, and so will Come-outer-ism, and some women will wear men's clothes, and the world will most likely survive it all, and go on with its progress after the correction of this retrograde motion. There will be a calm, even after this wind of doctrine shall have blown itself out.

Query–Will you throw some light on the importance of the words "many mansions?"

Answer–We think the expression, "many mansions," was simply intended to give the children of God abundant assurance that ample provision would be made for them. Certain it is, that the Lord did not intend this as an encouragement to party-ism. It is well enough to let the brethren see what the things sectarian cogitators are inventing.

5/8/60,v3,#19, pg.75

Query–Are there any circumstances under which the Christian is justifiable in going to law with a brother before the unbeliever? If so, what are the circumstances? If not, ought the church to take the matter in hand, and, when the brother will not promise that he will not do so any more, ought fellowship to be withdrawn? Can the Christian, without violating the law of God, bring suit against any one—believer or unbeliever?

Answer–That Christians ought not to go to law, one with another, is clear from Paul's first letter to the Corinthians. We can not see how there can be any circumstances making it justifiable for a man to do what he ought not to do. From the same Scripture it is clear that, when brethren differ, they should refer their differences to wise men among their brethren. When this is done, they should submit to the decision of those to whom the reference is made, the party refusing clearly becomes a subject of discipline.

We do not take the position that it would violate any clearly expressed law of Christ to resort to the civil law for the recovery of a debt from one not a Christian. But it is certain that Christians should not freely and readily resort to the civil law. We have twice, in the past five years, declined resorting to the law for the recovery of our dues, for small amounts (from $50 to $75 in each case), in clear cases, where the amounts would easily have been recovered, and the parties were not members of the church, and did so because we doubted, at least, the propriety of resorting to the law. In one of these cases the party shortly made an arrangement, voluntarily, by which he settled the full amount. In the other case we lost the amount. We are acquainted with a preacher, in excellent standing, with fair property, and one who transacts some business, who said he never had a lawsuit. He said he had three ways of settling: 1. He proposed a settlement on the ground that he had thought right. 2. He proposed an arbitration. 3. He proposed to settle according to the will of the other party. In some one of these ways he had always succeeded. There are but few cases that could not be settled in some one of these ways.

The requirement of the law of God is, that, "if possible, we *live peaceably with all men:*" that we "follow peace with all men and holiness, without which no man shall see the Lord." In doing this, we are not meditating how we can gain an advantage at the law over an adversary, to say nothing of a brother for whom Christ died, but how we can "*live peaceably* with all men"—"*follow peace* with all men." We are not to study how far we can go and not be excluded from the church, but how near we can live to the Lord—how we can do what is evidently right—how we can be at peace with all men. There is no extreme on the side of peace. We can not go too far. On the other side, we need all restraints. We need to watch that we follow not the desires and be not governed by the passions of the old Adam, instead of the law of the spirit of life in Christ.

2/4/73,v.16,#5,pg.36

Query–In case a church is about equally divided by serious difficulties, which threaten to be the ruin of the cause in a community, and repeated efforts have been made to settle the matter within themselves, and the disaffected request the church party (or the elders) to agree to have a disinterested committee to adjust the trouble, and they utterly and repeatedly refuse to agree to it, what can be done in that case? Bro. Franklin, I am confident you can see that all this question should be answered, though some of us think they have been answered some time ago, but some have forgotten it, I guess. Please give us your mind the first opportunity. This will oblige a great many.

Answer–We have any amount of patience and endurance to answer at almost any length and explain again and again, where we think we can relieve a case, do away any alienation or disaffection, or restore harmony, love and peace among children of God. But in many cases this can not be done. We have known of cases where the best counsels, the most affectionate reasoning and expostulations, the kindest entreaties, the most fervent prayers and streaming tears from those whose hearts were full of grief, all went for nothing—had no influence to reclaim the erring. What is to be done in these cases? We must not weary nor cease our prayers nor efforts to recover the erring and save men.

We must say a few things in the way of *generals* before we come to *particulars*. We visited a church some years since, and there was quite a general impression among the members that their preacher did not suit them—that he was not "the right man in the right place," etc. Many fine things were said as to the kind of a man they needed, etc., and the idea prevailed that they had better turn their preacher off and get another. We suggested to them in a circle one day that possibly they had not at all discovered the real malady; that possibly the main difficulty was not at all in reference to the kind of a preacher they needed, but to the kind of a church they needed; that possibly the change they needed could be effected by *turning off the church* and getting *another* and a *better one*.

It may be such as is the case where some such church difficulties as alluded to above occur. It is not a court of appeals that they so much need, nor committees of disinterested men, as *good members* who have the love of Christ; who want peace and harmony; who "follow *peace* with all men and holiness without which no man shall see the Lord."

We once acted on a committee with several others, heard testimony and arguments for a week, and had the parties bound in writing to abide the decision of the committee. When the decision was made, all parties in the matter agreed and there was shaking of hands over it, and we prayed over them and were all happy. But in a short time, we do not remember whether a week or a month, the whole matter was thrown aside and the parties stood as they did before. Our prayerful and patient working all went for nothing.

When brethren become alienated they frequently do not want to settle their difficulties, but to get an advantage over an opposing party. No court of appeal nor anything we can say will reconcile them. If we, in any part of the affair, agree with them, they *there* agree with us; but if we in any part of it differ from us. There the matter ends. Still, we will try and give a little attention to the matters in hand. 1. There are cases where nothing can be done. In other words, there are cases that can not be settled. Church members sometimes have been *crooked* so long that they will not become *straight*. They continue in their alienation so long that it becomes kind of habit with them and food for them. They continue in their alienation so long that it becomes a kind of habit with them and food for them. They can not do well without it.

If a church is about equally divided by a difficulty and can not settle the matter among themselves, and can not settle the matter among themselves, and will not refer the matter to a committee, it simply *can not be settled*. A case that can not be settled must remain *unsettled*. We answer that in *that case* nothing can be done. Some cases of difficulty will never be settled in this world, and will have to be referred to the last judgment for adjudication. It would be well, though, in such a case as stated, for the disaffected party to consider the matter well, and see to it that they have acted wisely and in the Spirit of the Lord in the whole matter. On the other hand, the church party should review the whole ground carefully, and see to it that *all they can do* to open the way for the disaffected party to become reconciled and brought into the unity of the Spirit and the bond of peace *be done*. Let no stone remain unturned, no effort untried and nothing remain undone that might bring peace.

4/15/73,v.16,#15, p.116

Query–If we are subjects to errors, interpolations, etc., in translating or transcribing either intentionally or accidentally and if language is unstable and liable to change and corruption, and if words are constantly losing their primitive meaning, and by the refining and discriminating processes by which they multiply themselves, are constantly losing their original significance and distinctness: I say, if all this be true, then is human language, oral or written, a perfect medium through which for God to reveal his will to man?

Answer–Human language, perfect or imperfect, is the only medium through which a revelation to man ever was or ever can be made. We do not claim for the *medium* that it is perfect, but the *revelation itself* is perfect. The imperfection of language and instability form the occasion for new translations and revisions. Revelation, when first given to man, was perfect, and the language employed to convey it to the mind of man answered the purpose. In the providence of God, the original languages through which revelation was made died, and consequently ceased to change. But, in the very nature of things, a living language is always changing. The circumstance, however, that language is an imperfect vehicle through which to convey divine things, is no objection to the divine things thus conveyed to us. It may be a reason why our knowledge of revelation will never be perfect in this life; but certainly no reason why revelation itself shall be considered imperfect. It may be alleged that revelation to man is more difficult on account of the imperfection and instability of language; but the same difficulty lies in the way of every kind of communications to men.

The true state of the case is that the medium of language is sufficiently perfect and entirely adequate for all the purposes of a revelation to mankind. The communication from God to man found in the Bible is sufficiently clear and intelligible for all the purposes of its original design. The man who will make an honest effort, can understand the will of God concerning him—can discriminate between good and evil, right and wrong, the way to hell and the way to heaven. But the man who will not make an honest effort, would not be a Christian if one would rise from the dead before his eyes. If he had seen the Lord in person he would have found occasion for caviling. The seed of the kingdom must fall into a *good* and *honest* heart.

It is useless to fall out with the medium through which revelation has come to man. The best medium in existence was employed, the very one through which we communicate man with man, and the one with which man is more familiar than any other—the medium of *language*.

8/9/59,v.2,#32, p.126

Query—Do I understand you to mean when you say that the disciples had work to do they found a way to do it, and we must do the same? Did not the disciples act directly under the influence of the Holy Spirit, as the New Testament was not written? Do you mean we must do the same?

Answer—The disciples acted under the influence of the Holy Spirit anciently and do yet, but that does not prove that the Holy Spirit, when he commands us to feed the hungry, tells us whether we shall buy the food, take some that many may possess, whether we shall carry to him or send it to him; whether we shall cook it for him or let him cook it for himself. The Lord leaves some room for the exercise of common sense, and consequently only reveals what man could not know and do without revelation.

5/1/60,vol.3,#18,pg.71

Query – By what means are we to ascertain what the disciples did that is not written? Or do you have any testimony that they did any thing but what is written? And if so, what is it?

Answer – The Apostles, in all their work, had to determine where they could go, when they would go, where they where they would preach and how much they would preach in each place and at each time.

5/1/60,vol.3,#18,pg.71

Query – Do I understand you to mean, when you speak of anti-means theories, that God has not given us a sufficient revelation of his will to conduct his church with, or that it is necessary for the churches in the present day to do a great many things for the advancement of his kingdom that it is not written?

Answer – We do not mean that God has not given a sufficient revelation. The revelation is sufficient, and goes just as far as it should. It is perfectly right that there should be some room left for common sense, and what we mean by "anti means theories," is that some men are constantly looking for Scripture and calling for chapter and verse, in matters that must be decided and acted upon, before we can do any thing, which are purely of human discretion. The law of the Lord does not decide where any man shall preach, when he shall preach, how long he shall preach, with forty other things that must be decided before any thing can be done. A man who will cavil about the Scripture in all this minutia and refuse to do any thing is an *anti-means man*, and only a clog on the wheels.

5/1/60,vol.3,#18,pg.71

Query – Can the church permit a brother thus to withdraw himself from their fellowship without taking some notice thereof, or what course should they pursue in the premises?

Answer - We know of no precedent for granting withdrawals. One may go out from a church because he is not of it, but not with the consent of the church.

5/1/60,vol.3,#18,pg.71

Query – Are we authorized from Scripture to go outside of Christ's church to get evidence to exclude a brother or sister.

Answer–There is nothing in Scripture in regard to where the evidence shall come from. The only matter to settle is simply the question whether *the evidence is good.* Is the evidence sufficient to convince the church of the guilt or innocence of the party accused? If it is, take it no matter where it is from. It would be a pretty spectacle for a man to remain in the church who had been seen reeling and trembling in drunkenness simply because no member of the church had seen him drunk.

5/1/60,vol.3,#18,pg.71

Query–Where did Cain get his wife, and who was she? We read from Gen 4.16 that he (Cain) went out from the presence of the Lord and dwelt in the land of Nod on the east of Eden. Shall we infer that he found his wife in the land of Nod, or was she cast out with him from the presence of God? I have never been able to satisfy myself upon this.

Answer–Josephus says, Cain took his wife with him, which is evidently true, as there was nobody living in the land of Nod when he went there. This circumstance is the foundation of one of Paine's difficulties. He says that the Bible represents Cain as obtaining a wife in the land of Nod, where it is evident there was nobody living. But the Bible does not say this. It simply says, that he there *knew* his wife," or, to express it plainly, *there lived with her as his wife.*

5/1/60,vol.3,#18,pg.71

Query–You will doubtless be surprised at receiving a communication from one who is entirely unknown to you. Be assured my dear sir, that nothing but motives of the most vital and intense interest could have actuated me thus to address you. My object is to elicit concerning the most important theme that has ever agitated the mind of man—a theme, when compared with all things besides, swallows them up into perfect nothingness, and dwindles them into nonentity. I allude to Christianity. Before stating my difficulty, it may not be improper to relate, briefly, the circumstances which led to this letter.

Heretofore I have lived a life of recklessness, profanity and ungodliness, neither believing nor disbelieving Christianity, for the simple reason that I never examined the Bible, that I might decide whether it was true or false. Consequently, I knew nothing, believed nothing and cared nothing about the subject. I had not failed, however, to note the vain wrangling, disagreeable conflicts and heated animosities of the different "evangelical churches of Christ," as they style themselves, which served only to prejudice me against religion.

Happening accidentally upon a number of your valuable paper, (three or four copies of which are taken here, among the subscribers to which I shall name, N.D. Clark, a highly respectable and wealthy citizen of this place,) I was deeply interested in the perusal of it's contents, for it suggested thoughts to my mind concerning religion which I had not before thought of.

Time passed away, and I thought no more on the subject, until a few weeks since, when one of your excellent and talented ministers, J.R. Lucas, visited us at the request of one of our citizens, and held a meeting of days. I listened with profound attention to every sermon he preached during his stay with us; and I will here add, that in him I found reasoning that I ever saw anywhere; and as an eloquent speaker and powerful pulpit orator, he ranks among the most gifted. The result of my attending these meetings, was a determination to "search the Scriptures," and ascertain, if possible, "whether these things be so." Accordingly I set to work, and on reading the four evangelists about six times, and comparing them closely, the following difficulties or contradictions appeared, to which I invite your special attention: 1. The account of Herod destroying all the children in and around Bethlehem, under two years old, is related only by Matthew; not one of the other three evangelists mentions it. Now, it seems to me that the importance and universality of this matter must have made it known to them all; and it would have been too striking to have been omitted by either of them. Matthew says Jesus escaped by being warned of an angel, and fleeing into Egypt; but John was then under two years old; he was left behind, and yet he fared as well as Jesus, who fled. 2. Concerning the superscription which was placed over Christ when he was crucified, no two of these writers agree in reciting it *verbatim*. Matthew says, "This is King of the Jews;" Mark gives it, "This is the King of the Jews;" Luke relates it, "This is the King of the Jews;" John records it, "Jesus of Nazareth, King of the Jews." Now it would seem reasonable, from these circumstances, that those writers were not present at the scene, and only got it from here say. The only one of the Apostles who seemed to have been there; and he was accused of being one of Christ's disciples, *"he began to curse and to swear, saying, I know not the man;"* yet we must believe this same Peter, convicted of perjury! 3. Mark tells us that he (Jesus) was crucified at the third hour; and John says it was the sixth hour. According to John, the sentence was not passed till about the sixth hour, or noon; but Mark expressly declares that he was crucified at the third hour, or 9 o'clock in the morning. See Mark 15.25 and John 19.14. 4. The history of the circumstances attending the crucifixion are related differently in these four books. Matthew says, (chapter 27, verse 45) "Now from the sixth hour there was darkness all over the land until the ninth hour." Again, "And behold, the veil of the temple was rent in twain from top to bottom; and the rocks rent, and the graves were opened, and many bodies of the saints which slept arose, and came out of the graves after his resurrection, and went into the Holy City and appeared to many." (verses 51, 52 and 53) Mark, in relating the circumstances connected with the crucifixion, makes no allusion whatever to the earthquake, the rending of the rocks, the graves opening, nor to the dead men being brought to life. Luke is also silent upon these points. But John, although he details all the circumstances of the crucifixion down to Christ's burial, says nothing about the darkness, the veil of the temple, the earthquake, the rocks, the graves, nor the dead men. 5. In reference to the resurrection, Matthew says, "In the end of the Sabbath, as it began to dawn toward the first day of the week, came Mary Magdalene and the other Mary, to see the sepulcher." Mark says it was sun rising, and John says it was yet dark. Luke says it was Mary Magdalene and Joanna, and Mary, the mother of James, and other women, that came to the sepulcher; and John says that Mary Magdalene came alone!

The book of Matthew proceeds: (verse 2) "And behold there was a great earthquake, for the angel of the Lord descended from heaven, and came and rolled back the stone from the door, and sat upon it." But the other books say nothing about the earthquake nor about rolling the stone back and sitting upon it; and according to their account, there was no angel sitting there. Mark says the angel was *within* the sepulcher, sitting on the right side. Luke says there were two, and they were both standing up; and John says they were both sitting down. But I fear I shall weary you. More might be added of the same character, but as an answer to the above will obviate all difficulty in regard to the balance, I will desist.

If you will have the kindness to remove these difficulties, by reconciling the contradictions, you will oblige one who is in serious trouble, and one who is halting and fluctuating between two opinions, hesitating whether to embrace Christianity or skepticism.

Answer—The gentleman who "lived a life of recklessness, profanity and ungodliness; neither believing nor disbelieving Christianity; for the simple reason that he had never examined the Bible that he might decide whether it was true or false." This, we think, is the "simple reason," not only why a great many live reckless and profane and ungodly, but why *they do not believe* the Bible. There can be no better reason why a man should "know nothing, believe nothing and care for nothing," than the simple circumstance that he had never "examined the Bible." Thousands, for the same reason, are in the same condition.

Though our friend claims to have read the "four evangelists through about six times," we have some lingering doubts whether he would have found the difficulties he introduces, if he had read these books over "six times" more, if he had not read, or heard some one talk who had read *another book*, of infinitely less merit. Unfortunately for us we obtained and read that *other book* when we were twenty years old. It is a book not often found upon center-tables, upon the book-shelf, either in the studio, private family or book-store. A deep and general sense of its unworthiness keeps it in some dark corner, and induces those who have read it, or obtained its difficulties second or third handed, if they present them at all, to do so without giving the author credit. We found these same difficulties, and many others, in the reading of this book, and doubt not that our friend, either directly or indirectly obtained them from the same source. But this has nothing to do with the difficulties themselves. 1. The circumstance of one historian recording a fact and another writing it, involves not the credit of the historians. We may not see the reason why one should mention it and the other omit it, yet the one may have had a good reason for mentioning it, and the other an equally good reason for omitting it. The fact that Matthew mentions it, is a very strong evidence of its truth, seeing that his narrative was published in Palestine, in all probability about eight years after the crucifixion, when *it could* and *would certainly* have been refuted, if the statement had not been unquestionably true. Thousands of people knew when his narrative was first, published, as certainly as they knew any thing, whether it was true, and to have refuted it would have overthrown his whole narrative and shown him to have been a most willful falsifier. This shows that the statement was certainly true and the people knew it.

The extent of territory included in the words, "in Bethlehem, and in the coasts around," was not very wide, and the fact was of sufficient note to be mentioned in a narrative to the Jews, or for them, especially as they claimed to believe the prophecies, but not of the same importance to any other people, or any other country.

The difficulty respecting John may be obviated in two ways: 1. He may not have been in the bounds described. 2. He being six months older than the Savior, may have been over two years old. Our friend must not be too eager to find difficulties as to *assume*, without any proof, that *John was in the specified bounds*, and that *he was under two years old*. These two points need proof, and a failure in either case obviates the difficulty. 2. The circumstance that the record of the inscription is not given in the identical same words, militates nothing against the credibility of the testimonies of the four witnesses, but on the other hand, makes the evidence more convincing, as it shows that there was no collusion. It is substantially the same as given by each of them; but some of them give it fuller than the others. John embraces the words, "Jesus of Nazareth," omitted by the others.

Where does the writer refer to when he says, "those writers were not present"—"the only one of the Apostles who seems to have been present was Peter?" Does he mean at the crucifixion, where the inscription, in the Hebrew, Greek and Latin languages, was posted up? Then others, beside Peter was there, and he is mistaken about the place of Peter's swearing. If he means while the Lord was in Pilate's court, then he is mistaken about the inscription, for it was not put up there.

5/59, vol.2, #22, page 86.

Query–Unless you can be more profitably engaged, I wish you would give through the REVIEW the distinctive difference between the words *only* and *alone*. The only difference I know of is this: When I make the assertion that "justification is by faith *only*," I mean that nothing but faith can possibly do it. When I make the assertion that "justification is by faith *alone*." I mean that faith, unaccompanied with any thing else is sufficient to ensure justification. I heard a Methodist minister a few days ago, argue the difference, or what he conceived it to be, but I did not understand him. Whether it was from a want of comprehension on my part, or clearness on his, I do not know. The question is, is there a difference beside the one I have given above, or am I wrong in that.

Answer–Our brother will see by the reference to James 2.17, 21, that the apostle uses "only" and "alone," in the same sense. Faith only and faith alone, mean exactly the same—"faith without works." See James 2.20.

8/26/62, v.5, #34, pg.2

Query–What ought to be done with sisters, that with axes, sledges, and hammers, and have broke their way into a grocery, and destroyed the liquors, and some other things found therein, and burned up the barrels that had contained the liquor. ? Please give your scriptural views of the matter and oblige.

Answer–The above are pretty tough questions, especially to "give any scriptural views of the matter." We recommend the following: 1. Teach these sisters *forbearance* with those who sell liquor to their husbands, sons, and other relatives, thus robbing them of their time, money, and honor, thus sinking them in shame and disgrace, showing them that the poor rum seller has no other means for a living—that he is too lazy to work, too proud to beg and has not the honor to conduct any other business. 2. Teach them *patience*, so as not to fret when their husbands, sons, and other relatives have been enticed into the rum shop, spent all their money and much of their time, at the same time neglecting their families, and been made beastly drunk, and kicked out at the door and into the gutter by the rum seller, and thus *endure hardness* as good soldiers and Christian women. 3. Explain to them that their organ of destructiveness has become enlarged so as to endanger the business of rum sellers and be greatly detrimental to the convenience of rum suckers. 4. Expostulate with them, showing that if they do not repent of their destructive habits, but continue to persist in it, awful consequences will be, that the country will soon be deprived of a rum shop; their husbands and sons will find no place to get strong drink and thus suffer for the *good creature*. 5. Explain to them farther, that if they persist in their destructive habits, confining them, as they do, to liquor establishments that in a short space, their husbands, sons and relatives will find no filthy doggery where they can crawl in, spend their precious time, when they ought to be at work to support their families, participate in obscene language and profanity, quarrel, stab, shoot, smite with the fist, kick, knock out teeth and gouge out eyes. Reason and expostulate with them, showing them that unless they repent and desist their destructive course, that *gentlemen* will be deprived of these precious entertainments and be in danger dying of *very thirst*. 6. That they fall not into similar offences in time to come, for the benefit of rum sellers and security to their property, get up a petition, circulate it among the citizens and get them to sign it, male and female, requesting them to *shut up shop, close the business*, and turn to some other calling, informing them benevolently that the ire of the "sisters with others," is being kindled and that there is danger ahead. 7. If these remedies do not succeed, we recommend that the husbands and fathers of these sisters move them into a better, more refined and elevated community, where there are no rum sellers and consequently where the temptation to their destructiveness is not in their reach, and, in this way, we think they may be saved. 8. If, however, any of them should prove impossible, we would recommend that some preacher of fine ability, unquestioned piety, and one who can give a "scriptural view of the matter," to devote "a sermon to the subject, pointing out to them the consequences if they persist, such as that it will ruin the rum-making business, the rum selling, the rum buying, rum drinking, the loafing about rum shops, etc., and in a short time we shall have no drunkards, much less disorderly conduct on the streets, few affrays, stabbing, shootings and fisticuffs, the business of the police, courts, lawyers and magistrates will be greatly curtailed. Men whipping their wives, abusing their children, neglecting their support, will be much fewer, the number in the houses of refuge, asylums and poor houses, will be greatly diminished. The *unpaying* practice of Physicians and all the other *unpaying* parties will be greatly curtailed. In one word, every business, no matter how profitable, founded on the rum traffic, and all *the proceeds* from it, of every sort, must inevitably be curtailed if their destructive sisters shall persist in their work of ruin.

Aside from all irony, we deliberately say that while no one can justify Christian sisters or brothers, in any such work as described in the above question, these sisters are not as far in the wrong, or as highly accountable before the Lord, as the men, in any town, where *they can,* in a legal way *stop the rum traffic, and have not the moral courage and manliness to do it.*

9/2/62 v.5, #35 p2.

Query–Does the fore part of Hebrews 6 justify the conclusion that a person, after apostatizing, is irretrievably lost?

Answer–The allusion to those whom it was impossible to renew again to repentance, was especially to those who turned away from Christ—from the gospel—and returned to the law. Those, in thus rejecting Christ, put him to an open shame, abandon him, turn away from the holy commandment delivered to them and do despite to the spirit of grace. For them, there remains no more sacrifice for sin, seeing they have rejected Christ the only sin-offering, and nothing remains for them but fiery indignation which shall devour the adversaries. There is a vast difference between this character, and the man who has been overtaken in a fault," surprised into sin, or partially led away by the enticements of the world, and neglected to some extent his obligations. Many of this description may be, and actually are brought back to their religious obligations, to their former appreciation and enjoyment.

9/2/62, v.5, #35, pg. 2

Query–Will you please tell us, through the REVIEW, what you think is meant by the seven spirits of God, spoken of in the Revelations, and oblige the Bible Class at this place.

Answer–We are of the opinion that the above is a little too tough a question for a Bible Class, as we know it is for us. We are yet spending much of our time on Matthew, Mark, Luke and John, Acts of the Apostles, and the Epistles, and only occasionally have time to look *so for over* in the book of Revelations. It is not very easy to tell what any spirit is, even our own spirit, much less the seven of the Apocalypse. It may be that some one else can tell. If so, we have the space....

1/6/63, v.6, #1, p.2

Query–For many weeks, or I could say months, for within the last 15 months our mail facilities have been suspended and welcome visits of the ACR and HARBINGER have failed to reach us as in other more peaceful days.(date: Feb. 9,1863, Civil War days. kdf.) I feel like crying to you as the anxious inquirer did who called to the watchman out of Seir, "Watchman, what of the night?" And as the watchman did, are you as ready to cry from Zion's watch-tower, "The morning cometh," and say what the signs of promise are? Surely, this must be an eventful period through which we are passing. A dark and gloomy hour overshadows us, whether portentous of evil, or pregnant of good, we wait to see. What think you of the signs of the times? Many interpreters of prophecy for a great number of years have pointed to this period as the time for the fulfillment of prophecy. Has the time come for all human governments to be extinguished, or rolled up as a scroll, and is the joyful hour at hand when the Sun of Righteousness shall come to reign as King of Kings, and Lord of Lords; or have we yet a long night through which we must pass before we see the bright dawning of a better day.

Answer–So far as the stupendous movements of the world are concerned in our great and once happy country, we know not where we shall land. The Lord knows. We are in his gracious hands and he will do right with us. We do not profess to have much foresight into these wonderful matters, nor are we making it our work at all to advise or try to control in the matter, any more than if a pestilence, hurricane, or tempest were raging in the land. We should, in that case, feel bound to do all in our power to alleviate the condition of those suffering from its consequences. Our mission is to take care of the church of God during the storm, and to call sinners to repentance. We have a kingdom that can not be moved; a kingdom not of this world. We have a government that can not be shaken. We have a king that is unerring. He is the Sun of righteousness. He is the King of kings and Lord of lords. We must keep our eye on him and do his bidding. We know not how long these trials are to be upon us. One thing we know, and that is, that we need not expect any permanent peace, comfort or happiness in this world. The people of God never have enjoyed any permanent rest in this world. They have been harassed by the wicked, driven from place to place, buffeted, their goods spoiled, destitute, afflicted and tormented. We know not when the end of these troubles shall be; but we know this, that all things shall work together for good to them who love God, the called according to his purpose, and that these light afflictions work out for us a far more exceeding and eternal weight of glory. Let us study to do the will of God, so that whether we sleep, live or die, we shall be the Lord's. We shall soon pass to where the weary will be at rest and the wicked shall cease from troubling. Let us pray that righteousness may prevail; that wicked men and all their wicked machinations may be put down; that peace and happiness may be restored. The Lord have, mercy on all the holy brethren and keep them in the love of God.

3/10/63, v.6, #10, p.38

Query–Please give your views on the following Scriptures: Matthew 11th chapter, and 11th and 12th verses. We are searching after truth. We differ as to when the kingdom was taken by the violent, and the violent took it by force.

Answer–We have no doubt that during the Savior's personal ministry was the time when the kingdom suffered violence, and when the violent are said to have taken it by force. The kingdom, in the life-time of Jesus, only existed in "the eternal purpose" of God, at one period—that is, his eternal purpose to establish the kingdom. At a later period it existed in the promise to Abraham, which really contained the Messiah, the Gospel, and the entire New Institution, in promise, not unfolded or explained, but in a secret, afterwards to be revealed. At a still later period, the kingdom existed in prophecy not understood or comprehended, and consequently in a mystery. It existed in the predictions of the prophets as good things to come, and not as good things already come, or for the people of that time. In the time of John the Immerser, it existed in the men through whom God would unfold it to the world; but in its full developed state, established form, clearly revealed and unfolded to the world, it was only "at hand." This was the state of the case in the Savior's life-time. The belief too, that the kingdom was at hand was general; but the popular idea was, that it would be an earthly kingdom—a splendid civil government, that the kingdom would be restored to Israel, as in the time of Solomon and David, only greater and more glorious. With this view they all pressed to into it; tried to find out to find out about it; the most violent were as clamorous as any, and, at one time, determined to take Jesus by force and make him a king. This is what we suppose was alluded to by the violent taking it by force. After they ascertained that *it was not of this world*, they abandoned it, and turned against the King and put him to death.

5/12/63, v.6, #19, p.74

Query–Upon what condition was a Gentile admitted to the privilege of a Jew? Did they have to be circumcised in order to be a proselyte of the gate?

Answer–The Judaizers among the first Christians maintained that the Gentiles "must be circumcised and keep the law of Moses." See Acts 15.5. Genesis 17.13, it will be seen that those purchased with Abraham's money, who were Gentiles, had to be circumcised.

5/5/63, v.6, #18, pg.70

Query–Although unknown to you by face, I have been one of your readers for the last two years, during which time I have learned that you are profound at unraveling knotty questions; I therefore take the liberty of presenting the following query, viz: If a man, by evocating primitive Christianity, Universal Liberty, Temperance, Congregational Independence, Christian Union and Education, is a man of *one idea?* What would a man be who advocates only a part of the above-named subjects? Would he be a man of less or more than *one idea?* Please answer this through the REVIEW, as many of your readers would like to be enlightened upon this subject, and oblige your brother in Christ

Answer-1. No one, that we know, says that a man who advocates all the above items, is a man of one idea. 2. The writer of the above appears to think that "primitive Christianity" does not include "universal liberty, temperance, congregational independence, Christian union, and education," hence he adds these to "primitive Christianity." 3. We do not think that the man who advocates all these is a man of one idea, but the man who hitches all these on for a *show*, and at the same advocates *but one*, and shows that he cares for none, only as they will answer for hobbies, is a hobby rider and a man of *one idea, if he has even that.*

1/4/59, vol.2, #1, page 3

Query—Who are the *two witnesses* spoken of in Rev 11.3? Please give us your views on this subject through the REVIEW.

Answer—We do not know. Some of the commentators think they are the Old and New Testaments. Some think they are Moses and Jesus. We have not got so far over in the book as that; we may some day.

10/59, vol.2, #42, page 167

Query—If a brother in full fellowship in the church refuses to partake of the Supper, and claims that there is no command for it, and maintains that all institutes ceased with the Apostles—that there is no necessity for baptism—that a man can be a Christian as well out of the church us in it—and walks uprightly. What is to be done with him?

Answer—Most certainly such a man can not remain in the church, or desire to do so. Put him out in the world where he belongs, and if he has a plan of living a Christian without keeping the ordinances, or ever belonging to the church, let him practice on his own plan. We have no such custom, neither has the congregations of the saints.

12/18/60, vol.3, #51, p206.

Query–In Matthew 24.3, we read, "Tell us when shall these things be? And what shall be the sign of thy coming and of the end of the world?" In looking at the answer, Christ gave to these questions, you will please let us know what you understand by the expression in the 14th verse of this chapter, "And then shall the end come." Also the 29th and 30th verses, and if this alludes to the final coming of the Savior, how can you reconcile the language of the 34th: "This generation shall not pass till all these things be fulfilled?"

Answer–We cannot go in depth on this matter but we think the expression, "Then shall the end come," refers to the final coming of the Savior and the end of time, or the end of the dispensation of grace. "This *generation*," is simply "this *race*," the Jewish race, "shall not pass away till all these things be fulfilled." The preservation of the Jews, as a nation, or distinct race, when all other nations are mingling and losing their nationality, so far bids fair to fulfill that idea, and we think the soundest and best criticisms justify the conclusion, that the Lord meant *this race*, and not the generation then living, or a period of thirty years. But we can not now give the subject any extended notice, nor quote authorities now.

12/58, vol.1, #49, page 195

Query–What course would be proper to pursue in regard to a young brother whose walk had been orderly for several years, but in the last year had fallen into bad company and become dissipated, being drunk and swearing on the street, and seen in that state by an officer of the church? Would it be right or scriptural on report of such officer and others to withdraw from the erring brother, without making an effort to turn him from the error of his way, because it was a public sin. Is there any Scripture for dealing thus? If so, please refer to chapter and verse. Please answer in the REVIEW.

Answer–The proper course would be, on hearing of the first instance of the young brother turning aside, for an overseer to see him and expostulate with him and try to reclaim him. Attention should be given to him constantly, and long before a year passes away, if he forsake not the error of his way, discipline should be enforced. It is a terrible thing to permit such a case to run on for a year, disgracing the church and cause at large. Still, every means possible should be used to induce him, as the offense was public, to make a public acknowledgment and promise of amendment before exclusion. But no such disorder should be endured for a year. It is a scandalous state of affairs when such grossly disorderly persons are permitted to pass without discipline for a whole year.

3/19/72 vol.15, #12, page 92.

Query—Will you please explain the following passage of Scripture: "For the gifts and calling of God are without repentance;" Rom 11.29. I want to know what those gifts and calling are on when bestowed, and for what purpose. If the gifts and calling are on when bestowed on one, why not on all.?

Answer—We presume that the gifts and callings alluded to in this scripture are such as apostolic and prophetic gifts, and not that they are bestowed upon *men who do not repent;* but that the purpose of God is immutable that he does not repent that he has bestowed these gifts in any case. Or when God calls a nation, or dispenses gifts to a nation, for a certain purpose, as he did to the Jews, his purpose is so immutable that he does not repent.

10/60, vol.3, #40, page 161

Query—It is a self evident fact, that an individual cannot be an adopted son of only one man at the same time. This being so, how can a man be a son of Temperance, and retain his son-ship with the Lord at the same time?

Answer—The above "self evident fact" is not evident at all, nor is it true; for a person may be an adopted son of some man, and an adopted Son of God, at the same time. I will now tell you how one "can be a Son of temperance and a son of the Lord at the same time," is the most plain case in the world. It is simply for a Son of Temperance to be adopted into the family of the Lord. He is still a Son of Temperance and a Son of God. We would advise the writer of the above query, not to trouble himself about the Sons of Temperance, as none will insist on him to become one, but by all means. What he surely is, *a man of temperance in all things,* would he will do well.

Western Reformer 1848, vol.6, # , page 34

Query—Is it lawful for Christians, when assembled for divine worship, to unite instrumental music with vocal in the worship of God?

Answer—Religious worship falls under three heads, viz moral, instituted and discretionary. 1. MORAL. Prayer is a moral duty, and the singing of praise appears to be so. Col 3.16. Psa 104.33. There may be appendages to moral duties which are *not morally obligatory*. Thus, under the Old Testament dispensation, incense was an appendage to prayer, and instrumental music to singing, but neither was of a moral nature. *No one says that it is* SINFUL NOT *to use instrumental music in divine worship*. 2. INSTITUTED. Instrumental music was instituted under the Old Testament dispensation. In the time of Moses were used the trumpet and coronet; David added many other instruments by the divine command. 2 Chron 29.25. *Instituted worship ceased at the death of Christ*. Instrumental music was not instituted by Christ or his Apostles; *"they sang a hymn."* Matt 26.30. Singing is not only a *moral duty;* but it is instituted under the New Testament. Eph 5.19. Col 3.16, etc. 3. DISCRETIONARY. When a moral or an instituted duty admits of being performed in a variety of ways, none of which are inconsistent with its morality or with the divine appointment, there is room for the exercise of discretion in the selection of the *mode* of performing it. Thus every church must judge for itself at what hour to begin public worship; what tunes to sing; how often singing shall be performed, and other similar circumstances. If *music* as a GENERAL TERM, were either a moral or an instituted duty, *instrumental* music, being included in it, *might be lawfully used*. But, under the gospel dispensation, *singing only—like immersion only*—being instituted, instrumental music—*like sprinkling and pouring*—is unlawful, because excluded. If it should be objected that we read in the Revelation of 'harpers harping with their harps," we answer, it is true; but we also read in that book of the golden altar, of the offering of incense as an appendage to prayer, and of other imagery borrowed from the Jewish dispensation. But no Protestant will argue hence that incense ought to be used in divine worship by Christians.

The above is copied from the English *Baptist Magazine,* published in London, in November, 1818. It would seem that the question considered agitated that denomination at the beginning of this century. We should like very much to know whether any immersionist attempted to answer the *argumentum ad hominom* the reply contained, and to see how any of *our brethren* can handle it without depriving himself of the use of the strongest critical argument he employs in defense of immersion as an instituted act. Will some advocate of instrumental music try it?

12/24/72, v.15, #52, p.402.

Query–Is it contrary to a professor of the religion of our Lord and Savior Jesus Christ, to belong to either the Odd Fellows or Free Masons?

Answer–We put Masonry, Odd Fellowship, etc., on the same footing as politics—we know nothing about them, and have nothing to do with them *in the church*. Paul said, "Circumcision is nothing and uncircumcision is nothing, *but a new creature*." That is, the grand matter, in Christ, or in the church, is to be *a new creature*. Masonry is nothing and Anti-Masonry is nothing; Odd Fellowship is nothing, and Anti-Odd Fellowship is nothing; *religiously*, nothing, not to be known, but the matter is, *to be a new creature*. We have never been inside of any of the secret societies of our country, but when those who have, or who will belong to them, become Christians, we are not to annoy them about these other organizations. If we can live better lives than they do, all right. Otherwise let alone and not trouble ourselves about their societies.

5/24/62, v.5, #25, pg.2

Query–Should Christians attend social parties, and participate in dancing and card-playing for amusement?

Answer–It speaks but poorly for religion when it is necessary to ask or answer such a question as the above for the sake of any religious community. Why do we not have questions like the following: Should Christians attend social parties, and participate in religious conversation, reading and singing sacred pieces for religious edification and improvement? For the good reason that nobody doubts the propriety of such social parties. We do not think that the holy faith of the gospel has made much impression on the heart where the *desire* still remains for dancing, playing cards, or theater-going. In such hearts the *world* has the ascendancy. Dancing, card-playing and theater-going members of the church are not only dead weights, but worse. They do the church more harm than they could possibly do if they were outside. We may preach, pray and weep till our hearts break and we are worn out, to try to save sinners over the pernicious influence such members, but all will be in vain. They will sink themselves and us with them if they remain in the church. Mere worldly establishments, depending on the increase from unconverted children, baptized into the church, as they style it, before they know their right hand from their left, may succeed with all the wicked machinations of the world in but a church depending upon turning the world to God by argument—by preaching the gospel and the good deportment of the members can not tolerate such things without sinking. Feasting, dancing and card playing is *revelry*.

1/27/63, v.6, #3, p.3

Query–Upon what condition was a Gentile admitted to the privilege of a Jew? Did they have to be circumcised in order to be a proselyte of the gate?

Answer–The Judaizers among the first Christians maintained that the Gentiles "must be circumcised and keep the law of Moses. See Acts 15.5. Genesis 17.13, it will be seen that those purchased with Abraham's money, who were Gentiles, had to be circumcised.

5/5/63, v.6, #18, pg.70

Query–In reply to a query some two months since, you stated through your paper, that there is Scriptural authority for the present custom of standing in prayer. Now this is just what I have long been searching for; for having to disregard the established custom of Christian congregations, and even the requests of worthy and aged ministers, is very unpleasant; but until the authority is produced, (which I have never been able to find,) I shall be compelled to dissent, though it may subject me to scorn and ridicule. For I choose to "obey God rather than man." Then by producing the desired authority, you will confer a lasting favor on your humble brother and fellow laborer in Christ.

Answer–"And when ye *stand praying*, forgive, if ye have aught against any; that your Father also who is in heaven may forgive your trespasses." Luke 11.25

10/20/63, v.6, #42, pg. 166

Query–Cannot the Missionary Society send a good and exemplary preacher to Portsmouth for one year. I feel certain that by proper effort the cause could be built up in Portsmouth. Oh, will the brethren neglect so important a place.

Answer–We did not see this till the Missionary meeting was over, and, therefore, it failed of its object. As the best that can possibly be done now, we lay it before our readers, and appeal to the brethren to assist in saving this meeting house. It is a genteel house, and in a place of much importance, and should by all means be saved. *One Hundred dollars more will save it.* The brethren in Portsmouth are poor and have done more than they will be able to do. They at present can do no more. A few small remittances will help them out. Will not brethren make remittances as directed above? Or, if sent to us, it will be faithfully appropriated. Brethren, think of this and enclose a dollar, or a half dollar, and help these brethren out of a tight place.

1/17/63, v.6, #46, pg. 182

Query–I would like much to hear your views, through the columns of the REVIEW, "on dancing, as a social amusement, by Christians or their children" wherein the evil is, if any, as it is a subject of much debate and argument at present. Should Christians countenance the same in their residences?

Answer–The arguments generally employed by the advocates of "dancing for amusement," so far as we are posted, are as follows: 1. There is no harm in it. 2. It is not as bad, or no worse, at most, than some other things that professors of religion do. 3. It teaches young people, especially young ladies, gracefulness and accomplishes them for society. 4. It is a healthful exercise. 5. If young people are not allowed to dance, they will be at something worse. This forms about the sum of the arguments, so far as we have heard, in favor of the practice. Let us, for a few moments, look at these items: 1. *There is no harm in dancing.* This is a singular commencement. Did you ever hear any one commence arguments to prove that it is right to visit the sick, by saying, "It is no harm?" Surely not. Why not? Because visiting the sick is not under suspicion. No one thinks it is any harm. It is of universal good report. There is no harm alleged against it by anybody. But dancing is not so. It is under censure. Many hold it to be an idle and worthless folly. Hence it commences with the plea, that "it is no harm." The very circumstances, that this suspicion hangs over it—that it is under censure—is a sufficient reason why a Christian should have nothing to do with it. It is not of good report, and that is sufficient for any pious person.

But when we are about to enter into anything good, we do not commence by saying, "There is no harm in it." When we are about to do any-thing, the question should not be, "Will it do any harm?" But we should inquire, Will it do any good? It is not enough to him, who considers his life worth anything, to know that a thing will do no harm. It may be simply useless; but people whose time is worth anything should not al-low it to be spent in that which is useless. One of the hardest sentences we ever heard uttered, and one that we have felt more upon since than any other, was contained in the sentence of a judge pronounced upon a murderer. In alluding to his life, he called it, "Your worthless life." What is so horrible, to any one capable of doing good, being useful and making the world happier and better, as the thought of being *worthless*. Yet there is not a clearer proposition in the range of human thought, than that he who does no good is worthless. Dancing, therefore, if it could be shown to be no harm, might prove *worthless*. On this hypoth-esis, gentlemen and ladies, whose time is worth anything, should not engage in it. If there are gentlemen and ladies, nay, more, *Christians*, to whom God has given time that is useless, or in which they can find nothing good to do, and they must necessarily while away this time in something useless, and dancing is found to be no harm, probably they had as well dance. 2. *Dancing is not as bad, or no worse, at most, than some other things that professors of religion do.* The idea running through this, then, is worse than that contained in the previous one. That proceeded on the score of innocence—on the plea that dancing is *no harm*. But this plea proceeds upon the admission that *it is no harm,* but *not so much harm* as some other things. The hypothesis appears to be, that professors of religion must do harm; and about the best they can do, is to *choose that which is the least harm*. Dancing, therefore, is piously selected as a practice of least harm! We cordially grant that there are worse things than dancing; but, at the same time, there are but few snares that will more readily catch the feet of young disciples, and lead them to ruin. 3. *It teaches young people, especially young ladies, gracefulness, and fits them for society!* We never saw a *teacher* of dancing yet that was a pious man, a de-vout member of the church, or one that took any interest in church, and but very few that could be induced to conduct themselves gracefully in church or any other place. The teachers of dancing, and dancers them-selves, we have found the most graceless, disorderly and disrespectful in churches, of any class we know, so far as our observation has gone. We know of no evidence of its being an accomplishment of any kind, for anybody, either saint or sinner. 4. *It is a healthful exercise.* To make serious reply to this deceitful, deceptive and empty pretense, is a little hard to do. To see a person who cannot go three squares to the house of God on foot, especially if it should be a little unpleasant, who can dance till midnight, "for amusement," speaking of its being *healthful*, is ridiculous in the extreme. It may be, for anything we know, that for any person who has become so useless as to sit, day after day, and not move enough to circulate their blood, dancing would prove healthful. But there are a thousand things better for them. A visit to the sick, to the poor and the distressed, with something for their necessities, would be vastly better for both soul and body. Almost any kind of useful labor would be more healthful, and leave vastly less remorse of conscious. But if a person has such an aversion to labor, to visiting the sick, the poor and needy, or doing anything useful, they deserve no health, and the world will only be the better off when they are out of it. More health, permanent happiness and real enjoyment are found in an industrious and useful life than all the seekers of pleasure ever knew. The man of useful life has no time for pleasure and amusement. His time is taken up, wholly taken up, and he is so happy in it, that it appears short, in constant acts of usefulness. But pleasure-seekers are constantly devising how to while away time, to pass it off or murder it. Time appears the greatest burden they have, through their whole life, and, at death, the trouble is, that they have not more time. The good man appears pressed through life to do the good he desires to do, but when death comes, his work is done, well done, and he dies in hope of hearing the Lord say, "Well done, good and faithful servant; enter thou into the joys of thy Lord." 5. *If young people are not allowed to dance, they will be at something worse.* This does not proceed upon the principle, that young people are to do any good, perform any good work or be of any service. Nay worse; it proceeds upon the principle, that they must be of necessity do something bad, and if they do not dance, which is bad, they must do something worse. But this is not the case. Young people have their sphere in life, and can do good in that sphere. But before they will know useful enjoyment, they must realize the truth, that usefulness and happiness go hand in hand. The happiest life is that spent in doing good; and it terminates in the happiest death.

There is one trouble in writing for dancers. They do not read, and we never expect them to hear anything that we say. Besides, the most of them, with whom we have been acquainted, do not pretend to think whether it is *right* or *wrong*. They will dance because *they will*. That is an end to all reason and all law. But we put one matter to all that encourage dancing in any form. Did you ever know a pious, zealous, praying Christian that was a teacher of dancing?

We do not believe you ever did. Did you ever know a pious, zealous, praying Christian that was, at the same time, a dancer? We do not believe you ever did. Did you ever know a pious, praying parents who felt deeply concerned for the souls of their children, who desired them to dance? We do not believe you ever did. Are not all the more pious, zealous and prayerful of professors opposed to dancing? You know they are. This ought to satisfy any one seeking for the will of God. Are not the teachers of dancing, and the dancers, the giddy, the thoughtless, lighthearted and irreligious? Why do members of the church, when they have been to the dance, absent themselves from the Lord's table, take the back seats and generally refuse to participate in worship? Only from a consciousness that they have done wrong. Why do people of the world throw it in the face of the preacher when the members dance? Because they know that it is a stigma upon the church.

More apostasies among the young people commence with dancing, than any one folly with which we are acquainted. When they have taken one step, the way is paved for taking another. Dancing-masters would not only ruin our young people, but they dance upon our graves! In our cool, deliberate and most decided judgment, a more worthless set of men cannot be found prowling through respectable society than dancing-masters. If parents wish bitter repentance, deep sorrow and most solemn mourning over the follies of their fair daughters, we know of no more certain road to it, than to countenance those graceless butter-tongued, and useless, and worse than useless, men, who propose to teach dancing. There is infinitely higher happiness for our fair daughters, a higher road for them to travel, and transcendently nobler company than that found on the floor among a company of men and women, skipping over the floor like a flock of monkeys. We do not believe that any one truly acquainted with Jesus *desires to dance.* If young people belonging to the church dance, expostulate with them kindly, and give them to understand that they must cease.

1/26/58,v.1,#4, pg.14

Query–Is it right for members of Christ's body to join any of the secret societies of the present day?

Answer–The Church should not have any to do with such questions. In

Christ we know nothing about Masons, Odd Fellows, Good Templars etc. The church will be kept in continual confusion, if we are to be annoyed with questions about these societies. A man may be a Christian and be a Good Templar, an Odd Fellow or a Mason, or be a Christian and not be one. We have no use for any of these societies, for if a man is a Christian in the full sense, he has all the good there is in any of these, or all of them. But the question whether a man shall join any one of these societies, is no Church question, but a mere question of propriety and expediency, which every man has the right to decide and must decide for himself. If aside from this, a man has been constituted a Christian, and lives a Christian life, it is meddlesome ness, factionism, and mischief making to interfere with him simply because he belongs to one of these societies. Let those who do not belong to any of these societies, live better lives, show more piety and devotion to the cause, give more for its support, and thus show that they are better without these societies than the others are with them and they will do vastly more good than they can by creating contention in the Church on account of others joining.

7/28/63,v.6,#30, pg. 118

Query – Is it right for a minister or preacher of the Gospel to put on regalia or badge worn by some of the secret societies, and wear it while he is preaching, especially on the occasion of a funeral, or at any other time while he is representing the Church?

Answer – As to wearing regalia, many act simple and render themselves ridiculous in that way as well as in any other. Men do such things as unbecoming, little and childish, against which more wise and prudent persons might advise and persuade them; but it is showing greater weakness and folly than theirs, to create contention in the Church on account of their foibles. Great allowance must be made for the weakness, childish and frivolousness of the preachers who love these poor little worldly shows.

7/28/63,v.6,#30, pg. 118

Query – You say as to 11.16–17 of Jeremiah, The House of Israel therein mentioned, means nothing but the family of Israel, of the blood descendants of Abraham. But is it not true that they were nothing more, for it is plain that they were also God's Church. See Acts 7.38 "This is he that was in the Church in the wilderness." You say it is ridiculous to say and were sprinkled of him in Jordan. You also say that it is ridiculous for John to say, "I immerse with water. But there is one coming after me, he shall immerse you with the Holy Ghost." For further proof to establish our position concerning this olive tree, I propose to prove that God never established but the one Church, and that the same Church is in existence at this day. I see discussions in the REVIEW of less importance, therefore I am satisfied that you will comply with my proposition.

Answer–1. Stephen does not call it "God's Church," but, when translated into English, "the congregation in the wilderness," consisting of the blood descendants of Abraham, and nobody else. They were not in that congregation by faith, for many of them had no faith, nor by circumcision, for many of them had never been circumcised, but they were in that congregation, or the nation of Israel by virtue of a mere blood relation. 2. John never did say, "I immerse *with* water," when fairly translated, any more than "immerse *with* Jordan," or "immerse *with* Enon," but "I immerse *in* water"—"immerse *in* Jordan"—"immerse *in* Enon"—"he shall immerse *in* the Holy Spirit." 3. We suppose that our good friend intends to prove that the "congregation in the wilderness," Acts 7.38, is the church now in existence, and that God never established any other. This will strike out the church alluded to in the words, "On this rock *I will build my church,*" Matt 16.18, for it was not built when the Lord said this. That old "church or congregation, in the wilderness," or that was forty years in the wilderness, is in existence now, meeting in synagogues, on Saturdays, or Sabbath days, refusing to eat swine, and denying Christ, but our friend does not belong to it, nor would Christ benefit him if he did. We would, therefore, recommend him to undertake to prove some less ponderous and more profitable proposition than the one proposed by him. When he can prove that the Jewish Church, the Methodist Church, and the Church of Christ, all now visible on earth, are one, but one, and the same and identical, he can succeed in proving his proposition, and not before.

11/24/63, v.6, #47, pg.188

Query–Is it right for us as the followers of Christ to open the doors of the Church for political and Temperance Speakers who blaspheme the name of *God*, after which have a tune played by the brass band? Now if this be the way Christ intended his house to be used, I should like to be cited to the "Thus saith the Lord" for it, and I will comply with such with cheerfulness.

Answer–There is nothing in the material in a meeting house any more sacred than the material of a dwelling house, though the associations are different. A meeting house, however, is owned by the church, which knows nothing of politics, and has in it persons differing widely in politics. It always hurts the feelings of pious church members to have political speakers opposed to themselves, speak in their house. There are some pious church members who take a little of "good creature," whose feelings are greatly wounded by "political temperance speakers," and, upon the whole, it is generally, it is generally more prudent to keep all such meetings out of the meeting house.

We are perfectly aware, that there are some political speakers and temperance speakers, unfit to speak anywhere, but we find Christians endorsing the temperance speakers, if they are good Templars, and Christians endorsing the other, if politics are of *their own kind*. But they can not bear a temperance speech in a meeting house, if they have a dram, or a political speech if it differs from their politics.

We belong to no temperance society but the church and take no pledge but the Bible; but we preach and practice temperance as strict as good Templars. Temperance lecturers, some times, use blasphemous language and expressions unbecoming, but they never wound us in speaking *on temperance.* We prefer keeping politics out of preaching entirely, and think it profitable not to have political speaking in our meeting houses. But we are not so delicate on this matter, as to refuse to worship in the meeting house because a political speech had been made in it, even though opposed to our politics. The love of God and the Spirit of Christ are absent when church members become so huffy about these matters. It is a great thing to try to live In love and peace and maintain the unity of the Spirit and hold our religion above everything else.

1/21/67, vx, #3, pg. 21

Query–I notice that you answer queries in your paper, and, as I think, satisfactorily. I, therefore, thought I would mention to you a matter that has been troubling me for some time. When I was baptized (I have often feared since) I was not in a proper spirit. I went forward with a full determination to obey the Lord in all his appointments;

but on the morrow, seeing my husband opposed to it, I began to regret that I had so grieved him; but I would not, of course, decline. So I went ahead, almost faltering between two opinions. Now the question is this: Am I truly a Christian? It is now going on seven years since I was immersed, and the matter still troubles me. I have always been in the church since my baptism, and always attended when I could. I love the Lord with all of my heart, and have still tried to live closer to the Lord. My husband is still against me, and would still be glad if I would join with him, no doubt. Do not understand me to say, or intimate, that I am sorry I ever obeyed the Lord. I am only sorry that I was not in a better state of mind, and spirit when I obeyed the Lord. What I did, I did voluntarily, and I have tried to be faithful since I became a member of the church.

Answer—As a matter of course, we can tell nothing about cases of this kind any more than others. The revealed will of the Lord in the Bible, is the only source of light in all such matters. So far as we can comprehend the case, we can see no reason why this sister should feel in doubt or perplexity. When she was baptized, she believed with all of the heart, turned to God with full purpose of heart, and submitted voluntarily. The circumstance of the move not being agreeable to the husband, as a matter of course, would produce some little unpleasantness, but could not invalidate the profession made. When the first Christians lost their homes, their friends, their property and, as in many instances, were banished to strange countries, to desolate islands of the sea, for their profession, it produced much trouble, many sore trials and wonderful afflictions, but did not invalidate their profession. The trial of making a profession, in opposition to those we love, or the trial of going contrary to their will or the will of God, displeasing them or the Lord, is, to a person of proper feeling, a very great one, especially when it comes to the woman going contrary to the will of her companion. In the very nature of the case, such a step cannot be taken without unpleasantness. But in all such cases, it is a settled matter, that every accountable being must act freely, and not by constraint. The action in religion must be voluntary. All individuals have the right to act for themselves. We, then, should reason as follows, in such a case as the above mentioned; 1. It was, unquestionably, her right to resolve and act for herself according to her own light and understanding. 2. She was then, and is still, satisfied that she had the proper faith and repentance. 3. She went into her profession with a determination to obey and serve God. 4. She has been trying honestly to serve God ever since.

Why may she not, then, claim the promise of God, and, in full assurance of faith, come to God, trust in God, call upon him and enjoy the hope of the gospel? Our advice to her, is not to trouble about the past, at all, but to look to the present, and study now how to live devotedly, piously and truly in the service of the Lord. Many persons think of something done without a full understanding many years ago, and feel as if they wish to do that over again, with a better understanding. But the understanding the most of the first Christians had was that Jesus was the Lord, that Christianity was true, and that they could not be saved unless they submitted to it. The matter with her, and all sisters whose husbands are not in agreement with them, is to commend Christianity to them in their lives, showing them that Christianity has made them better, that they trust in the Lord, call upon him, love their husbands, love their children, and, in all respects, are better and happier since they are Christians. We hope our sister will trust in the Lord, call upon the Lord daily, if she has children, pray with them and for them. How many mothers there are now, *whose children never heard them pray!*

8/24/58, v.1, #42, pg. 134

Query–By what means do we learn that our sins are remitted, by the word, or by a direct revelation?

Answer–There are now no direct revelations. He who turns the hearts of the people to looking to direct revelations, or immediate revelations, or *new* revelations from God, for the evidence of pardon, or anything else, deceives them, and turns their hearts away from *divine evidence* to a delusion. The promise of the Lord contains evidence of pardon. "He who believes and in immersed *shall be saved*," or pardoned. When the penitent believer has been immersed, he has the promise of the Lord for pardon. If he will not believe that, he need not go to the Lord for a new revelation.

The immersion in the Holy Spirit and in fire was not to be administered by man, and man can not administer it. The immersion of John is done away, as all of any intelligence or note admit. The immersion of the commission, was to be administered by man. The apostles were to teach all nations *immersing them* into the name of the Father, and of the Son, and of the Holy Spirit." "Into the name" amounts to the same as "into

Christ," "into one body." It is the initiatory rite into the new institution. As long as any are to be initiated, it will continue, and is, therefore, the one immersion of Paul.

2/5/67, v.x, #6, pg. 45

Query–Has not the 21 chapter of Luke, beginning with 25th verse, reference to the second coming of the Lord? And when he comes to the 32nd verse, he says: "Verily I say unto you, this generation shall not pass away till all be fulfilled." Has he not reference to the generation that shall live to see those signs previous to His coming, and shall not pass away, until all be fulfilled?

Answer–We doubt not the coming alluded to here is the second coming of the Lord, which has not yet transpired, at the resurrection of the dead. "This generation," simply means "this race"—the Jewish race or nation—shall not pass away, or lose the nationality, till all these things be fulfilled. In accordance with that prediction, that race continues, or has not yet passed away, and, shall not till the Lord comes.

1/7/62, v.5, #1, pg.3

Query–Do I understand you to be opposed to the missionary work of our state and others, or merely to the organization of such societies?

Answer–We do not desire any brother to understand us to be opposed and have been incessantly engaged in missionary work for thirty-one years, and we are engaged in it now as much as at any former period, both in our personal efforts in the field and the labor of a continual correspondence with preachers desiring fields of labor and brethren desiring to employ them. It is not *missionary work* to which we are opposed, but empty plans, schemes and organizations, after sectarian models, which have proved failures; expensive, cumbrous and lamentable failures in *doing missionary work*, filling our publications with speeches, reports and resolutions, as also unpleasant controversies, and discouraging the brethren. From the day we entered the faith of Christ till now, we have been unwaveringly for missionaries, missionary men and missionary work, and were never more so than we are now. The work of evangelizing the world is of transcendent importance. Indeed, we do not see how a man can be a *living Christian* and not be a missionary, and decidedly for missionary work, or, which is the same, for the evangelization of the world. But we keep in our mind a clear distinction between *mission work* and so-called *missionary societies*, which have proved failures in doing the work; between genuine *missionary men* and *mere society men*. The missionary men either go into the field of work, or contribute of their substance to support those who go into the field and work and many of them do both. We do both. We are not at home in a fine editorial chair, with a cigar or pipe in our mouth, opening the letters and telling others how and where to work; but we are in the field, reading and writing about five hours a day, visiting and talking as many more hours, and preaching on an average a sermon and a half a day from one end of the year to the other, and then, besides all the labor of correspondence, procuring places for other preachers, specially our young preachers, we give more than two hundred dollars a year of our hard earnings to sustain others. Please pardon these lines. They are in self defense, in view of the effort being made to get the impression that we are not for mission work. We are trying to show our faith by our works, and thus make a record that will stand in the day of judgment.

We are for the *missionary men* in Kentucky, our dear brother's state, who are in the field *doing the work*, for the *missionary work* which they are doing, and for those who are sustaining them in this good and noble work. We are for the same sort everywhere else. But we are not for the *society men*, who *stay at home*, except on anniversary occasions, perform-ing little or no missionary work, but *talking* and *writing* about mission-ary societies, and trying to prove that those of us in the field all the time are not missionary men. Men who are *missionary men indeed*, can find plenty of missionary work, and should be at it all the time either in person or sustaining some other person. But there is one thing certain, viz: That we can not all *stay at home* and evangelize the world. We can not in every instance send some *one else*. We must *go ourselves*. A little talk favorable to *societies*, and now and then a donation for societies, may ease the consciences of men who should be in the field, but will not make much show in the last judgment.

Our brother is, in the true sense, a missionary man, in the field, in his advanced years, and if we understand it, largely at his own charges. The Lord bless him and all like him, honestly laboring to spread the gospel and save men. We want *missionary work,* and not *societies.* We want living, working churches, preachers and members, as the Lord ordained, and not societies, as the Lord did not ordain. The brethren in Kentucky, if we understand them, are aiming at this, and coming to it.

3/12/67, v.x,#11, pg. 84

Query–Is it scriptural to eat the flesh of swine?

Answer–Touching eating meat, Paul says, "Every creature of God is good and nothing to be refused if it be received with thanksgiving." 1 Tim 4.4

3/5/67, v.x, #10, p.76

Query–Will you please favor me with an article on the subject of *Dancing*. Does the word of God tolerate it or forbid it?

Answer–We feel more like our labor is lost in writing on dancing than almost any worldly folly of our time, for the following reasons: 1. Dancers rarely read any religious publications. 2. They do not care what we write, nor even what the Bible says.

There are some, however, who are not *dancers,* but who have been incidentally, and in an evil hour, led into the dance, who love the Savior, tremble at his word, and will listen to friendly reasoning, expostulation and entreaty. 1. There are but few persons who dance *merely for the dance,* or for the *exercise* obtained in it. A person does not go into a room alone and dance! Why not? A person could dance as well alone as before a company, and get as good exercise. But a dancer would not thank you for a dance in a room alone. Why? Because something more than the dance is desired. Put a company of young men into a parlor alone, or young ladies alone, and tell them to dance, and they would not thank you for the privilege. Give them the music into the bargain, and they still would not go forty rods for it. Why? Because the main thing is wanting. What is wanting? The *men and the women in the dance together,* in the general whirl, *clasping hands, shuffling feet together, embracing and kissing!* This is the exercise that is sought, so conducive to health and gracefulness! Those who delight in this healthful, graceful, and innocent exercise, inquire, softly and pleasantly, "What harm is there in dancing?" "Where is the Scripture against dancing?" Many flexible preachers reply: "It is no worse than playing sister Phoebe, or many other things that are done." We answer too, that it is no worse than many other follies, sins and transgressions, which lead to ruin. Still, feasting, drinking, and dancing to music is reveling, and the word of God says, "Those who practice such things shall not inherit the kingdom of God." The companies in which dancing is practiced, are full of levity, jesting and foolish talking. They are invariably accompanied with feasting, and almost invariably drinking and swearing. There is no word in the English language will express the whole thing so well, or that comes so near being a proper name for it as *reveling*. The common manner of speaking of it, simply speaking of *dancing* is evasive, avoiding much of what is done. When a father or mother is thinking of permitting daughters to attend these places, they should not be deceived, nor allow their daughters to be deceived, by mere talk about *dancing*. That is folly and worse than mere folly; but that is not all, nor the half. The dance is merely the means of reaching something else more desirable. All that trouble and expense are not merely for the *dance*. The dance itself is only a means of reaching another object.

Does the reader reply, that respectable people dance, and teach their children dancing as an accomplishment? They do sometimes, we are sorry to be compelled to admit. They go to the theater, the race, fairs, and even and gambling saloons, and many of them are lovers of pleasure more than lovers of God. Many of these are on their way to ruin. Must our sons and daughters be permitted to follow these through their follies, their mirthfulness and pleasure-seeking, down to the bottomless pit? The voice of love and warning from heaven is against all this. The voice of God, the love of God, the warnings of God; all the threatenings of heaven are against all this. The very place, the associations, all the surroundings of these reveling companies are simply and manifestly irreligious. Who ever read of a *pious dancing master?* We care not who talks of his "gracefulness," his "politeness," his "accomplished manners," etc, etc. We have never seen one that we could keep in order in the house of God, to say nothing of his being *religious*, or *pious*. The dancing masters and their admirers are the notables who grumble if the preacher of Christ addresses his audience over twenty or thirty minutes. They are the gentry that are bored with "long service." They are the refined *elite*, who complain of "dry sermons," "tedious preaching," and that push out of the church as if they were escaping prison, and walk away, "I did think that man would preach all day!" They too, can turn up the lip, if a few dollars are needed for the support of religion! But they never grumble a word to be kept in the ball-room till midnight, nor to pay $10 for the expenses of one night. These are the folks who say "It is no harm to dance!"

Who ever knew a pious dancer? Who ever knew of a pious and devoted member of the church who loved the dance? Who ever, thought of such a thing as the love of God dwelling in a person, who loves the feasting, drinking profanity, the downright foolishness; the whirl and twirl, shuffle and scuffle; the prancing, skipping and scampering, the promiscuous hugs squeezes and kisses of the ball-room? Day and night, light and darkness, heaven and hell, are not more unlike than the ballroom and the sanctuary of the Lord. The one is the place for sensual pleasures and the other for spiritual enjoyment, the one is the development of the spirit of the world, the carnal mind and the lusts of the flesh, and the other the development of the character of Jesus and the spirit of God. They are perfect antipodes.

If the people of the world, please to dance, we have nothing to say. They are of the world, and seeking *of the world*, food, gratification and satisfaction, for an inner man, created in the image of God. This, they will never find. Those who love those merely sensual gratifications, worldly follies and amusements, whether in the church, or out of it, *are simply of the world*, and if they are to continue in the practice of all these follies, they ought not to corrupt and disgrace the church, nor to deceive themselves by remaining in it. It is transcendently less censurable to at once, or throw off the mask; away with all profession, and go out of the church and into the world, thus letting all know that no pretense is made to religion, but that a man is out in the broad road to interminable ruin, than to be in the church, without any piety or love for the Savior.

4/2/67, vx, #14, p.108

Query–SOCIETIES—Why can not societies be formed for the promotion of religion, morally, intelligence and true politics? We have agricultural societies and fair, societies for the promotion of arts and trades, but societies for the highest things we have not. We are groveling among the lowest things of this world, and forget the highest.

Answer–Have we not already *societies* almost without number? We should like to know in reason's sacred name, what kind of a *society* the writer of the above would have that he may not find. Among all these societies the Lord has one, and if this zealous friend of societies would rise higher, and do something noble, it strikes us that he might find room for all his zeal and benevolence in that old fashioned society called the church of the living God.

4/1/62, v.5, #13, p.2

Query—What do you think of a person who has been baptized when quite young, who did not repent and realize the need of Jesus Christ before being immersed? I fear I have not started right in this great work, which makes me unhappy.

Answer—Without the faith of Christ, the repentance required in the gospel, a realization of the need of the Savior, immersion is no more to a person than sprinkling water on the face of an infant. It is the faith in Christ, the repentance to life that makes immersion into the name of the Father, and of the Son, and of the Holy Spirit, valid. Without the realization of our lost condition, our need of the Savior, full confidence in union, as our only hope and Redeemer, neither immersion, prayers, communion, or membership in the church are anything. Without faith it is impossible to please God. He who comes to God must believe. If the writer of the above had not the faith and the repentance required in the New Testament, the way is clear. The work is to be commenced at the first by believing in the Savior, repenting and being immersed.

4/9/67,v.x #15, p.117

Query—Is it necessary to give the right hand of fellowship to induct one into a certain congregation?

Answer—We do not say it is necessary, or at least indispensable to receive them by extending the right hand of fellowship. The practice in this particular is not uniform. The practice most general is for all the members to come forward and extend the hand. In some instances the officiating brother extends the hand on behalf of the church. In St. Louis the whole church rise to their feet, while the officiating brother, on behalf of the church, gives the hand accompanied with a few impressive words of advice and exhortation. The precise form of recognizing members, when introduced into a particular congregation, is not a matter of special importance, and is therefore not prescribed in the law of the Lord. Where the brethren are trying to become a little fashionable and aristocratic, they do not like to come forward *themselves* and give the hand. When they are full of the love of God, and not paying much attention to what they call "style," they like very well to come *themselves* and give the hand specially to poor, cast down and heart-broken of the earth. They love to give them a cordial greeting a hearty welcome to the church and all within it. We notice, in many churches, the sisters not only give the hand, but many of them greet those of their own sex also with a holy kiss. We love to see members received with such a cordiality as to make them feel welcome. In many places, after the audience is dismissed, the members gather around persons who have come out, and give the hand and bid them Godspeed.

4/16/67, v.x, #16, p.125

Query–Is it right for parents, or other instructors to teach little children to pray or to say prayers? Is it right for us to instruct children of any age to pray, prior to coming into the kingdom?

Answer–This question may be answered by asking some other question. Which comes first, becoming a Christian, or the practice of a Christian? Which comes first, the worship which is in the body of Christ, or coming to Christ and entering the body? Which should we teach children first, the way into Christ, or to worship as if they were in Christ? Evidently, not only children, but all others, should be taught first how to become Christians, how to worship as Christians. Why not teach the children to commune before they are in Christ? Because the communion is in the body and for the members of the body. The same is true of all acts of worship. They are all for the children of God. The first thing to teach children is, how to come to God—how to become children of God; how to be constituted worshipers. Then teach them to worship in spirit or in truth.

3/18/67, v.x,#13, p.52

Query–We are somewhat troubled here with Spiritualists. They claim that the amount of transfiguration is a model circle—four spirits in the flesh and two out of the flesh, conversing together, this showing that spirits can come back and hold converse with the living. Those that Christ cast out, they claim, were bad spirits—thus arguing that good and bad spirits go where they please. We wish your explanation on this for we need light. Please give it through your paper.

Answer–1. We put it to these persons to say squarely whether they believe the Bible. If they do not, they have no business with the transfiguration. We know nothing about that event aside from what the Bible says. If they believe the Bible then, we show that they are necromancers and that Moses punished such with wrath and that Jesus excludes these from the kingdom of God. 2. If they do what they say they do receive communications from the dead; they are what the Bible styles necromancers, witches, wizards, sorcerers, persons possessed with unclean spirits and ought to be utterly rejected by all good people. If they do not what they say, they are lying pretenders and ought to be rejected. 3. In the mountain of transfiguration who was the medium, the rapper, table-tipper? Our Lord was there, spoke for himself, but acted no part of the medium. Peter, James and John were there, but not engaged in the stupid tricks, the shameful and disgraceful manifestations of table-tippers. They were there as witnesses of the grandest event in sacred history. They were there in the flesh, but not under the influence of demons, or spirits of dead people, good or bad, but as witnesses of Jesus.

Moses was there not speaking through some spirit medium, tipping tables, producing raps, or untying some man bound with a cord, nor in any of the silly tricks of the spirit, circle; nor in the dark, but in open daylight; not in *body*, but in *person*. Yes, Moses was there, identified as much as when he was here in the flesh, fifteen centuries after he died, saw, heard and conversed with our Lord, on the stupendous events shortly to occur in Jerusalem. He was not in the body for Christ was the first-born from the dead of every creature, and this event was before he rose from the dead. Yet Moses was there, not peeping and muttering, through some miserable medium, tipping tables, rapping, making music on some instrument in the dark, making tables, chairs, etc., dance around a room; not in the circle of spiritualists, who deny their Savior and the Bible, but in a conversation on the sufferings of Jesus soon to occur. He was not there *invisible,* but *visible;* not tipping nor rapping, but talking *audibly* ; not performing insignificant tricks, but acting the dignified man of God, in company of the Mediator of the better covenant, upon better promise.

Elijah was there, not in the flesh; nor separated from the body, but in the spiritual, immortalized and glorified body, in the presence of three eyewitnesses of Jesus, a specimen of redeemed, immortalized, glorified and happified humanity. God took him for ought we know, for this very occasion, without ever dying, that he might thus exhibit him glorified before three witnesses of Jesus.

This was a grand occasion. Three selected witnesses of Jesus were present. Jesus was glorified in their presence. They saw him in divine majesty as we would see him now, if we were standing before the throne in heaven. Here, at his side, stands the Mediator of the Old Covenant,

244 | *Queries & Quandries*

recognizing the Mediator of the Old Covenant. By his other side stands the old prophet, who had been gone from the earth for ages past, for God took him from the east bank of the Jordan. They are in conversation with Jesus about the momentous events about to occur in Jerusalem. What a sublime grandeur there was in this transcendently glorious scene. Moses could point to the Messiah, and exclaim to Peter, James and John "there is the prophet to whom I pointed you fifteen centuries ago, whom the Lord your God should raise up of your brethren, like to me. Elijah could also say, "here stands the Prophet of the prophets, of whom I spoke ages past." The feeble men in the flesh are overcome with the grandeur of the imposing scene, and one of them exclaims, not knowing what he is saying, "Master, let us make three tents, one for thee, one for Moses and one for Elijah."

The man whose mind is sufficiently carnal to lower this grand scene down till he can see nothing in it but spirit circle, and compose it to these modern jugglers, should fear to take the immaculate name of Jesus into his corrupt and unhallowed lips. Have not the lying pretenses of Spiritualists been refuted times without number? Look at the following: 1. Did not Horace Greely offer them $500 a week during the Crimean War for the war news in advance of the mail? Did they furnish the news? They did not. During our late war, (the Un-Civil War kdf.) their lying pretenses were all over the North. Where and when did they ever furnish intelligence in advance of the dispatches? If they can not reveal the events transpiring in this world, what reason have we to credit their shallow pretenses in reference to the world of spirits? 2. The assumption that they can call up spirits at will, and any spirits that may be named, involves the idea that they are not local beings, but omnipresent, and know everything! Who believes this? 3. The pretence that they can answer questions simply propounded *mentally*, or only *asked in the mind*, assumes that spirits are omniscient and know the thoughts of men as God does. It is as silly a farce as Romanists of a half dozen continents, all praying to the Virgin Mary, as if she were omnipresent, so as to hear all these prayers. 4. Admitting that they have communications with spirits how do they know that they are the spirits they claim to be? They admit that there are *lying spirits*. Could not a spirit pretend to be a father, mother or child, that was not, and deceive them? Do they reply, that they speak of things that nobody but the father, mother or child knows? How do they know that? They assume that spirits know the thoughts of the living. If they know your thoughts, they could get the things from *your own mind*, that you have been gulled to think came from your father. How do you know it is the devil himself dealing with you? We know one thing about it, viz.: That whatever the influence may be, fleshly or spiritual, of this world or *hades*, of man or the devil, it leads men and women to despise Moses and the prophets, Jesus and the apostles, the confessors or martyrs, the Bible and the church; it severs husband and wives, parents and children, leads to licentiousness and insanity. It has not made a man or a woman better on the face of the earth. It has not reformed a single community on the footstool of God. It is as base as any form of infidelity ever known. It is as degrading as drunkenness. Their silly and pretensions to answer questions are as false as Satan. A "writing medium," proposed to us to answer any question we might propound *mentally*. We wrote the question on a slip of paper. "When did my mother die?" He was at his table writing answers, but did not see the question, and wrote "Yes," for an answer. We wrote: "Of what disease did my mother die?" He again wrote the answer, "Yes." We continued, till we wrote some forty questions, such as could not be answered by a *yes* or *no*, not one of which was answered. Our mother, at the time was not dead. Look at the following Scriptures: "And when they shall say to you, Seek to them that have familiar spirits and to wizards that peep and that mutter; should not a people seek to their God? For the living to the dead? To the law and to the testimony: they speak not according to this word, it is because there is no light in them." Isaiah 8.19. "Now the Spirit speaks, that in the latter times some shall depart from the faith, giving heed to seducing spirits and doctrines concerning demons; speaking lies in hypocrisy; having their conscience seared with a hot iron. 1 Tim 4.1–2.

The Bible is safe, or nothing is safe: hold on to the Bible. At the close of the sacred volume, the Lord says: "If any man shall add to the words of this book of this prophecy, God shall add to him the plagues that are written in this book." "If any man shall take away from the words of the book of this prophecy, God shall take away his part out of the book of life and out of the holy spirit." The Lord have mercy on the people.

6/4/67, v.x, #23, p.181

Query–Are the disciples of Alexander Campbell disciples of Jesus Christ?

Answer–There are no disciples of Alexander Campbell. The disciples are not of man, but of Christ. He is the Lord, their teacher. They hear his voice, and learn of him.

6/4/67, v.x, #23, p.180

Query–Where did A. Campbell get his authority to start a new sect, and when?

Answer–A. Campbell did not get authority to start a new sect anywhere, never claimed any, and never started a *new sect*, nor propagated any *old sect*, but went back to the church which the Lord said, "I will build," and which he called his church—the "one new man," or church, which God made. In this Mr. Campbell lived, labored and died.

6/4/67, v.x, #23, p.180

Query–Are not all human institutions sectarian?

Answer–All human institutions, substituted for anything in the kingdom of Christ, or added to it, are innovations.

6/4/67, v.x, #23, p.180

Query–What is the kingdom thou talks so much about in the RE-VIEW, of coming into the kingdom, and being in the kingdom? Is it the kingdom of A. Campbell? An answer to this will greatly oblige thine, etc.

Answer–The kingdom of Christ, that we talk so much about, is the body of Christ, or the church of Christ, the family of God. There is no kingdom of A. Campbell. He was a subject of the kingdom of Christ—an honorable and faithful subject of the kingdom of Christ.

We recommend to the writer the foregoing to read carefully Matthew, Mark, Luke and John, and see if he can settle his mind in the belief the Jesus is the Christ, the Son of the living God. If he can settle his mind in this belief, he should read Acts of the Apostles carefully through, and see if he can learn what a believer had to do to become a Christian. If he can learn this, let him put it to his own heart to settle the question, whether he will do this, and become a Christian. If he will honestly and faithfully do this then he may turn his attention to the epistles, written to Christians, to show them how to live Christian lives, to serve God, and be finally saved in heaven.

6/4/67, v.x, #23, p.180

Query–Will you please give me your principal reasons for believing that man is not naturally totally depraved?

Answer–1. We are not taught in Scripture that man is totally depraved. 2. If a man were totally depraved, there would be no good in him. The demons can be no worse than totally depraved. The devil is no more than totally depraved. The worst man has in him some good traits. While in a bad, the bad greatly preponderates, but there is still some good. 3.Those who talk of total depravity, also talk of total hereditary depravity. They do not speak of this as the condition of *some men*, but of all unregenerate men. This we know, if we reflect, is not true. For, if all unregenerate persons were *totally depraved*, they would all be precisely alike—no good to them. We positively know, from common observation, than all unregenerate men are not precisely alike. Some of them are better than others. Hence our Lord in the parable of the sower, finds the way-side ground, stony ground, thorny ground, and *good* ground. There could be no good ground if all were *totally depraved*, to say nothing of hereditary. He makes a difference even in the bad ground. The thorny ground is not as bad as the stony ground, and if it is not as bad as the way-side ground. The thorny ground is *bad*, the stony ground is *worse*, and the way-side is *worst*. He defines the *good* ground to the man who receives the word into a *good* and an *honest* heart. That can not be total depravity. He then divides the good ground into three classes, *good*, *better*, and *best*. Some of it brings thirty-fold that is *good*. Some of it brings sixty-fold that is *better*. Some of it brings a hundred-fold, that is *best*.

Instead of "total hereditary depravity," take the Bible teaching that all are under sin, guilty before God, in unbelief, and lost, and without the Savior not a soul could be saved— that Christ is lifted up to draw all men to Him—that no man comes to the Father, but by Him—that without mercy, the grace of God the cleansing of the blood of Christ, no one could be saved at all. This is true, Scriptural and right. But sinful as man is, in his unregenerate state, he can hear the Word of God and believe, or he could not be justly punished for unbelief if he can repent and turn to God, or *he can* not be punished justly for impenitence. In the nature of the case, man can not be justly held accountable for what he *can not* avoid.

But the man who preaches that the sinner is so depraved, or disabled, naturally, in any way, call it hereditary natural, or what you please, be-yond his own control, that he can not believe furnishes a better *excuse for unbelief than* Thomas Paine or Robert Owen and to preach that the

Holy, the Just the True, will punish a man *for unbelief,* when he *could not believe*, is simply to repulse the common sense of mankind.

To preach that the Lord, the righteous Judge will punish men in hell for *their impenitence,* when they *could not be penitent*, is to reach for climax of inconsistency and absurdity. The thing is utterly revolting. This kind of preaching finds no reason for man being lost in anything he can avoid, but in an innate depravity, over which he has no more control than he has over the climate of his place of nativity, or the complexion of his skin. According to this view, it is no more difference whether you are Calvinistic or Armenian, than there was in the man's proposition to the Indian: "You may take the buzzard, and I will take the turkey, or I will take the turkey and you may take the buzzard. The Indian's sensible reply was: "You never said turkey to me once." The Arminian says, salvation is conditional—that it is on the condition of faith, but he says the sinner *can not* believe—that faith is an immediate gift of God. God, than *elects* the man when he will give faith, and saves him on condition of faith; but leaves the man standing by his side, who can not believe, gives him no faith, and damns him for his unbelief! This is the way the gospel is nullified, and sinners are excused and hardened in their unbelief. The Lord does not say, you can not, but "you *would not* come to me that you might have life."

6/11/67, v.x, #24, p.188

Query–If a sinner believes, repents, and is baptized, and adds to his faith all the Christian virtues named in the gospel, without attaching himself to any religious congregation, is he a true Christian—such an one as will be saved? or in other words—Is the attaching of oneself to a congregation of disciples a necessary step in our salvation?

Answer–If all the disciples would follow the example of the disciple who stands separated from the church, where would the church be? There would be no congregation, or church. Can a man be "a true Christian and such an one as would be saved," while living in such a way as would destroy every congregation in the world, if all the disciples would do as he does? Where would the meetings, the communion, the fellowship, the preaching of the gospel or anything the Lord has appointed be, if all would do as he does? The man who stands off from it, is in disorder and a dead weight to the cause.

Those who are immersed into the general body, ought at once to be added to the congregation most convenient to them, and never from that time forward be out of the congregation. Letters ought all to be so given that persons are not dismissed from the church giving the letter, till united with another.

Then they should be held as responsible to the church given the letter, after the giving of the letter as before till they are received into another church.

A man had as well never have been immersed, for his own salvation, and better, so far as the cause is concerned, than to have been immersed, and then refuse to unite with his brethren, for he pledged himself to the Lord in immersion and has ever since set his appointment at naught. This recreant to his covenant entered in immersion.

7/2/67, v.x, #26, p.213

Query–Please answer through your paper (the REVIEW), if not too much trouble, who Melchizedec, King of Salem, was, where he was from and where he is at present, as Hebrews 7.3, says that he is without father, without mother without descent, having neither beginning of days, nor end of life; but made like unto the Son of God, abideth a priest forever.

Answer–1. He was "King of Salem, priest of the Most High." See Heb. 7.1. 2. We do not know where he is now. We have seen no history of him since he left this world. 3. We suppose he was without priestly descent, father, or mother, his priesthood not having the same beginning of days and end of life as the Aaronic and Levitical priesthoods.

7/2/67, v.x, #26, p.213

Query–I read in the New Testament, Acts 2, that fifteen languages were spoken on Pentecost. I would like to know if the Greek was one of them? At what time in the history of the world, did the Greek language become a dead language?

Answer–We can not now write an essay on this subject, and can only give a word of comment. Owing to commercial, political and religious changes and revolutions in the world, certain languages are introduced, prevail, and become dominant. The literature of the country is mainly written in them and they are the languages of the schools. Other languages are crowded out of their countries, and cease to be spoken or written. They are, then, in those countries, styled *dead languages*. In this way the Hebrew and the Greek languages have been destroyed from some countries, and, in others, have never been the language of the people. In all those countries, they are styled dead languages, not known except by a few scholars. But all living languages are constantly changing, hence the Greek and Hebrew spoken five or six centuries before Christ, differ from the Greek and Hebrew in the time of Christ. But neither were properly *dead languages*, in Palestine, either six hundred years before Christ, or in the time of Christ. In some countries, the Greek language has never been dead; but it has changed immensely. In all those countries where the literature and schools are not in the Hebrew or Greek, those languages are called *dead languages*. In the time of the apostles and where the New Testament was written, the Greek was the living language. To understand the meaning of the Greek word, in that language as then used, is to understand the meaning of that word in the New Testament.

The Greek words for *sprinkle* and *pour* were in use in the time of the apostles, as used by them in their true sense, as in other writings, and are rightly translated in the common version, but never applied to the ordinance or the initiatory rite of the New Institution.

We suppose that the logic of the preacher alluded to above, was that the meaning of *baptizo* is lost, and therefore, it means *sprinkle*.

8/7/67, v.x, #32, p.253

Query—"Blessed are the meek, for they shall inherit the earth." Matt 5.5. Is it in the present life that the meek are to inherit the earth, or after the first resurrection? If it be in the present life, is it a blessing at all, more than they would receive if they were wicked?

Answer—We have for many years supposed it most probable that the Lord here alluded to the "new earth," or the regenerated earth, as it shall emerge from its immersion in fire. The "new heaven and new earth," evidently are for the righteous.

10/15/67, v.x, #42, p.333

Query—In the third chapter and eighteenth verse of John: "He that believeth on him is not condemned." Does this apply to the person who accepts Jesus as the Christ, believes all that is said concerning him in the Bible, but has not obeyed the gospel?

Answer—In all such Scriptures as the one here referred to, the believing carries with it the idea of *full submission*. It is not merely to *believe on him*, or to *believe what he says*, but to so believe with the heart, or the affections, as to *bow in complete submission to him*. Hence we have the following; "He came to his own, and his own received him not. But as many as received him, to them gave he power to become the sons of God, even to them that believe on his name." See John 1.11–12. Those who "received him," "believed on his name." were still not *sons*, but he gave them *power*." Or *privilege*, to become, what they were not, "sons of God." See also the following: "Nevertheless, among the chief rulers also many believed on him, but because of the Pharisees they did not confess him, lest they should be put out of the synagogue; for they loved the praise of men more than the praise of God." John 12.42–43. Do we have persons who "believed on him," but "did not confess him," for the reason that they "*loved the praise of men more than the praise of God*." These were not "*sons of God*," and yet "believed on him." "Faith without works is dead." See James 2.26. *Dead faith* never saved any body.

7/4/71, v.14, #27, p.212

Query—Please give your views of the following Scripture: "I am the door; by me if any man enter in, he shall be saved, and shall go in and out, and find pasture." John 10.9. The two *ins* and the *out* I can not understand.

Answer—The difficulty in your way of understanding is in pressing the figure beyond what was intended. No points or resemblance or of comparison are made between the entering in and the going out. "Christ is the door: *by him*, if any man comes to the Father, he shall be saved." The false prophets who appeared before him were not the door of the sheep. None could enter the divine favor by them. As he compares his disciples to *sheep*, he compares the blessed state of the Christian to the *pastures* on which the sheep grazed, entering in and going out, as they did, but makes no comparison of the *entering* in and *going* out to anything in the kingdom.

8/1/71, v.14, #31, p.244

Query—As I am a seeker of the truth and take the Bible alone for my guide, I address you for information. Is man a free moral agent according to the Scriptures—that is, is it a scriptural phrase?

Answer–Man is *free*. We do not say "*free moral agent*." That is redundant. He can not be an *agent* and not be *free* to act as an agent. On the idea that man is *free* rest all our ideas of praise and blame. It is had in view in all laws for man, both human and divine. It is the ground for all rewards and punishments. It is the very basis of accountability. Every man who says, "I will," or "I will not," says so on the ground that he is *free*, that he *can do* or *refuse to do* this or that. In view of this the Lord says, "You *will* not come to me that you might have life." It would be mockery for the Lord to invite men to come to him, *knowing* that they *could not*, or to command men, as he does, to *turn*, knowing that they *can not* turn away from sin.

8/1/71, v.14, #31, p.244

Query–Can the elders of the Church of Christ be justified, under any circumstances, in voting for and giving their influence to sell whisky in an incorporated village?

Answer–Neither "the elders of the church," the private members of the church, or anybody else can be justified in voting for and giving their influence in favor of license to sell whisky. The Lord, the righteous Judge, will open the eyes of some men to the immense mischief in which they have participated, and on the side of which they have given their influence, when it will be too late to correct their mistake. How can men dream of heaven while they are acting a part in the scheme of traffic that is destroying the bodies and souls of men? What moral sense can a man have when giving his vote for license to sell the destroying element? or when favoring it in any way? Who would want to appear in the presence of the Judge of all immediately after giving such a vote, or in any way favoring such iniquity?

8/1/71, v.14, #31, p.244

Query–Please point out to me the chapter and verse in the New Testament that directs or permits church-members to join any worldly institutions, such as Odd Fellows, Free Masons and Good Templars(?)

Answer–In matters purely secular we do not look for Scripture authority. In these things the Lord leaves us simply *free*. We are not directed by the Bible, but by human wisdom. We do not look for authority in the Bible for becoming a trustee of a school or college; for joining a stock company, a railroad company, a banking company, etc. etc.

The Bible gives no direction in many matters of this sort legitimate and proper. A man may be a Christian and join such company or not join it. He is simply free in such matters.

We belong to no secret society and never did, and have no reason to frame an excuse for our self. Our reasons for declining to join them have all the time been sufficient to keep us from doing so; but they are *prudential* reasons, and not that we think men violate the Scriptures in so doing. There is simply *no Scripture about it*. It is a secular matter entirely. The question about joining a secret society is a mere *prudential one*, and the reasons for and against it are merely prudential. It is not a question of *Scripture authority*. It is not a question of faith or even a religious question. It may be considered and decided by the same considerations, both by a man who is a Christian and one who is not a Christian. It is not claimed that men are required by religious obligations or religious authority to join one of these societies. The question of joining it may be considered by a religious man or a man who is a member of no church. He may inquire merely as a citizen. Can I do more good by joining than without joining? Can I do more good by joining than without joining?

In this view of it our reasons, if we advise any one to try to influence him to join or not join, are simply *prudential*. We do not attempt to bring Scripture authority on one side or the other. It is not a question to be settled by Scripture authority. If, however, you can show that a Christian will leave the meeting of the church to attend the meetings of his secret society; that he has more money for the society than for the church, or money for the society and none for the church; time to attend to the society and no time to attend to the church; time to attend to his secular human organization and no time to attend to the divine institution, the church, he is making a bad record for the Christian.

There are not very many zealous members of any of these societies, and zealous members of the church at the same time. A man is apt to become cold and careless either in the one or the other. It is never wise nor good for a man to have too many irons in the fire at a time, or to have the attention divided among too many things. If a man joins a society and continues as zealous and faithful as ever in the church, we have nothing to say.

4/2/72, vx, #14, pg.108

Query–1.Does the law of Christ require a brother to forgive another sin, offense, or injury against him without repentance, restitution, or reparation to the utmost of his ability? 2. In Matthew 17.21–22, when Jesus replied to Peter's inquiry, "How oft shall my brother sin against me and I forgive him? until seven times? Jesus saith unto him, I say not till seven times, but until seventy times seven." Does not this even presuppose the conditions of repentance, restitution or reparations? 3. Does God ever forgive the sinner who "has known the law" without these conditions? If not, how can it be expected of us who do so? 4. Would God require of us a passive submission to insult and injury, and thus to assassinate the dignity of human nature and sink man into a spaniel?

Answer–The law of the Lord, in a case of trespass, requires us, if a brother says he repents, to forgive him. But we were not dealing in a case of *discipline*, but dealing with the brother alluded to *as an editor*. The case was before us as *an editor* and we had to dispose of it in some way. We simply stated how we would dispose of the case. We have no authority over him in his church relation, nor were we dealing with him in any way only *as an editor*. We leave him to the Lord, the Church of which he is a member, and the opinion of an intelligent brotherhood. We appreciate the intended injury and the bad spirit manifested, but the Lord does not allow us to resent or retaliate, nor have we any disposition to do so. If his course can injure us, we submit and bear it. Of course, we were grieved, wounded and mortified. We reviewed the matter carefully to see how much blame attached to us, in what it consisted, and what had aroused such a spirit, and think we comprehended the case, much more so than we have expressed, but did not desire— and do not know—to say much.

We should not have been surprised to have been criticized, strictured with freedom and in plainness, but such a document as the one we printed we have no reason to expect. This, we find, is the sense of the brotherhood generally. There was one security against such attacks. An intelligent brotherhood, after having time to mature the matter will render a proper decision. To that decision we submit till He who judges righteously shall decide on all our actions. If Stephen could say, when sinking in Death, in reference to his persecutors, "Lay not this sin to their charge." And if Jesus, when in the agonies of death, gave us an example in exclaiming, "Forgive them, they know not what they do," we certainly can and ought to bear the insult added to the injury in the case at hand. Our code of honor is of a higher order than that of the world, and it is good for us to have an opportunity to exhibit in practice what we have taught others in words many times. When our Lord was reviled, he reviled not again; when he was persecuted, he threatened not. We have endured much of this kind of abuse, and by the grace of God, can endure much more.

6/3/73, v.16, #22, p.172

Query – You will do myself and others a great favor by giving your advice on the following questions: 1. Should there be a trouble between two or more brethren of the same congregation, and should they meet each other in the presence of other brethren and agree to forgive each other of all the past, and live as brethren of one common cause ; then, after such agreement, should one or more of the same brethren violate such obligations, and engage, in alienating these same brethren, what course should be pursued with such persons? 2. Should a committee of other churches go to a congregation where there is trouble and investigate said trouble with-out the consent of a majority of its members, would such a course be right ? 3. Should this committee effect a decision that in some way affected the moral standing of one or more members of the congregation, who had no knowledge of the investigation, and were not notified to appear, and consequently were not present to defend themselves, would said decision be worthy of regard

Answer – 1. The church should withdraw from them. They are covenant breakers and factionists. 2. By no means, unless solicited by the church to do so. All other churches should stand clear and avoid their difficulty unless solicited to aid them and the church consents to the decision of a committee from other churches. We know of no more unwise counsel than that which would set adjoining churches to sending committees to adjust a difficulty in a church without its solicitation or consent. No surer plan could be adopted for invoking all the churches in the vicinity in the difficulty, and creating general alienation. 3. No committee has any authority to meddle, with the discipline, as administered in a church, unless invited and the church agrees to put the case into its hands. Then, such a procedure as described in this question would not be approved by intelligent people anywhere. We are constantly surprised to learn of obtaining in different cases occurring.

It is the result of the demoralizing teaching becoming common.

Nothing could, be more demoralizing and mischievous than some of the teaching setting aside the authority of Christ in the church and the encouragement to establish tribunals that have no authority. Nothing but confusion can grow out of such procedure. We do not doubt that a church can do no wrong, but the church is the tribunal, and there is no tribunal above it this side of heaven. We do not doubt the propriety of a church, in a difficult case, or a case where she has failed to give general satisfaction, agreeing to a reference to good men selected from other congregations, or the same congregation. But no other church has any right to meddle unless solicited to do so by the church in trouble.

6/24/73, vol. 16, #25, pg. 196

Query–A very singular affair has taken place in one of our churches, which has resulted in the exclusion of one of its oldest members. This old brother was a widower and wanted a wife. His son had died and left a widow. The old gentleman and his son's widow were married. For this offense the church disfellowshiped him. The question is this: First, Did he violate any law either of the Old or New Testament? If so, where is the law recorded, and by whom? Second, Does our law forbid any such marriage? As this to me is, and perhaps to others, a now case requiring discipline, your views are respectfully solicited.

Answer–The case mentioned above is certainly singular. We do not remember of ever hearing of a case of the kind. There is simply nothing in the New Testament about any such case, and we do not think of anything about it in the Old Testament. We do not know what Scripture said church acted on, or grounded their charge on. Indeed, we do not see how they would word the charge. We know a case where a man eighty years old married a woman of but little more than twenty years. No man could expect anything only that such a thing would be a subject of remark; that it would be regarded as very unnatural and unwise; but we do not see any ground for a church charge. When old people do such weak and unwise things they are more subjects of pity than of censure. A man must have but little respect for public opinion, even if he has not the ordinary impulses repelling such an idea, to marry the widow of his deceased son. We should think, too, that both the parties would be greatly wanting in self-respect to do such a thing, if they have ordinary intelligence. But we should not have thought of making it a case of discipline. The impulses of men are blind, and, in many instances, not under control of judgment. Such unequal, unnatural and unwise alliances can but result in evil to all concerned, and certainly ought to prevented if possible.

6/24/73, vol.16, #25, pg. 196

Query–Will you please explain through your paper what is meant by the "Apostles' Creed?" Had the apostles a creed ?

Answer–The Apostles' Creed, so called, is evidently a creed the apostles never saw, a creed made by uninspired men, and called "The Apostles' Creed" to give it weight and authority. It is a pious fraud, a forgery, and not what it claims to be at all. We have not the means at hand where we now write to give the information accessible about it, and only say what we do from memory.

The New Testament in the only book that is indorsed by apostolic authority, and that is not a popular book in our time. It is quite insufficient without some uninspired creed to expound it. If men want apostolic authority and will go to the New Testament they will find it. But the Apostles' Creed goes down on the same list as the Apocryphal books, bound up in some copies of the Bible, and the Apocryphal New Testament has some of the most ridiculous things in print. Prof. Stowe has given some five samples, to show how they compare with the genuine books of the New Testament, in his "History of the Books of the Bible." The Apostles' Creed is of about the name authority as those Apocryphal books, and deserving of about as much credit. If we can think of it, when we are where we can lay our hand on, the proper works, we will give more information about the matter.

6/24/73, vol. 16, #25, pg. 196

Query–If a man and wife separate, has either a right to marry another person while the former companion is living?

Answer–A man who is a Christian is forbidden to put away his wife, in the law of Christ, except on a certain condition, specified by the Lord himself. If an unbelieving man shall leave his wife because she is a Christian, for she is not bound. Where the grounds for separation exist and the parties separate, whether they may marry again is not so clear. It has generally been permitted among us; but where parties have applied to us for advice, before forming such relation, we have invariably advised them, if we advised them at all, to stand clear of ground that is doubtful. This is safe, to say the least of it.

7/1/73, vol.16, #26, p.204

Query—If two sinners marry and become dissatisfied with each other, and separate without assigning a scriptural reason, and then each of them marry another person (without a divorce) and one of the four come forward to confess his or her faith in Christ should the minister take the confession and immerse the person, and the church receive him or her into full fellowship with them, or should he or they not?

Answer—The unscriptural things done before we are Christians all go together as "old sins," and are "blotted out." What they can not undo must be left to God. We would take the confession and immerse the person. No doubt numerous persons received by the apostles were entangled in unlawful marriages, but their profession looked forward to a good life in time to come, and not back to the unreasonable things in their past lives.

7/1/73, v.16, #26, p.204

Query—Has a Christian a scriptural right to marry a sinner or unbeliever? If so, what does Paul mean in 2 Cor 6.13? If not, has a Christian minister a right to marry them?

Answer—It is clearly implied that Christians should not marry unbelievers. In numerous instances apostasies have been occasioned by such alliances, and numerous other evils have followed them.

7/1/73, vol.16, #26, p.204

Query—We have a practice of the church in this place of extending the "right hand of fellowship" to persons who have been but recently baptized, or, in other words, the new converts are seated conveniently, and the brethren and sisters, while singing a familiar hymn, commence marching around single file and shaking each convert by the hand until all have passed by, when the ceremony is over. Do all the congregations of Disciples practice this? Is it in conformity with the teachings of the New Testament?

Answer—Our attention has been called to this matter many times and we have frequently spoken of it. We heard of a tree once so straight that it leaned a little the other way. We have seen some near friends come up when persons would come forward and confess and embrace them or kiss them. But where is the Scripture for it? There is none. It is not a requirement at all. It is not a matter of law. It is only a voluntary thing. Many others do not do it. The same is true of the members coming up and giving the new convert the hand. It is a voluntary thing. It is only an expression of their love to the new convert. If any do not feel like thus expressing their love to the converts there is no law requiring them to come. In this the churches are not uniform, and, for any reason we can see, they need not be.

In some congregations all come up, or pretty much all, and give the hand, in congratulation or cordial greeting, as soon as one confesses. In others this is not done, but on receiving the members into the church all give the right hand as a recognition of their membership and fellowship This, however, is also a voluntary thing. All are not required to come. There is no law in the case. In other congregations the members do not give the hand at all. The officiating brother or the overseers of the church extend the hand in receiving them into the congregation, or what is usually styled "right hand of fellowship." It is true we are immersed into Christ, or into the body or kingdom, but immersing a man into Christ does not identify him with any local congregation. Every member of the body of Christ should be a member of some local congregation where he is amenable for his conduct, where he meets regularly to worship. "As many as gladly received his word were baptized." This brought them into Christ, or into the kingdom. But the history proceeds, "And the same day there were added to them about three thousand souls."

This was a further procedure after baptizing them—it was adding them to the church. This adding to the church, not the general body, but the local church, must in some visible and tangible form. There is no law prescribing how it shall be done; it may, therefore, be done in any fitting matter. Where the law of Christ leaves us free let us be free, and where the law prescribes let us follow the law implicitly.

We know of a worthy lady once to object to coming up and giving the hand. When others were to be received we stated that if they were any a little cold and that did not like to be so conspicuous as to come up and give the hand that we did not know of any law requiring them to come, and we thought they might be excused. She came up and gave the hand. We love to see the brethren move harmoniously, with one mind and one judgment.

9/30/73, v.16, #39, p. 308

Query–I wish to ask you a few questions, through the Review, in regard to Sunday or the Lord's day. We have brethren here who have held membership with the church for many years in good standing who try to justify themselves by God's work in cutting down hay and grain, raking and gathering up the same, because they think it is necessary. Ask them for Scripture for it and they refer to sleep in the pit. Now I wish to know, first, if Sunday or the Lord's day is set apart for any particular purpose and in memory of any certain event? And, second if the Lord's day is to be observed by the Lord's purpose? And, third, if the Lord's day can be observed in the field, engaged in manual labor? Please inform us.

Answer–We regret the necessity of being called on to answer any such questions as the above. We regret exceedingly that the practice should obtain anywhere among Christians calling forth such questions, and are thankful to know that such practice receives no countenance anywhere among well informed Christians.

Referring to Scripture that relate to the Sabbath is entirely irrelevant. Such Scriptures have no references to the Lord's day, or the first day of the week. The Sabbath was the seventh day of the week, or Saturday, and the Lord's day was the first day, or Sunday. The Sabbath was given by Moses to the Jews, and to nobody else. When the law was abolished the Sabbath went with it, its observance, penalty and all. The Lord's day is not of Moses but of Jesus, not of the law but of the Gospel, not for the law but of the Gospel, not for Jews but for Christians. It had its origin, not in the rest of the Almighty after six days' work in creation. The assembling of the saints for the worship on the first day of the week, in consummating the resurrection of the Christian's Lord on that day, and the breaking of the loaf and pouring the wine on that day commemorate the sufferings and death of the Lord on that day. This has the example of the first Christians as a precedent, which is divine authority with those who understand the Scriptures. The cutting of hay and grain, gathering and putting up hay and grain on the Lord's day has no precedent in the example of the first Christians, no divine authority, and does not work is in shape to lay over on that day. We make this necessity ourselves and will be accessible for it. We speak not of accidents that necessitate work.

9/23/73. 16, #38, p.300

Query – Is it right and scriptural for brethren to build large and commodious halls, and understandingly and intentionally to rent them to sinners for the purpose of dancing? Please answer at your earliest convenience through the REVIEW.

Answer – Not for men under the Jerusalem and who follow the Jerusalem Church as a *model*; but when we depart from the old gospel and follow Doctor Progress, we can make money by *base methods*, such as renting halls for dancing, training horses for racing, bet on them, dance a little ourselves, participate in innocent games, attend the theater, circus shows, attend the races, take a little strong drink, sell liquor, and "such like" things; but all who do such things will find their influence cut down to nothing in the Church. Indeed, they are dead weights on the Church. They are simply people of the world; it may be, pretty creditable and respectable. They may be tolerably civil and moral people, and behave themselves well, as the world would consider it. But if a Christian had a hall, and believed he was on his dying bed, but in his right mind, would he rent it for a ball room? Not a word of it. There are two things that will ruin many souls 1. The love of money. Those under this influence will do anything that will bring money. 2. The love of pleasure. Those under this influence will do anything that will give pleasure. Their love of pleasure must be gratified even at the expense of their souls. Pleasure is their god, and they seek him, find him, and are devoted to him. They never complain of the *lengthy* service at his altar, nor of the *expense*, nor of the *unworthy worshiper* in the same pew.

10/28/73 v.16, #43, p.340

Query – Does the Bible teach that there are degrees in heaven or in hell? Do all receive the blessing alike? Do all receive the punishment alike?

Answer – We have never preached or taught that there will or will not be degrees in happiness in heaven, or that there will or will not be degrees of punishment in hell. We never had a doubt but that He who has promised the happiness of heaven was able and willing to make it what it ought to be, or that he who shall lose that happiness will lose all that is dear to him; nor did we ever have a doubt but that He who has threatened the punishment of hell will inflict what ought to be, and that he who shall be a subject of it will find it equal to the language in which it is threatened. In all the promises of God fulfilled in this world, their fulfillment has never fallen below the expectations of those who relied on the promises. In all the threatenings of the Lord fulfilled, their fulfillment has never fallen below what the believers in the word of God expected.

The penalty annexed to the violation of the law in Eden was certainly equal to what any one would have understood from the threat. The same was true in the cases of the antediluvians, Egyptians, the Jews and all others. The main matter, then, is not to speculate about degrees, but to "strive to enter into that rest"—the happiness promised to escape the punishment threatened; the fiery indignation which will devour the adversaries—the *sorer* punishment than *death without mercy*.

It is no feature of the progressionists that we are aware of, but an offshoot from *Restorationism*, or *Universalism*, in their efforts to modify the divine penalty pronounced on those who shall prove incorrigible, utterly reject Christ and die in their sins. We want nothing to do with any tampering with the law of God, specially the promises that relate to the eternal happiness or the threatenings which relate to the eternal punishment. Instead of preaching or teaching about degrees in happiness or misery, in the world to come, we ought to be "hungering and thirsting after righteousness," studying how to live nearer to God, more faithfully to do his will; to do those things that are pleasing in his sight. Those who do his will are safe, no matter how many degrees there are in punishment. Those who do not his will are not safe, no matter about degrees in happiness or punishment.

The great matter is to please the Lord. He went about doing good, not doing his own will, but the will of Him who sent him. Let us meditate on his truth and faithfully believe it; meditate on his commandments and faithfully do them; meditate on his promises and hope for them. Eye has not seen, ear has not heard, neither has it entered into the heart of man, the joy that God has prepared for them that love him. The angels desire to look into the things brought to us in the gospel. Good men look into them, look forward and hope for them with joy.

10/28/73 v.16, #43, p.340

Query–Ought Christians to unite with a secret political society—a society aiming to overthrow the powers that be? Is it in accordance with Scripture? Please answer, with some explanation, on Romans, 13th chapter, through the *A. C.* REVIEW

Answer–We know not what *society* is meant, nor does it matter ; but it would hardly admit that it *aims to overthrow the powers that be*. Of course no Christian ought to unite with any society with *such an aim*. It would be in direct violation of the authority of God, as found in the 13th chapter of Romans. "The powers that be are ordained of God." " He who resists the power, resists the ordinance of God." It is a poor comment on a man's religion to engage in insurrectionary movements to subvert legitimate authority. Such movements are wholly incompatible with such commands as the following: "Follow *peace* with all men, and holiness, without which no man shall see the Lord."

Nothing speaks more loudly again Romanists and Mormons than the *political scheming*; their insidious attempts to subvert *rightful authority*; the machinations of the Jesuits; the continual collisions with civil authority. At the close of the first century the were six million Christians in the Roman empire, and there is not an account of their ever having had the least collision with civil authority, or engaging in any political schemes. If men are not pleased with the course in affairs are taking, let them come before the people in the usual way and plead for reform. But let there be no *secret* movements.

12/9/73, v.16, #49, pg. 388

Query–Please excuse this letter, as it is written in all good faith to find out the truth: 1. What day is the Sabbath? 2. Are we; as Christians, commanded to keep the Sabbath to the Lord, as holy? 3. When was the Sabbath changed from the seventh to the first day of the week? 4. By whose authority was it done? I desire to know the truth in this matter, and whether we, as Christians are obeying God or man. If we are following the traditions of men, we should lay them aside and obey God. May the Lord teach us the right way and give us strength to walk therein.

Answer–1. Saturday, or the seventh day is the Sabbath. 2. By no means, nor are there any that keep it (as required in the law of Moses, the only law that ever gave it divine authority), in this country, except the Jews, and they only *profess* to keep it, but *do not do it.* 3. It was not *changed* to the first day at all. There in not one word about it ever being *changed* at all to any other day. 4. It was not done by any authority, and is not done at all. In the civil law, the first day of the week is called *the Sabbath*, and we are required to observe it, but *not as required by Moses.* Still there is nothing burdensome in the requirements of the civil law, nor wrong for a Christian to observe. As Christians, we want the *first day* of the week free from all secular pursuits, for the assembling and worship; as also religious instruction both for those in and out of the church. It is the day on which Christians are required to meet to break bread. The civil law is about as favorable to us, as Christians, as it could be. We can, in strict accordance with the civil law, do all the Lord requires, and the civil law does not require us to do anything inconsistent with our profession. It is an incalculable blessing to have the strong arm of the civil law to protect us in the assemblies of the saints, to worship and teach according to the Scriptures. We assemble on the first day of the week in memory of the resurrection of the Lord, and celebrate his sufferings and death. This day has nothing in it the nature of the Sabbath. It is but a feeble observance of the first day to rest from all labor, from making any fires doing any cooking, as required in the law of the Sabbath.

The first day of the week brings all the hallowed memories of the resurrection of our Lord, and the communion commemorates his sufferings and death. These are higher and grander then than any of the associations of the Sabbath; more spiritual and happy than the mere idea of *rest.*

12/16/73, vol.16, #50, pg. 396

Query–A case in point in this: A few years ago the Government of the United States passed what is known as the "Bankrupt Law." Some of the brethren of the congregation of Christ that is near me took advantage of said "Bankrupt Act," and paid several thousand dollars. Since then the same brethren have become considerable moneyed men, and own several thousand dollars' worth of property, lands, etc. We have preaching tolerably regular, but no one seems disposed to obey the gospel, although their known sentiments are for us and our teaching. A short time since I conversed with several persons on the subject of obeying the truth, and received the reply in every instance that "we can not fellowship-and know that they have paid debts in this manner, and even owe me, and will not pay it, although they owe thousands to my hundreds." What shall we do with such stumbling-blocks, who impede the prosperity of Zion in this way? Give us a full, plain Franklin answer to this if you can, for I am disposed to think that this is not the only congregation that may be afflicted similarly. Many brethren are desirous of seeing a full and lucid solution to this difficulty.

Answer—We have known instances in which men took the benefit of the above named law, in which we had no doubt it was right; but, in some cases, they forgot the purpose they alleged when they took benefit of said law. When a man is exhausted and still owes heavy amounts that may be pressed at any time, he has no chance to pay, nor to do anything for himself and dependants. In such cases we have known men who were in the prime of life and had fine business capacity who would allege that if they could have their way clear for a few years they could make enough to pay all and would do it. If they had remained as they were, liable to be harassed at any time for the amount they owed, they could not have made money to pay ; but by the benefit of the law in a few years they could pay. This appeared to be about the best they could have done. But in some cases, they made the money and much more, rose into opulence and wealth, but forgot the old debts. Yes, and forgot their promise to when they made money. In this case, they were legally clear, but morally bound by their promise that if they were successful they would pay. We do not say if by unforeseen events men of business talent, acting honestly fail and are reduced to poverty, they may not take the benefit of the Bankrupt Act. This law was made for such men and for the good of the country. It was considered that it can work good capacity for business to remain crushed down on account of a failure that he could not avert or foresee. That would pay no debts, but ruin the man and cut his enterprise and energies off the operations of the country at large. In a case of that kind, if the man gives up every thing honestly, according to law, and takes the benefit of the law, we see no ground for complaint. But if he lays away an amount to start on after he takes the oath, he is a perjured man, and morally ruined. But if he gives up all honestly, according to law, and then starts anew and prospers he ought to remember his old creditors who have disappeared and deprived of their dues a long time and come to their relief. But, in these evil days, men are not legally bound at all. We do not now think of a case where a man has taken the benefactor of the Bankrupt Act, then prospered and afterward paid off the old indebted no matter how wealthy he became. We have known some cases where men promised that in case they ever became able they would do this, but not one where they did it.

The change in circumstances produces a wonderful change in the view of men. If some of these men who have taken the benefit of the law, and have since became wealthy, were placed in the shoes of those who have lost their dues, they would see the matter in a very different light, in a moral point of view. The man of the world who has lost his money looked at the professor of religion who owes him but wipes the debt out by going into bankruptcy, in a different light from those who stand off.

A follower in Christ should certainly feel granted to learn that any transaction of his was in the way of men turning to the Lord and being saved. We should maintain the highest moral standing possibly that we give no occasion to the adversary, and because it is right in itself to do so. There are several things involved in bankruptcy in viewing it morally such as the following: 1.There is something in the way a man becomes involved. Was it by extravagance, prodigality and inattention to business? These are wrong in themselves, and must, in the nature of the case, bring a man to grief.

Many times, indebtedness is involved in this way and in such cases a man must reproach himself. But in many instances indebtedness is incurred by turns in commercial operations that no man can foresee, or changes in monetary matters. In cases of this sort there can be no moral blame. 2.When a man becomes involved hopelessly by some means over which he had no control, and he honestly gives up everything, according to law and goes into bankruptcy, we see no blame. It may be the best thing that can be done, taking every thing into the account. The law was made for such men. 3.But here comes the temptation to commit the great sin; to lay away something secretly, commit perjury, and go into bankruptcy. This has, no doubt, been done many times. In a few years the man appears to prosper wonderfully, and is rich. Or, some son or son in-law at once becomes rich and creditors are swindled. In such a case as this there is no use in talking of morality. Villainy is the name for it. Many cases of this sort occur where legal proof can not be had, and yet men acquainted all round pretty well are morally certain how the matter is. But if legal proof can not be found the corruption, we do not see how the church can obtain proof that will convict. Where conclusive proof can not be obtained, and persons are under suspicion, the Church has no alternative only to carry the load, and the individual must bear the suspicion. There is no possibility to remove it. There is one thing that Christians can do, and that is, not to make haste to get rich; not to be governed by the love of money; not to be reckless; but to be careful; be content with a moderate and safe business.

The great matter needed is the economy. As a people we should cease our extravagance and live in moderation. This will not relieve the matters of the foregoing inquiry, but will have much to do in preventing the occurrence of other cases of the kind. Let us be careful and deal honestly. It is a terrible thing for a Christian to involve his honor and profession in doubt and be held under suspicion a lifetime; to be regarded as a dishonest man.

12/16/73, v.16, #50, pg. 396

Query–When we see in the controversy now going on over missionary societies that there is quite an array of talented and able scribes that are not only advocating such societies by the use of the pen, but are really engaged in active operation in carrying on such work, and while, on the other hand, we see quite an array of equally able and talented scribes that earnestly and actively condemn and oppose such societies and denounce them as useless, unscriptural and a cause of strife, how, I ask are we that are illiterate to decide which side is in the right?

Answer–The questions mentioned above are not to be settled by men great or small, learned or unlearned, but by the word of the Lord, the only authority of the Church and the highest authority of the universe.

2/2/75 v.18, #5, pg. 34

Query–Can a congregation use their weekly contributions for any purpose that may be thought best for the benefit of the church and the cause of Christ, or is it designed for the poor and the Lord's table only? If you will please answer through the REVIEW you will oblige many brethren.

Answer–If the congregation should specify when a contribution is about to be made that it is for the poor saints, it would be bad faith to appropriate to any other object. But if the contributions of the first day are made in the general way for the cause, without any particularly specified object, we see not why they may not be appropriated to the first good object that may come.

3/9/75, v.18, #10, pg. 76

Query–It is said: "They continued steadfastly in the apostle's doctrine, and in fellowship, and in breaking of bread and in prayers." Does the word "fellowship" mean finance, money or anything of that kind, or is it love, or sympathy for one another? Some of the ministers say it means money, and some that it means the other.

Answer–We have no doubt that it means the contribution. The writer is speaking of *specified acts* performed in the worship, and not *emotions*, but specified *items performed*. The items were the following: 1.The apostles' teaching. The teaching was an *item*, or an *act* performed. 2. The fellowship, or contribution. This was an *item* or *act* performed, and not a mere emotion felt or enjoyed. It was something, and not merely an impression in them or on them. 3. Breaking of bread. This was an item done, or an action performed. It was not an invisible emotion or impression. 4. Prayer. This was an item in worship, or a thing performed, and not an emotion or an impression in them.

3/9/75, v.18, #10, pg. 76

Query–1. Is it right for those from whom the Church has withdrawn their fellowship, and that, too, by special request, to organize themselves into a congregation in a small village, where there are not more than sixty or seventy members? 2. Ought our preachers to give them encouragement in such a course, to the pulling down of the cause of Christ, in said place? 3. Is it right for neighboring congregations to recognize them as a Church? 4. Ought the brethren of a sister church give them encouragement by their presence? 5. If our prevailing encourage such a course, are they making full proof of their ministry?

Answer–In the disordered state of affairs in *sectdom*, instead of Christendom, we have to encounter every imaginable form of difficulties in undertaking to bring light out of darkness, order out of chaos, and peace out of confusion. We find all the weaknesses of human beings, the sinfulness common to our race everywhere, and widespread ignorance to encounter. Then there are the proud, fashionable, and pleasure-seeking, as well as the envious, restless and factious, with whom we have to deal. We have also the sectarian education and example misleading the people. We may also add, that we live in a time of general insubordination and disrespect for rightful authority and rule. The establishment and maintenance of parental authority instead of being the rule constitute the exception. The school government is much the same. We have good civil laws as were ever enacted, but no moral sentiment to maintain and enforce them. The moment crime is committed up rises an abounding sympathy with the criminal, and the dignity and majesty of the law are forgotten, as also the security and safety of society and property, and the just penalties of wise and good laws are evaded and not enforced; the hands of transgressors are strengthened, and their hearts hardened and encouraged to persist in crime, with the assurance that they, too, if they should be overtaken, will have the sympathies of the people and may escape. In the midst of all this what can we expect but insubordination in the Church? People that did not obey their parents when they were children, or the school-teacher when they were in school, and who, if they obey the civil law themselves, sympathize with the criminal and aid him in evading the penalties of the law, will not rest quiet under the rightful rule of King Jesus. They can talk all day about principles and expediencies, but they know no rule and recognize no authority. They do not realize that they are disgraced in violating the law of Christ and becoming subjects of discipline. But when they disobey the law and it is executed, fellowship is withdrawn from them, to work they go with more zeal than they ever before showed, not to set themselves right before the violated law and the great Lawgiver, but to rouse a sympathy in their behalf, that will justify them in the eyes of the people and condemn the authority of Christ in the Church that had been executed.

But we will not continue to moralize in this general way, but will come directly to the matters in hand. We have no authority to settle matters of this kind, and man can not give an opinion worth as much as those who know the parties; the circumstances and surroundings. Indeed, we can give no opinion at all, only in view of certain contingencies. When a division arises, the cause of it is always sought if a new congregation is formed in a community where there are not more than sixty or seventy members, any one outside will inquire for the cause of it. From the instances above, we gather that the immediate cause of forming the new congregation was that the congregation of which the leaders in forming the new congregation had been members; had withdrawn fellowship from them. If this is correct and the old congregation proceeded on scriptural ground in excluding them, they are not under the jurisdiction of the Church, and it is not worth while to inquire about any religious action of theirs till they retrace their steps and set themselves right. Their action is clearly without the Church. It matters not where they were, who they were how many or how few members there were in the community. This much appears to us entirely clear.

But what if the ground of the exclusion was not scriptural? We know of a case that occurred some years ago, where an overseer in a congregation wrote out some rules to govern them in their meetings or, it may be, in business meetings, and required the members to sign these rules. Eleven members, if we remember, refused to sign these rules, but never disobeyed them. For refusing to sign them they were excluded, we think, without any other charge. Several of these were men of ripe years, much experience and public men, and of unquestionable standing. What shall we say of those? Must such exclusion be regarded? These eleven went to another place of meeting, and others went with them, making some thirty in all at the start. They have since built a house, sustained themselves, and now number about two hundred. This is the only instance we know of where an excluded party have had the time to test the matter and succeeded. This case furnishes but little encouragement for *any*, and *none* for but few others, for the following reasons: 1. They were clearly excluded without any scriptural ground, but simply because they would not sign some rules written by an unscriptural man, and not because they would not sign some rules written by an uninspired man, and not because they did not obey these uninspired rules. The case is probably without a parallel. 2. The unimpeachable character, the intelligence of the persons excluded, and piety, commanded the respect of the good and the true. 3. The Church, in the transaction, clearly abandoned the ground of a congregation of the Lord in excluding them, and on that account forfeited its claim and respected. It was not merely an *error* in its action, but a repudiator of the very principles of the churches of the Lord, in requiring the members to do what all the churches refuse to do, to *indorse uninspired rules.* The persons disobeyed no law of God, nor even the law the overseer had written, but refused to *indorse what he had written.* In requiring them to indorse an uninspired rule, the Church violated its fundamental ground and thus *revolutionized itself.* 4. Where a movement is clearly a factionary movement, no church or individual ought to encourage it in any way, but all ought to exhort to encourage them to return to the true ground. We have before us an extract from the pen of President Pendleton, taken from the *Christian Standard* of May 16, 1874, as copied in an article before us. He says: "A wide acquaintance with ecclesiastical affairs, for over the third of a century, enables us to speak with some assurance on this subject; and we believe on the conclusion of our observation will be confirmed by that of many others, when we say, that we do not now recall a single instance of one who has yielded to the spirit of faction and become the agent, or the willing instrument even, of dividing a church, destroying its peace, and crippling its influence, upon whom there has not fallen, sooner or later, signal tokens of the divine displeasure, in the loss of standing with the brethren, the withdrawal of the confidence of the churches, and general degradation in all that ennobles and honors the Christian profession and rewards the Christian life. And this experience goes to confirm our faith in the sleepless oversight of the great Head of the Church, in keeping her against the wiles of her constant enemies, and fulfilling, to those who confess his name, the blessed promise that the gates of hades shall not prevail against her. Let those who defile her and bring her into reproach, and despise her discipline, take heed lest the threatened curse fall upon them and they perish in the way.

4/27/75, v.18, #18, pg.125

Query—If the Church was aware of the circumstances, and such an individual was to present himself for the purpose of making the confession, could he be received into fellowship, if he did not, in passing through the second change (or change of life), amend his life, or restore what properly belonged to another, if he was able to do so. It is seemed to think, and perhaps correctly too, that the individual would have to be received and time and opportunity given for an exhibition of the fruits; but would not this enter into and constitute a part of the change of life necessary to pass through in order to forgiveness of sins?

Answer—We have for many years admitted that repentance is not the change of life, or reformation itself, but is a change of mind or character. But if this change of mind or purpose that leads to a change of mind or purpose is such as this meant by the word repent, it will result in the change of life. If the subject had defrauded another it would require reparation, if reparation was possible.

8/24/75, v.18, #34, pg. 268

Query—If it takes a brother to sanctify an unbelieving wife in order that the children may be holy, I want to know what is the condition of the children where neither of the parents are Christians. What are the means by which they are to be made holy?

Answer–The Scripture referred to is 1 Cor 7.14. It is not easy to tell precisely what is meant by the believing party sanctifying the unbelieving. It is evident, however, that it has no reference to any religious sanctifying other than making the marriage relation proper or legitimate. The idea was evidently in existence among the early Christians that where the husband or the wife was an unbeliever the marriage relation would be improper the children would be illegitimate, and, therefore, they should separate. The Apostle opposes this, and maintains that the relation is proper; that the children are legitimate, and that they should not separate unless the believer forcibly leaves. In this case the believing party is not bound to the other. The sanctifying can not have reference to anything more than the marriage relation, the setting apart the unbelieving party to it, and constituting it lawful and right, and the offspring free from any reproach on account of the unbelieving parent. It can have no such signification as that the circumstance of an unbeliever being married to a Christian, *making a Christian*. It is true that being married to a Christian might be a means of bringing the unbelieving party to hear the Word, understand it, turn to God, and bring forth much fruit. But the simple circumstance of being thus united with a Christian does not make the party thus united a Christian. Nor does the children be*ing holy* mean that they are *Christians*; but simply that they are pure in the sense of being *legitimate*. The main point in the argument of the Apostle is to show the believing party that they may not depart from the unbelieving simply on the ground of unbelief, that their relation is legitimate and lawful, and their children legitimate and free from reproach. This is the sum of what there is in it.

This is a commendation to the religion of Christ. It comes not breaking up family relations, separating husbands and wives, but sanctions marriage, and makes it right and honorable. If there is any separating the unbelieving must be the cause of it, and not the believing who obey the Lord. Touching the children of them who are not Christians on either, no religious scruples arise about their relation, or that of their children. While their marriage relation in proper and legitimate, they are outside, and not in any doubt about their marriage relations, nor seeking any apostolic instruction. There is no trouble about their children, but the matter in their case is simply that they are not Christians—not in the covenant at all.

Query–Was John cast into prison before or after Christ had chosen his disciples? Please reconcile Mark 1.14, John 3.22–24

Answer–Mark 1.14 reads as follows: "Now after that John was put in prison, Jesus came into Galilee, preaching the gospel of the kingdom of God," John 3.22–24, we have the following: "After these things came Jesus and his disciples into the land of Judaea; and there he tarried with them, and baptized. And John also was baptizing in Aenon near to Salim, because there was much water there."

We suppose that the words, "chose his disciples," in the above, mean "chose his apostles." If that is the meaning we think, though we have not made through examination, that the apostles were evidently engaged in their first mission, or under their first commission, before John was imprisoned; otherwise how could it have been said that Christ "made and baptized more disciples than John through Christ baptized not, but his disciples?" John's mission lasted but a short time, but Christ was baptized by John, and entered at once on his mission, and called the apostles, and they commenced while John was still in the field. We do not see what we are requested to reconcile. The two Scriptures referred to do not refer to the same time, place or things. The statement that Jesus came into Galilee, and the other statement, that "after these things came Jesus and his disciples into the land of Judea," do not refer to the same time, the same place, or the same transactions, and therefore need no reconciling. Jesus and his disciples came into the land of Judea before he went into Galilee. He chose his apostles while in Judea, before John was imprisoned, but went into Galilee after John's imprisonment.

Query–Is it right to retain in the church a member who advocates the following doctrines? 1. Denying that the kingdom of God was set up on the day of Pentecost. 2. That Christ is to reign on earth, on the throne of his father David, in Jerusalem, as a literal King. 3. That the earth is man's only inheritance. 4. Soul-sleeping 5. Setting aside the eternal punishment of the wicked, and substituting annihilation. 6. Denying the personality of the Devil. 7. The right to belong to the Church of Christ; holding and advocating the above-named doctrines. Please inform us what course shall be pursued in the above case, as we have just such a one here. We have no preacher near who can visit us more than once or twice a year, who can explain these matters, and they are causing us some trouble.

Answer–1. The teachers alluded to not only deny that the "kingdom was set up on Pentecost, but that *there is any kingdom of God*." This is negative preaching—denying the existence of the kingdom. Nothing more false and pernicious than this can be taught. 2. The idea of a literal reign of Christ, on the throne of David, in Jerusalem, is simply error held by the Jews who believed on Christ, during his earthly ministry, and the one exploded when Jesus was crucified, and that they had in view when they "thought it was he who was to have redeemed Israel;" but did not understand *how*. Jesus is now reigning on the throne of David in the only sense in which he ever will. When he shall come again, raise the dead, and judge the world, he will deliver up the kingdom to God, even the Father, that God may be all in all. 3. The idea that the earth is the only inheritance of the saints, excludes the teaching of our Lord, that instructs us how we may "inherit eternal life," or the teaching of the apostle that sets before us "a building of God not made with hands, eternal in the heavens." 4. We never could see any reason for talking of "soul sleeping" among people that do not believe that a man *has any soul*. These men do not believe the clearest statements of Scripture. The Lord says, in the clearest language that can be uttered, "Fear not them who kill the body, but are *not able to kill the soul*." This passage not only settles the fact that man has a soul as well as a body, but that killing the body does not kill the soul. Man can kill the body, but *can not kill the soul*. There is simply no such thing as *soul sleeping* in the Bible. Sleep is used as an emblem, or figure of death; but in this case *sleep* is the emblem or figure, and it means *death*. Death is the thing meant. But it is simply the body that dies, not the soul. 5. Everlasting and eternal are from the same in the original. "Everlasting punishment," and not everlasting annihilation, nor everlasting extinction of being, nor everlasting nonexistence, is what the Lord threatens. Matt 25.46. At the same time the righteous enter into "life eternal," the wicked "go away into everlasting punishment." The original word *aionion* here is translated, in the common version, "eternal," in one place, and "everlasting" in the other. There is no reason for not translating this word the same way in both places. It means precisely the same in both places. At the same time we repeat, that the righteous enter into "life eternal," the wicked "go away into eternal punishment." The same word used by the Lord, in the same sentence, to express the duration of the life of the saints, is used to express the duration of the punishment of the wicked. It is as likely that the life of the saints shall terminate, as that the punishment of the wicked shall cease. There is no word in any language that more certainly expresses unlimited duration than this word *aionion*. It is used to express the duration of the life of the saints, the praises of God, and even the existence of God. A word may be used with less than its full import, but *never with more*. 6. Denying the personality of the Devil. Here we have more *negative preaching*—more *denying*. What a world of gospel there is in this! Who is to be saved by denying the personality of the Devil? Who is comforted and built up with this sort of stuff? The infidel laughs. The Universalist nods assent; but who repents? The scoffer is delighted. That is the man for him! But does he quit scoffing? We have recently heard of a man who had stripped his feet bare after a rain of a warm summer's day, and, walking up through the mud to an old preacher, denied the personality of the Devil; when the preacher, pointing behind the man, replied: "He must be *alive* and *personal, for there is his track fresh in the mud*! Another preacher allowed that when the Devil has a man so completely blinded that he does not believe there is any Devil, or that he is a personal being, he never expects to have any more trouble with him. He will never listen to the truth any more. 7. The right to belong to the Church of Christ, holding and advocating the above doctrines. What does any man want to belong to the Church of Christ, holding and advocating such theories as these for? These theories would destroy any church. Let men who want to advocate these things go out and preach them, and see what they will *build up*. They may *destroy* a church with such preaching, as has frequently been the case; but they will never *build* up anything to it. No church should permit any such unbelief to be advocated in it.

Query—Is it right for cousins to marry? Some contend that it is a sin against God and a violation of the laws of nature, and in proof of the latter point to the degeneracy of some of the offspring of cousins. Is there any Scripture in the Old Testament prohibiting the marriage of cousins?

Answer—We do not now think of any Scripture that forbids cousins to marry, but there is no necessity for it, and we think the fruits of it have proved, at least, that it is not for the best. We would greatly prefer that it should not occur.

11/7/71, v.14,#45, pg. 356

Query—It is conceded that singing sacred songs, with the spirit and understanding, is a part of worship. Sacred songs are sung by Christians in the home circle, with the "organ" accomplishment. Then, if such singing, with the use of the organ, constitutes a part of worship at home, why not in the public assembly? Or, if is it wrong to use the organ in singing sacred songs in the public assembly, and the Lord's day school, why not at home?

Answer—We answered the above not more than a month ago. We make no difference between the use of the organ *in worship*, in the family, or any-where else. The same objection lies against it *in worship* anywhere, public or private. We have no objection to an organ, or any other instrument, as a secular attraction, or entertainment, in public or private. But there is nothing *spiritual* or *religious* about it, any more than there is about grammar or arithmetic, nor has it any more to do with *worship*. It is purely secular, and should be laid aside when we worship. It can not sing, to say nothing of *"singing with the spirit and with the understanding also."* It can not *teach* and *admonish*, the precise things we are commanded to do in worship—in song. If we are not worshiping, but simply entertaining ourselves, or company, we can do so, at suitable times by secular reading vocal or instrumental music, or any other ways entirely right and admirable. Or we may do in talking on geography, geology, astronomy, the arts and sciences. But certainly these would out of place in *worship*. The same is true of instrumental music, or mere *vocal music*. If there is nothing but the *music*, it is not *worship at all*. Worship in song must *teach* and *admonish*, and this must be done by the *sentiments uttered*, that are required to be sung with *the spirit* and with the *understanding*. This is applicable to all worship, both public and private, in the church or in the family.

1/8/78, v.21, #2, pg. 12

H‎ERITAGE
OF FAITH LIBRARY

The **DeWard Publishing Company Heritage of Faith Library** is a growing collection of classic Christian reprints. DeWard has already published or has plans to publish the following authors:

- A. B. Bruce
- Atticus G. Haygood
- H.C. Leupold
- J. W. McGarvey
- William Paley
- Albertus Pieters
- B. F. Westcott

Future authors and titles added to this series will be announced on our website.

www.deward.com

DEWARD
PUBLISHING COMPANY